Achieving Financial Stability and Growth in Africa

This book explores how the financial system should be regulated and structured to achieve the twin goals of inclusive growth and financial stability, with a focus on African low-income countries (LICs). The subject and content of this book is original in that it attempts to draw on the lessons and radical rethinking on the financial sector in developed and middle income countries, arising in the wake of the international financial crisis. It includes four in-depth country case studies, of Kenya, Ghana, Nigeria and Ethiopia, but also analyses the empirical evidence for Sub-Saharan Africa as a whole, evaluating the relevance (or not) of such major changes for the very different financial sectors and economies in LICs.

Achieving Financial Stability and Growth in Africa has major academic and policy implications, especially for LICs, but also more generally, on broader issues. These include the desirable size of the financial sector, as well as more specific issues, such as the high cost of borrowing of small and medium enterprises in LICs, and possible measures to reduce it. Highly topical subjects like the appropriate regulation of the financial sector and management of capital flows are discussed in depth. Though drawing on comprehensive reviews of the literature, this book has the virtue of the large comparative academic and policy experience of researchers, as well as in-depth case studies, that take account of institutional and economic features of LICs.

Written by senior academics and policy-makers, this book is a must read for those researching or participating in the financial sectors of LICs, as well as in developed economies. It is also suitable for those who study political economy and public finance.

Stephany Griffith-Jones is Associate Fellow at ODI, Financial Markets Director at IPD, Columbia University and Emeritus at IDS, Sussex, where she was Professorial Fellow for a long time.

Ricardo Gottschalk is an Economic Affairs Officer at the Division of Globalization and Development Strategies (GDS) of UNCTAD, Geneva, Switzerland.

'Ahead of the 2008 crisis many economists assumed that financial deepening – including increased private credit as a percent of GDP – was always positive for economic growth. We now know that there can be too much finance and too much private credit. But good finance is still crucial to economic development, and low-income countries must use the lessons of the global financial crisis to help identify which forms of financial development are most beneficial. This book will play an important role in the debate, combining sound empirical analysis, informative case studies and thoughtful synthesis of the overall insights and implications.'

Adair Turner, *former chair of the UK Financial Services Authority and author of* Between Debt and the Devil

'This is a compelling factual study about a critical dilemma for policy making in LICs – delicately balancing the trinity of financial inclusion, financial stability and growth agendas. This is even more challenging in the face of globalisation, inadequacies within domestic jurisdictions, ongoing reforms to global regulatory architecture and new rules like Anti Money Laundering that pose unintended consequences.'

Louis Kasekende PhD, *Deputy Governor, Bank of Uganda*

Routledge Critical Studies in Finance and Stability
Edited by Jan Toporowski
School of Oriental and African Studies, University of London, UK

The 2007–8 Banking Crash has induced a major and wide-ranging discussion on the subject of financial (in)stability and a need to revaluate theory and policy. The response of policy-makers to the crisis has been to refocus fiscal and monetary policy on financial stabilisation and reconstruction. However, this has been done with only vague ideas of bank recapitalisation and 'Keynesian' reflation aroused by the exigencies of the crisis, rather than the application of any systematic theory or theories of financial instability.

Routledge Critical Studies in Finance and Stability covers a range of issues in the area of finance including instability, systemic failure, financial macro-economics in the vein of Hyman P. Minsky, Ben Bernanke and Mark Gertler, central bank operations, financial regulation, developing countries and financial crises, new portfolio theory and New International Monetary and Financial Architecture.

Achieving Financial Stability and Growth in Africa

Edited by Stephany Griffith-Jones and Ricardo Gottschalk

LONDON AND NEW YORK

First published 2016 by Routledge

2 Park Square, Milton Park, Abingdon, Oxfordshire OX14 4RN
52 Vanderbilt Avenue, New York, NY 10017

Routledge is an imprint of the Taylor & Francis Group, an informa business

First issued in paperback 2019

British Library Cataloguing in Publication Data
A catalogue record for this book is available from the British Library

Library of Congress Cataloging in Publication Data
Names: Griffith-Jones, Stephany, editor. | Gottschalk, Ricardo, 1964– editor.
Title: Achieving financial stability and growth in Africa / edited by Stephany Griffith-Jones and Ricardo Gottschalk.
Description: New York : Routledge, 2016.
Identifiers: LCCN 2015035499 | ISBN 9781138123731 (hardback) | ISBN 9781315648668 (ebook)
Subjects: LCSH: Finance—Africa—Case studies. | Africa—Economic policy. | Economic development—Africa.
Classification: LCC HG187.5.A2 A25 2016 | DDC 332.096—dc23

ISBN: 978-1-138-12373-1 (hbk)
ISBN: 978-0-367-87565-7 (pbk)

Typeset in Times New Roman
by Keystroke, Station Road, Codsall, Wolverhampton

Contents

Figures

Tables

Preface

This book aims to explore how the financial system should be regulated and structured to achieve the twin goals of inclusive growth and financial stability, with a focus on African low-income countries (LICs).

The book builds on original research carried out in a three-year international project, funded by the UK Economic and Social Research Council (ESRC) and the Department for International Development (DFID). We are very grateful to both bodies for their financial and other support of all the research. The project included two workshops in Sub-Saharan Africa (Ghana and Senegal) to reach common understanding among the different authors, and to draw lessons from other regions, including both developed and emerging economies from Latin America and Asia. Public events were organized in Ghana, Washington for the IMF/World Bank Spring Meetings and Senegal, where many African senior policy-makers and academics gave us the benefit of their valuable and crucial perspectives. The first two were co-organized with Dirk Willem te Velde and the DFID-ESRC Growth Research Programme (DEGRP); we therefore warmly thank Dirk Willem and the DEGRP team at the Overseas Development Institute (ODI) for their excellent support at the meetings. Dirk Willem te Velde has also provided extremely valuable insights and overall support to the project since its inception to the end. Mobolaji Babalola has provided excellent administrative support, combining great efficiency and charm.

We are very grateful to Dr Usha Thorat, former Deputy Governor of the Reserve Bank of India and Professor Akio Hosono, senior advisor of Japan International Cooperation Agency (JICA), for their valuable contributions in Ghana, as well as to the Governor of the Bank of Ghana, Dr Kofi Wampah, for his excellent keynote address. Our public event in Senegal was a plenary panel at the Annual Meeting of Making Finance Work for Africa; many thanks to Alessandro Girola and Stefan Malletanby for their support for our participation. Dr Anand Sinha, former Deputy Governor of the Reserve Bank of India and Dr Caleb Fundanga, former Governor of the Bank of Zambia, kindly spoke at our plenary panel in Dakar.

The subject and content of the book is original in that it attempts to draw on the lessons and radical rethinking on the financial sector in developed and middle income countries, arising in the wake of the international financial crisis, and see the relevance (or not) of such major changes for the very different financial sectors and economies in LICs. It therefore has major academic and policy implications, especially for LICs, on broad issues such as the desirable size of the financial sector, as well as far more specific issues, such as the high cost of borrowing of small and medium-sized enterprises (SMEs) in LICs, and possible measures to reduce it. Though drawing on the econometric literature, the book is based on large comparative policy-experience of researchers, as well as in-depth case studies, that take account of institutional and economic features of individual LICs. Charles Harvey generously and thoroughly reviewed most of the draft chapters, which was extremely useful.

The book and research was structured in three parts. First, broad issues on desirable size, structure and regulation of the financial sector are discussed in an introductory chapter, which also sets the agenda and questions for the country case studies. This introductory chapter presents the latest thinking on central issues for a financial sector that delivers both growth and stability, and asks what their policy implications are for African LICs. The second chapter is an in-depth survey of the theoretical and empirical literature on the relationships between domestic financial structures and financial regulation, both domestic and external (focusing on the former) and their implications for inclusive growth and stability. The third chapter reviews the literature and evidence on capital account management issues in LICs. The fourth chapter explores issues of implementation of regulation, in a LIC context, building not just on the literature, but on extensive interviews with policy-makers in Africa, especially in Ethiopia, Kenya and Lesotho, which were especially visited for this purpose. In the second part of the book, four in-depth country case studies (Kenya, Ghana, Nigeria and Ethiopia), written by senior African researchers with extensive policy experience in these countries, have been written, representing chapters five to eight. These chapters are written based on a common research framework and have original empirical data, including that based on extensive interviews. In the third part, the concluding (ninth) chapter integrates the theoretical and empirical country analyses, compares in detail the countries studied and draws policy lessons for the countries and for other low-income and lower-middle income countries, especially but not only in Africa.

Drawing on the broader analysis and the literature reviews, as well as consultations with senior policy-makers and academics, we framed the research in the case studies around the following questions:

1) What features and what vision of development may one have for the country in the next ten years? What main opportunities (such as in some cases new natural resources) and main challenges (such as continued lack of access and high cost of credit, especially for SMEs)?

2) What sort of financial system is needed to support that vision and seize new opportunities, as well as manage key challenges of potential risks to financial stability?

3) What scale of financial (and especially banking) sector is desirable? Above all, what pace of growth of the financial sector is desirable? In each case study country, is the key challenge one of expanding access for certain sectors and social groups, and too little credit growth, or are there also challenges to maintain financial stability?

4) As regards access to credit, there are two issues. Is there enough access to credit, especially for SMEs; is it of enough maturity? The second issue is that of the excessive cost of credit. If it is or has remained high, even in the face of changes within the banking industry, that should have increased competition, why has the cost not come down or why has it fallen so little? If the answer is high costs in banks, what are the main factors explaining them? Is there collusion amongst the banks? Last, but perhaps most importantly, what are the policy solutions to deal with this issue? What are possible barriers to implementing such solutions, and how can these be overcome?

5) As regards the structure of the banking sector, what is the role of foreign and public development banks? How well have these particular categories performed, for example in terms of providing access to credit to SMEs, as well as other parts of the private sector? Is there a need for a greater role for good public development banks, to cover gaps in financing in key sectors, essential for inclusive growth? What are the experiences of public development banking in your country? How can GOOD development banks be expanded or created? As regards foreign banks, what are the key challenges for regulating such banks, both foreign ones in host countries and home banks in other countries?

6) More broadly, on domestic financial regulation, what might be the role of micro-prudential and macro-prudential regulation? How important is implementing Basel II and III for ensuring financial stability with inclusive growth? What aspects are particularly essential of Basel II and III? Are levels of capital adequacy in your countries' banks sufficient to ensure financial stability? If they are increased, could this raise the cost of credit further?

7) Is the regulatory toolkit in your country more reliant on other variables such as structure of banking assets, which may be more relevant for LICs? Should thus regulation be more tailored to LICs needs? What are capacity and other constraints in your country for implementing different regulation and supervision? Should counter-cyclical regulation be introduced? How should it be done? At the aggregate level of total credit expansion, or focused on specific sectors, e.g. those to whom credit grows the most, or specific sectors such as the real estate?

8) What institutions/mechanisms are available in the banking system for financial inclusion? How successful are they in providing access to the poorer segments of society? Do they pose sustainability risks for the individual users and/or financial stability risks in the macro sense? Is regulation adequate?

9) What is the structure and level of capital flows to your country? Has your country seen a recent expansion of foreign capital flows, e.g. via bonds?

What can be done to encourage long-term capital flows that enhance development potential? What are desirable levels of sustainable foreign debt in your country? How can the capital account best be regulated to avoid future currency or banking crises? Should it be done through regulating currency mismatches in lending to banks and companies? Or should counter-cyclical capital controls on inflows of short-term capital also play a role?

1 A financial sector to support development in low-income countries[1]

Stephany Griffith-Jones with Ewa Karwowski and Florence Dafe

Introduction

Designing a financial sector and its regulation, in a way that promotes development, provides a particularly challenging area for policy design and research. The policy challenges and research needs are very large, due partly to a major rethinking of the role, scale and structure of a desirable financial sector, as well as its regulation, in light of the major North Atlantic financial crisis. This crisis challenged the view that developed countries' financial systems and their regulation should be emulated by developing countries, given that developed countries' financial systems have been so problematic and so poorly regulated. Furthermore, it is important to understand the implications of the major international policy and analytical rethinking, including on regulation, for low-income countries (LICs) in Sub-Saharan Africa (SSA).

The financial sectors of African LICs are still at an early stage of development so that lessons from the crisis could inform their financial sector development strategies. They have the advantage of latecomers. Moreover, their financial sectors, while generally still shallow, are experiencing fairly rapid growth. Combined with African countries' existing vulnerabilities, such as limited regulatory capacity, and vulnerability to external shocks, this might pose risks to financial system stability. Despite the infrequent appearance of systemic banking crises on the African continent over the past decade (see below), fast credit growth in many economies – even if at comparatively low levels – calls for caution, signalling the need for strong, as well as countercyclical, regulation of African financial systems. For policy-makers and researchers, this poses the challenge of applying the lessons from the crisis in developed and previously in emerging countries to African LICs, while paying careful attention to the specific features of African financial systems.

There are also more traditional policy challenges and research gaps on financial sectors in LICs and their links to inclusive growth. To support growth, there are a range of functions that the financial sector must meet in African LICs, such as helping to mobilize sufficient savings; intermediating savings at low cost and long- as well as short-term maturities to investors and consumers; ensuring that savings are channelled to the most efficient investment opportunities; and helping companies and individuals manage risk. There are also large deficiencies in these areas originating from specific market failures and/or gaps. For example, there is a lack of sustainable lending at relatively low spreads, including with long maturities to small and medium-sized enterprises (SMEs), which is particularly constraining for growth in LICs.

This chapter presents two key areas for a policy, as well as a corresponding research agenda for the four case studies on finance and growth in SSA: 1) the desirable size and structure of the financial sector and 2) new challenges for financial regulation. Discussions in these two areas are important to advance understanding of the links between the financial sector and inclusive as well as sustainable growth, and any possible trade-offs.

Financial sector development and growth

Central bankers and financial regulators in African LICs have always faced major conceptual and institutional challenges in striking the right balance in their policy design to achieve the triple aims of financial stability, growth and equity.

These challenges acquired a new dimension in the light of numerous financial crises, initially in the developing world, but recently in developed countries. The latter led to a major re-evaluation of the role of the financial sector, its interactions with the real economy and the need for major reform of its regulation, especially in developed and emerging economies (see for example, Griffith-Jones et al., 2010, as well as IMF, 2012b). Among proposed regulatory reforms, Haldane and Madouros (2012) point in particular to the need to simplify regulation, which resonates very well with LICs.

It is important to note that the number of banking crises on the African continent has overall been remarkably low over the past decade (2000–2010), potentially indicating increased resilience of African financial systems, particularly in comparison to the 1990s (see Figure 1.1).

In this context the Nigerian banking crisis, the only fairly large crisis in that period – discussed below – is seen by some as a "sporadic outlier" (Beck et al., 2011:3). There is, nevertheless, the danger that absence of recent crises can lead to policy-makers' and regulators' complacency (as well as that by the financial actors), which precisely could increase the risk of future crises. This phenomenon, known in the literature as "disaster myopia", has in the past contributed to increased risk of crises in all other regions.

There has been relatively little research and policy analysis on the implications of the Global Financial Crisis for African countries and LICs more generally, with some valuable exceptions (see for example, Kasekende et al., 2011, and Murinde, 2012 for good analyses of regulatory issues in LICs). As African financial sectors are growing quite quickly, they may be more vulnerable to threats to their financial stability. This book, and the research that gave rise to it, attempts to contribute to help answer the question of how the need to ensure financial stability interacts with the need of a financial system in LICs that assures enough access to sustainable finance for the different sectors of the economy, including long-term

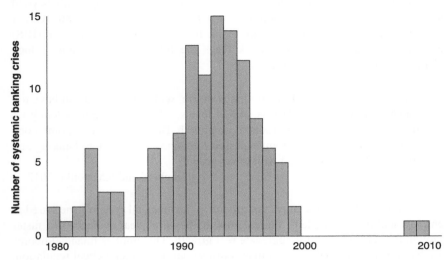

Figure 1.1 Systemic banking crises in Africa, 1980–2010

Source: Laeven and Valencia, 2008 and 2012.

finance to fund structural change, as well as different segments, such as SMEs and infrastructure.

The key issues

There are two areas of issues for understanding the links between the financial sector and inclusive, as well as sustainable, growth: 1) what is the desirable size and structure of the financial sector in LICs?; and 2) what are the regulatory challenges to maximise the likelihood of achieving financial stability, whilst safeguarding inclusive and more sustainable growth?

Size and structure of the financial sector

At a broad level, what is the desirable size and structure of the financial sector in African countries, to maximise its ability to support the real economy? What are the desirable paths of development of the financial sector in Africa to help it maximise its contribution to growth, considering the features of African countries and lessons from recent crises?

The traditional positive link between deeper as well as larger financial sector and long-term growth, that started in the literature with Bagehot and Schumpeter, but then was reflected in quite a large part of the empirical literature, such as Levine (2005), is being increasingly challenged. Authors like Easterly et al. (2000) had already early on suggested that financial depth (measured by private credit to GDP ratio) reduces volatility of output up to a point, but beyond that, it actually increases output volatility. More recently, a number of papers are showing an inverse relation between size of financial sector and growth, especially beyond a certain level of financial development, which is estimated at around 80–100 per cent of private credit to GDP. Thus, Bank for International Settlements (BIS) economists based on empirical work reach the following conclusions, which challenge much of earlier writing:

> First, as is the case with many things in life, with finance you can have too much of a good thing. That is, at low levels, a larger financial system goes hand in hand with higher productivity growth. But there comes a point – one that many advanced economies passed long ago – where more banking and more credit are associated with lower growth.
>
> (Cecchetti and Kharroubi, 2012:1)

Secondly, looking at the impact of growth in the financial system – measured in employment or value added – on real growth, they find clear evidence that faster growth in finance is bad for aggregate real growth. This implies financial booms are bad for trend growth. Hence, macro-prudential or countercyclical regulation, discussed below, is important.

Finally, in their examination of industry-level data, they find that industries competing for resources with finance are particularly damaged by financial booms. Specifically, manufacturing sectors that are R&D-intensive suffer disproportionate reductions in productivity growth when finance increases.

Similarly, an IMF Discussion Paper (IMF, 2012a) suggests empirical explanations for the fact that large financial sectors may have negative effects on economic growth. It gives two possible reasons. The first has to do with increased probability of large economic crashes (Minsky, 1974; Kindleberger, 1978 and Rajan, 2005) and the second relates to potential misallocation of resources, even in good times (Tobin, 1984). De la Torre and Ize (2011) point out that "Too Much Finance" may be consistent with positive but decreasing returns of financial depth, which, at some point, become smaller than the cost of instability. It is interesting that the IMF Discussion paper (IMF, 2012a) results are robust to restricting the analysis to tranquil periods, confirming that the "Too Much Finance" result is not only due to financial crises and volatility, but also misallocation of resources.

It is also plausible that the relationship between financial depth and economic growth depends, at least in part, on whether lending is used to finance investment in productive assets or to feed speculative bubbles. Not only where credit serves to feed speculative bubbles – where excessive increases can actually be negative for growth – but also where it is used for consumption purposes as opposed to productive investment, the effect of financial depth on economic growth seems limited. Using data for 45 countries for the period 1994–2005, Beck et al. (2012) and Beck et al. (2011) show that enterprise credit is positively associated with economic growth but that there is no correlation between growth and household credit. Given that the share of bank lending to households increases with economic and financial development and household credit is often used for consumption purposes whereas enterprise credit is used for productive investment, the allocation of resources goes some way towards explaining the nonlinear finance–growth relationship. In African countries, only a small share of bank lending goes to households. However, as financial sectors and economies grow, this will change, as has been the case in South Africa.

Rapidly growing credit to households – even though desirable and potentially welfare enhancing when strengthening reasonable levels of domestic demand and financial inclusion, in a sustainable way – might, however, cause financial instability, as well as harm poorer people, if not regulated prudently.

Excessive lending to the construction sector is another important source of financial instability, particularly when it creates a housing bubble. The two most advanced African economies – South Africa and Mauritius, both upper middle income countries – have recently experienced or are currently experiencing a construction boom. Both economies possess relatively deep financial markets with strong private domestic lending, including significant consumption credit extension. Figure 1.2 shows that private credit in high income economies was around 100 per cent of GDP on average in 2010 while it accounted for 70–80 per cent of GDP in Mauritius and South Africa.

South Africa was the country in Africa which experienced the strongest real house price growth between 2004 and 2007, by far exceeding even the price growth in the booming residential property markets of the US and the UK. In South Africa the ratio of household to business credit is approximately 1:1. The large majority of household borrowing takes on the form of mortgage finance. During the early 2000s this led to an unprecedented housing boom in South Africa, as growth in housing loans was over 150 per cent in real terms between

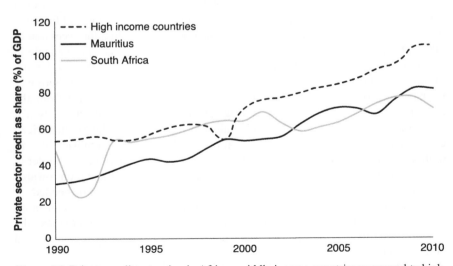

Figure 1.2 Private credit extension in African middle income countries compared to high income countries, 1990–2010

Source: The World Bank, 2013b.

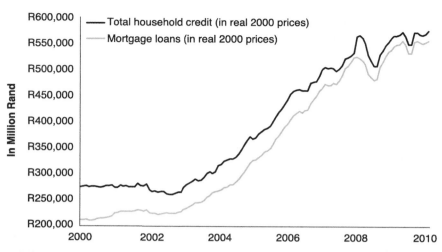

Figure 1.3 South African private sector credit extension by purpose, 2000–2010

Source: SARB, 2013.

2000 and 2010 (see Figure 1.3). This was largely absorbed by upper income South African households accounting for three-quarters of total household credit created during the period (DTI, 2010). In an attempt to reduce inflation, asset price increases and potential macro-economic over-heating, the South African Reserve Bank gradually initiated monetary tightening in June 2006, accelerating the rise in interest rates in the following year.

The subsequent economic slowdown in South Africa was to a large extent caused by measures to correct domestically accumulated economic and financial imbalances, while the Global Financial Crisis merely intensified the recession of 2008/09. The fact that credit and consumption-led growth was unsustainable in South Africa was illustrated in almost one million jobs shed in 2008/09, largely in low-skilled consumption-driven sectors. A positive aspect was that there was no banking crisis, perhaps because of the positive policy response from the economic authorities. However, as mortgage credit picks up, and especially if it does at a very fast pace, care has to be taken to regulate this. The South African experience lends support to the view that private sector credit expansion at very high levels might lead to output volatility and adverse growth effects. In order to prevent future crises and foster economic development, a re-orientation towards more business credit, particularly for productive investment, might be needed.

Limited data availability makes it difficult to measure to what extent consumption credit is on the rise in most African economies. This would seem to make the case for more disaggregated credit data, as well as monitoring by regulators and policy-makers, more urgent.

One of the few low-income SSA countries providing disaggregated domestic lending data is Mozambique (Banco de Moçambique, 2013). Private sector credit has increased significantly between 2000 and 2010 in the Southern African country – from 15 per cent to 23 per cent of GDP (see Table 1.1 later). During this period consumer borrowing almost tripled as share of total credit while it grew almost eightfold between 2001 and 2012 in real terms. Mozambique has had a strong growth performance implying a robust medium-term economic outlook (IMF, 2012c). Nevertheless, falling consumer price inflation has been accompanied by potential price pressures present in urban housing markets. Central areas in Mozambican towns and cities have been observed to experience property price growth of 100 per cent annually (CAHF, 2012).

More broadly, as we began to discuss above, of relevance for growth is thus the link between the structure of the financial sector and growth. The IMF in its Global Financial Stability Report (IMF, 2012b) has interesting further empirical analysis of the relationship between the structure of the financial sector and economic growth, as well as the volatility of this growth and financial stress. This is a fairly under-studied area, and one which has hardly been applied to LICs. The preliminary empirical results of the IMF report suggest that cross border connections through foreign banks may, during crises, be associated with instability, though their role may be more beneficial in normal times.

Crucial in the context of policy-making and research on finance in Africa is the extent to which the findings on the relationship between the structure and size of the financial sector and growth in more developed economies are relevant for and apply to African LICs because their financial systems are markedly different. In particular, these countries' banking systems are small in absolute and relative size, many of them reaching the size of mid-sized banks in high income countries. Beck et al. (2011) report, for instance, that if measured in relative size based on the claims on the private domestic nonfinancial sector to GDP (private credit), the median for African countries as a whole (i.e. including North African countries) was 19 per cent in 2009, while it was 49 per cent for non-African developing countries. African financial sectors also show that levels of financial intermediation and access to financial services have remained limited for large segments such as SMEs, the agricultural sector or poor households (as illustrated in detail in our country case studies in this book). Many of those use informal financial services.

Given the importance of SMEs in creating employment, the lack of credit supporting their activity in African financial systems is a major drawback for development. International financial indicators show that African businesses in general are disadvantaged due to less access to finance than competitors in other regions. Concurrently, SMEs enjoy a particularly poor access to sources of finance, leaving them with internal cash flow as the main source for investment finance. As a consequence, enabling African SMEs to have better access to financing sources has the potential to strengthen and accelerate growth if done on sustainable grounds and at reasonable cost, under adequate regulation.

The obstacles African SMEs experience in their domestic financial systems are mainly concentrated around the insufficient support by banking institutions, as well as lacking alternative sources of finance. Therefore, recent developments of deepening African financial markets might help SME growth if financial resources

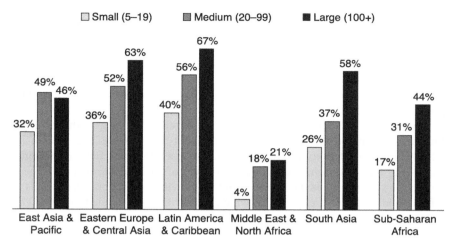

Figure 1.4 Regional per cent of firms by firm size with a bank loan/line of credit

Source: The World Bank, 2013a.

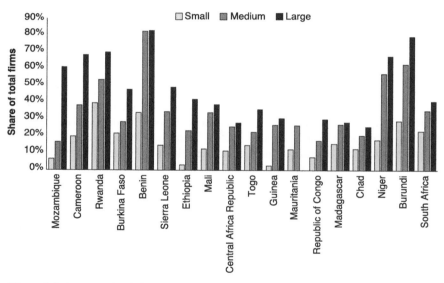

Figure 1.5 Access to bank loans and/or lines of credit by some SSA countries' firms

Source: The World Bank, 2013a.

are successfully and sustainably channelled into this segment. International indicators such as domestic analysis via enterprise surveys, by company size, support the view that African SMEs have limited access to finance.

Figures 1.4 and 1.5 illustrate the difficulties that African businesses and entrepreneurs have in accessing finance, in comparison to the average for all countries.

For a more detailed assessment of the ability of firms to have access to finance, the percentage of small, medium and large firms that have a bank loan or a credit line can be useful. Sub-Saharan African small firms have poor access to finance when compared to other developing regions (only 17 per cent of them do, as opposed to 40 per cent in Latin America and 32 per cent in East Asia), performing only better than the Middle East and North Africa region (see Figure 1.4). This analysis of access to credit by firm size is taken further for some Sub-Saharan African countries, by looking at firms of different sizes and their ability to have a bank loan or a credit line (Figure 1.5).

In general, between 60 per cent and 70 per cent of SMEs in SSA need loans, however only 17 per cent of small and 31 per cent of medium-sized firms actually have access to finance. As a consequence, firms in SSA have to finance a high proportion of investment through internally generated cash flows (82 per cent among small Sub-Saharan African firms, 78 per cent amongst medium firms and 72 per cent amongst large firms, according to The World Bank data). This reflects other findings, for example by the Milken Institute and their Capital Access Index (CAI), which found that African countries lack developed equity and bond markets, alternative sources of capital and that there are low levels of lending by banking institutions (with the latter two probably most appropriate forms of funding SMEs).

Not surprisingly, according to The World Bank, 48 per cent of small enterprises and 42 per cent of medium-sized enterprises in SSA have identified access to finance as a major obstacle to their business activities. This is an extremely high proportion, though some caution should be expressed, in that only creditworthy – and not all – SMEs should be granted credit.

In an effort to increase the level of participation of financial institutions to finance SMEs, public banks, such as the African Development Bank (AfDB), are undertaking a number of initiatives designed to encourage the participation of financial institutions. One notable initiative is the African Guarantee Fund (AGF), which is a for-profit social investment fund. The AGF is owned by the AfDB, the Spanish Agency for International Cooperation (AECID) and the Denmark development cooperation (DANIDA) with contributions of US$10 million, US$20 million and US$20 million, respectively (African Development Bank, 2012). Over the next three to five years, this share capital is expected to increase to US$500 million, giving the institution capacity to guarantee up to US$2 billion worth of SME loans. The additional capital will be coming from bilateral donors, private investors as well as from development finance institutions (DFIs) (African Development Bank, 2012). The AGF is selecting certain financial institutions to be partner institutions by assessing their commitment to grow their SME portfolio and improving financial product offerings to SMEs. For these partner institutions, the AGF will have two lines of activity:

1) Partial credit guarantees: the provision of partial guarantees for financial institutions on the African continent to incentivise them to increase debt and equity investments into SMEs.

2) Capacity development: supporting AGFs partner institutions enhance their SME financing capabilities through assisting to improve the capacity to appraise and manage SME portfolios.

(African Development Bank, 2013)

Operationally, the AGF will work on a risk sharing basis with financial institutions and the maximum risk coverage ratio will be 50 per cent. The balance of risk will be borne by the financial institutions (African Development Bank, 2013). The AGF is designed to achieve a triple-A rating in order to attract a zero per cent risk-weight on SME loans provided by partner institutions. This will allow these institutions to lend money with limited need to set aside regulatory capital because of the guarantee from the highly rated AGF.

It is worth noting that over and above the general consensus that SMEs lack long-term finance at reasonable lending rates, working capital facilities are also starting to be emphasised. The AfDB notes that: "SMEs . . . complain . . . how banks are hesitant to provide long-term lending and working capital facilities, both of which they need for growth" (African Development Bank, 2012:3). Currently, according to The World Bank (2013a), only 15 per cent of small enterprises in SSA use banks to finance working capital. Moreover, only a small proportion (6 per cent) of their working capital needs is covered by this type of finance.

The need for working capital from financial institutions is echoed by Standard Bank, which found that there is a need for working capital facilities for SMEs in SSA (Botha 2011). To this end, Standard Bank has launched a product called Quick Loans, which provides unsecured loans of between US$300 to US$30,000 for three to 12 months, as well as other forms of finance to traders (Standard Bank, 2013). Standard Bank (2013) has established SME banking in 13 African countries (excluding South Africa) and during 2011 provided financial services to more than 150,000 SMEs across these countries.

In general, data on the asset composition of banks across different regions shows that, unlike banks in other regions of the world, African banks hold a much smaller share of their assets in the form of private sector loans and a much larger share in the forms of government securities, foreign assets and liquid assets (Beck et al., 2011). Household credit constitutes only a small share in bank credit, except in countries where financial sectors are more developed, like South Africa.

Banking sectors in most African countries are highly concentrated. In many countries, banks are predominantly foreign-owned, many of them being regional banks from other African countries. Banks also operate very profitably, with subsidiaries of foreign banks in SSA having higher returns on assets than subsidiaries of the same banks in other regions (Honohan and Beck, 2007).

It is not clear to what extent the findings on the reverse link between financial depth and growth found in the context of developed and emerging economies is as relevant for LICs, with a much lower level of financial development, and with large parts of the population and companies lacking any access to financial services, as to countries with far deeper financial sectors. However, these findings will certainly be relevant for designing policies that will influence their future evolution. Furthermore, it may well be that in the near-term, the issue is more

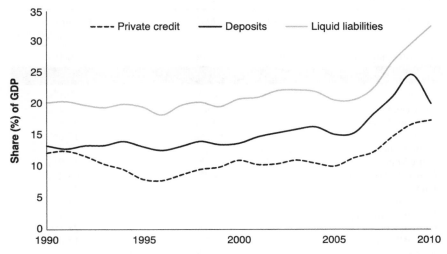

Figure 1.6 Financial deepening in SSA, 1990–2010

Source: The World Bank, 2013b.

related to avoiding excessive speed of growth of finance, that we have started to illustrate above, which may be a more significant threat to financial stability in the case of SSA. Indeed, as shown in Figure 1.6, financial deepening in SSA has accelerated in recent years. The amount of private credit as a share of GDP almost doubled from an average of 10 per cent during the 1990s to 18 per cent by 2010. Bank deposits as share of GDP grew from 13 per cent (in 1990–1999) to more than 20 per cent (in 2010), while liquid liabilities (also known as broad money or M3) to GDP rose by more than 10 percentage points over the same period from 20 per cent to above 30 per cent.

The above aggregate figures do not do justice to the fast pace of credit expansion in certain SSA economies. Table 1.1 provides country data about credit extension as share of GDP for all SSA economies individually. It highlights countries which have experienced a doubling of private credit to GDP within the past decade (2000–2010) in light grey. Economies where private credit tripled or increased up to tenfold over the same period are highlighted in darker grey, while SSA states that saw a rise in lending to the private sector of ten times or more are highlighted in black.

This analysis shows that in the recent decade there were a considerable number of SSA countries with very rapid credit growth, namely:

- Benin and Swaziland where credit to GDP (almost) doubled;
- Malawi, Mali, Niger, Nigeria, São Tomé and Príncipe, Sierra Leone, Sudan, Tanzania and Uganda where credit to GDP increased threefold and more (but less than tenfold);
- Angola with private credit growing by a factor of more than 15-fold, or 1,500 per cent.

Table 1.1 Credit extension in SSA by country, 1990, 2000, 2010

Country	1990	2000	2010	Credit growth 2000–2010 (%)
SSA (developing)	9.2%	11.0%	17.5%	59.1%
Angola	n/a	1.1%	18.1%	1545.5%
Benin	n/a	11.1%	22.1%	99.1%
Botswana	7.8%	13.9%	22.3%	60.4%
Burkina Faso	16.2%	10.8%	16.5%	52.8%
Burundi	7.4%	17.3%	20.0%	15.6%
Cameroon	27.1%	7.7%	11.1%	44.2%
Cape Verde	4.0%	37.5%	59.2%	57.9%
Central African Republic	7.4%	4.4%	7.4%	68.2%
Chad*	6.5%	3.4%	5.0%	47.1%
Comoros*	n/a	8.3%	12.2%	47.0%
Congo, Dem. Rep.	n/a	n/a	n/a	n/a
Congo, Rep.	n/a	5.7%	4.1%	−28.1%
Côte d'Ivoire	36.4%	15.2%	17.3%	13.8%
Eritrea	n/a	n/a	n/a	n/a
Ethiopia*	1.6%	18.2%	17.2%	−5.5%
Gabon	n/a	8.3%	8.1%	−2.4%
Gambia, The	10.0%	11.6%	17.7%	52.6%
Ghana	5.0%	11.7%	13.7%	17.1%
Guinea	n/a	n/a	n/a	n/a
Guinea-Bissau*	13.0%	7.6%	5.8%	−23.7%
Kenya	17.7%	25.6%	30.6%	19.5%
Lesotho	13.8%	14.0%	12.6%	−10.0%
Liberia*	n/a	n/a	13.8%	n/a
Madagascar	14.5%	8.0%	11.1%	38.8%
Malawi	9.2%	4.5%	14.2%	215.6%
Mali	9.2%	4.5%	17.4%	286.7%
Mauritania	31.1%	n/a	n/a	n/a
Mauritius	30.1%	54.2%	82.3%	51.8%
Mozambique	n/a	15.4%	23.2%	50.6%
Namibia	n/a	39.1%	43.7%	11.8%
Niger	12.8%	4.3%	11.8%	174.4%
Nigeria	8.8%	11.1%	30.3%	173.0%
Rwanda	7.4%	9.5%	n/a	n/a
Sao Tome and Principe*	n/a	4.1%	33.2%	709.8%
Senegal	27.5%	16.5%	24.5%	48.5%
Seychelles	7.0%	15.2%	22.9%	50.7%
Sierra Leone	3.3%	1.9%	9.2%	384.2%
Somalia	n/a	n/a	n/a	n/a
South Africa	49.1%	65.0%	71.7%	10.3%
South Sudan	n/a	n/a	n/a	n/a

Country	1990	2000	2010	Credit growth 2000–2010 (%)
Sudan	4.3%	1.8%	10.9%	505.6%
Swaziland	14.2%	12.6%	23.1%	83.3%
Tanzania	12.4%	3.9%	14.6%	274.4%
Togo	22.7%	15.7%	20.7%	31.8%
Uganda	2.5%	5.3%	13.4%	152.8%
Zambia	6.8%	6.7%	10.7%	59.7%
Zimbabwe	0.0%	0.8%	n/a	n/a

Source: The World Bank, 2013b.

Notes:
* Where 1990 or 2010 data were unavailable 1991 or 2009 data were used if possible.

Countries where private credit extension has (almost) doubled between 2000 and 2010 are highlighted in light grey.

Countries where private credit extension has increased threefold or more (but less than tenfold) are highlighted in dark grey.

Countries where private credit extension has increased tenfold or more are highlighted in black.

Though this is a rough indicator, countries in the last two categories would seem more vulnerable to potential crises, so they may need to examine whether they need to introduce tighter regulations, in general, or in particular sectors.

Financial systems in many African countries share features which seem to increase their vulnerability to shocks in the economic and financial system, including limited financial regulatory capacity (see Chapter 4), macro-economic volatility linked to the economic structure of the countries (e.g. natural resource dependence, and concentration of exports, which implies volatility of their terms of trade) and political pressure for financial deepening with a view to developing the real economy.

Fast credit growth might exacerbate vulnerabilities and enhance the risk of financial crises, as it has done in all other regions of the world. In the African context, the case of Nigeria provides a recent illustration that banking crises might mean a negative causation link between financial deepening and growth, even at relatively low levels of financial development. In 2004/05 the Central Bank of Nigeria (CBN) mandated a steep increase in the minimum level of bank capitalisation with a view to creating large internationally competitive banks and increase financial depth (Soludo, 2004). Banks achieved this capitalisation, which was high even by international standards, by means of equity investment, mergers and acquisitions, resulting in the consolidation of the banking sector, whereby the total number of banks declined from 89 to 25. The consolidation in the domestic banking sector, along with abundant capital in the wake of rising oil prices, increased the speed of credit creation with significant flows to sectors with little growth impact. Between 2006 and 2009 private credit tripled from 12 per cent to

36 per cent of GDP. In real terms (2002 prices) this meant that domestic borrowing by the private sector grew almost fivefold.

This growth of credit included loans used to finance share purchases, clearly an undesirable practice, setting the stage for a financial asset bubble particularly in bank stocks (Sanusi, 2010). The financial sector boom ended in a bust with a systemic banking crisis, accentuated by the impact of the North Atlantic crisis in 2009, as financial sector growth was excessive, partly because it had not been accompanied by the corresponding regulatory and supervisory upgrade. Consequently, non-performing loans as percentage of gross loans rose sharply from 9.5 per cent in 2007 to almost 30 per cent in 2009. Finally, nine financial institutions that were close to collapse had to be rescued at the cost of US$4 billion (for a more detailed analysis, see Chapter 7 on the Nigerian case study). The cost of cleaning up the balance sheets and recapitalising the banks concerned has been estimated at about 2.4 trillion Naira, equivalent to almost 8 per cent of the country's GDP (Navajas and Thegeya, 2013). The Nigerian crisis shows that there is no reason for complacency about the need for rigorous financial regulation in the African economies, especially in the face of rapid credit expansion.

With respect to the effects of foreign bank presence on financial stability and growth in Africa, the existing evidence is somewhat ambiguous and requires further research (for an interesting recent book, see Beck et al., 2014). There are indications that foreign banks can bring in experience from other regional economies and can help exploit scale economies in small host countries. Yet, the benefits for financial access remain ambiguous, partly because of the greater reliance of foreign banks on so-called "hard" information about borrowers as opposed to soft information, which often implies a focus on prime borrowers (Detragiache et al., 2008; Sengupta, 2007).

Furthermore, it seems that foreign banks are fundamentally different from domestic banks. As argued by Rashid (2011), foreign banks seem less inclined to lending and their loans are likely to be more volatile than those offered by domestic banks. Despite strong foreign bank presence, the effects of the global financial crisis on African banks have been limited. In part, this is due to the relatively limited presence of banks from developed economies in Africa (with a high proportion of foreign banks currently being regional ones, which is different from previous decades when foreign banks were predominantly developed country ones – see Brownbridge et al., 2011) and the fact that existing subsidiaries mostly fund themselves locally and not via their parents. This, however, limits the contribution that these foreign banks make to national savings (Fuchs et al., 2012a). In addition, reportedly large capital buffers – often above levels required by Basel III – have served to increase the resilience of African banks during the global financial crisis, although this may have involved some costs for intermediation (Fuchs et al., 2012b).

The fact that financial sectors in LICs tend to be relatively smaller and simpler provides an advantage in that governments have more policy space to influence the future nature and scale of their financial system. Furthermore, the fact that the financial sector is smaller may imply that it is politically less power-ful; thus, potentially, this gives more autonomy to regulators and – more broadly governments – to shape the financial sector.

Thus, LICs have, on the one hand, the advantage of being latecomers to finan-cial development and can benefit from positive and negative lessons from experi-ences and research on other countries. On the other hand, the incompleteness of LIC financial systems means that important challenges remain on extending access (to all types of financial services) to those excluded, such as a high propor-tion of poor households, microenterprises and SMEs. More generally, it is diffi-cult to fund working capital and investment, especially for SMEs (and particularly at low spreads and longer maturities) crucial for growth and employment genera-tion. The financing of infrastructure is a well-known problem in LICs, and the mobilisation of sufficient long-term finance, as well as the most effective way to channel it to investment in that sector, is a key area of policy.

The challenges of financial regulation

A key lesson from recent crises has been the need for regulation to be both countercyclical and comprehensive to avoid the build-up of systemic risk (Griffith-Jones et al., 2009; Saurina and Repullo, 2011). Though there is agreement on these principles, there is far less consensus on how these should be implemented. A great deal of research and policy analysis is being carried out in the BIS, the IMF, the Basel Committee on Banking Supervision and the Financial Stability Board on these issues.

One of the key problems is that LICs are not represented at all or are heavily under-represented in these bodies. Therefore, there is insufficient focus in their work on how relevant these issues are for LICs and how they should be implemented in such countries.

Macro-prudential or countercyclical regulation

As discussed above, over the past decade, there has been rapid credit growth in a number of African countries. Rapid credit growth can give rise to systemic financial and macro-economic risks, making the design and implementation of appropriate macro-prudential regulation and supervision a policy priority in Africa. For example, the *Final Report of the Making Finance Work for Africa Conference*, in collaboration with the Association of African Central Banks (AACB) and the Bank of Uganda (2011), defined as most relevant and urgent for African LICs – within Basel III – the incorporation of macro-prudential supervision.

In the case of macro-prudential regulation, an important research issue is how can it be complementary to monetary policy in LICs? Macro-economic volatility, for instance, remains a problem, partly because many African countries' exports are concentrated in a few commodities, which makes their economies vulnerable to the large price shocks characteristic of commodities.

Comprehensive regulation in LICs

The international analyses of comprehensive regulation should be modified for the LIC context. This requires taking into account the different nature of the financial system in LICs, where, for example, very complex derivative products are not an issue, but where many financial transactions go through informal channels, or financial services are provided by non-banking institutions like retail shops or mobile service providers. The mobile payment service M-Pesa, developed in Kenya, is a case in point. M-Pesa was launched to target mobile subscribers who were un-banked and now has over seven million customers, both banked and un-banked. Light regulation in the testing phase of the financial product, on the principle of proportionate supervision, contributed to M-Pesa's rapid growth. However, at a later stage of product development and at a higher level of outreach, regulation may need to become significantly more stringent for M-Pesa's success to be sustainable (see Chapter 5 on Kenya for a more in-depth discussion). Therefore, the challenge of comprehensive regulation has a very different institutional character in LICs.

Also of high priority are regional/cross border issues. This refers not only to regulation of traditional international banks, but also to the rapidly emerging pan-African banks. As Fuchs et al. (2012b) point out, recent reforms of the international supervisory architecture concentrated on creating colleges of supervisors for all internationally operating banks. Representation of African supervisors (especially LICs) is very limited. This is a source of concern as an international bank may have a small part of its portfolio in an African country, but implies a very large share of their market for a particular LIC country. The role of the LIC supervisor in these colleges becomes too small, if any at all, with potentially serious consequences for financial stability and growth impact in the LIC country. A key issue is the political economy of how to enhance in practical terms the "voice" of LIC supervisors in cross border supervisory processes that have strong impacts on their economies, so as to overcome asymmetries of power, whose persistence often leads to economically inefficient outcomes for LICs.

A key source of macro-economic volatility, as well as of financial systemic risk, is generated by certain types of capital flows. As a result, there has been growing recognition, in the IMF and the BIS, as well as in the academic literature (for example Stiglitz and Ocampo, 2008; Korinek, 2011; Gallagher et al., 2012) on the need for management of the capital account. One of the newest research and policy challenges is how to most effectively combine regulation of capital flows and national countercyclical regulation? Again, discussion in LICs has been more limited (see Chapter 3 in this book for a review of the literature and policy issues for LICs). Are capital account management measures needed also in LICs and under what circumstances? In terms of best practice, when are capital account regulations more effective, and when are domestic prudential regulations, which focus on currency mismatches? How best can they complement each other? The large volume of bond issues by Sub-Saharan African sovereigns recently implies access to new sources of capital, but poses new risks, especially as monetary policy becomes less loose in the US. Past international experience tells us that there are surges and reversals of capital flows, often linked to developments in the advanced economies.

The analysis on capital account management has focused more on discouraging excessive short-term capital flows when they threaten to cause macroeconomic over-heating, over-valued exchange rates and increase financial sector systemic risk. However, there is also the important issue of attracting long-term capital flows, especially where it can provide technology transfer and access to new markets.

Conclusion

While the 2007/08 crisis originated in, and strongly hit, developed economies, financial systems in African LICs did not suffer crises, except for Nigeria. However, there is no reason for complacency in regulating African financial sectors. Fairly rapid credit growth in the context of limited regulatory and supervisory capacity, especially in some countries, suggests that the time is now to draw appropriate lessons from the North Atlantic crises for African countries. There is also no reason to believe that if major private financial crises have hit all other continents, Africa would be an exception, unless it proceeds very cautiously with financial liberalization and financial development, and accompanies it as well with strong and effective regulation.

Regulation of the financial sector should be countercyclical to prevent boom-bust cycles which can lead to developmentally costly crises, and comprehensive, to include all institutions that provide credit. Capital flows should also be prudently managed, and where appropriate, capital account regulations should complement domestic financial regulation, as is increasingly recognised by institutions such as the IMF and the BIS. Furthermore, the rapidly growing borrowing on the international bond markets by SSA sovereigns could lead to future problems, so this trend needs careful monitoring.

The fact that African LICs' financial systems are still relatively small in relation to the size of their economies allows more space for African policy-makers and regulators to try to shape their financial systems so that they serve well the needs of development, by helping support inclusive and sustainable growth (for example, by supporting much needed lending to the SMEs), as well as desirable structural change.

Furthermore, the fact that the financial sector is smaller in SSA countries, as a proportion of GDP, may imply that it is less powerful politically; thus, potentially this gives more autonomy to regulators and – more broadly – governments to shape the financial sector to serve the real economy.

A key issue is not just the size but also the structure of the financial sector. Because financial sectors are riddled with market imperfections and market gaps, it is important to have government interventions to correct these market imperfections (for example, the pro-cyclical nature of private lending) and institutional arrangements to fill market gaps (for example, sufficient long-term finance for helping finance private sector investment). Furthermore, to implement a particular vision and strategy of development, it is valuable for governments to have institutions and mechanisms to help finance development of particular sectors. In this context, it is important to design instruments and institutions that can perform such functions. Public development banks have worked well and often played a very important role in the development of many successful countries, such as Germany, Japan, South Korea, Brazil and others.

There is also growing consensus that smaller, more decentralised, banks may be more appropriate in LICs, especially to lend to SMEs, partly because they can know their customers better, reducing asymmetries of information. Overall, a more diversified banking system, with large and small banks, as well as private and public development banks, seems to offer benefits of diversification – and thus less systemic risk, complementarities in serving different sectors and functions, as well as increased competition for the provision of cheaper and appropriate financial services to the real economy.

Note

1 We are very grateful to Joseph Stiglitz for valuable comments on an earlier draft. We are also very grateful for very good comments received at the two ESRC/DFID workshops, in Ghana and Senegal, and at the IPD Africa Task force meetings in New York and Yokohama. Charles Harvey also gave detailed comments. We thank ESRC/DFID for their support for the research leading to this paper. We are grateful to Nshalati Hlungwane for excellent research assistance.

References

African Development Bank (2012) *African Guarantee Fund for Small and Medium-Sized Enterprises Information Memorandum*. Tunis.

African Development Bank (2013) *Our Operations: African Guarantee Fund.* Tunis (available online under: www.africanguaranteefund.com).

Association of African Central Banks (AACB) and the Bank of Uganda Financial Action Task Force (2011) *Final Report of the Making Finance Work for Africa Conference.*

Banco de Moçambique (2013) *Statistics, Overall Credit Statistics by Purpose.* Maputo (available online under: www.bancomoc.mz/Default_en.aspx).

Beck, T., Munzele Maimbo, S., Faye, I. and T. Triki (2011) *Financing Africa. Through the Crisis and Beyond.* Washington, D.C.: The World Bank.

Beck, T., Buyukkarabacak, B., Rioja, F. and N. Valev (2012) "Who Gets the Credit? And Does it Matter? Household vs. Firm Lending across Countries." *BE Journal of Macroeconomics*, 12.

Beck, T., Fuchs, M., Singer, D. and M. Witte (2014) *Making Cross-Border Banking Work for Africa.* Bonn and Washington, D.C.: GIZ and The World Bank.

Botha, A. (2011) *Interview Titled: Finance Strategies for SME Development.* CNBC Africa, May 5.

Brownbridge, M., Harvey, C. and F. Gockel (2011) *The Impact of Financial Sector Reform Since Independence* (available online under: http://svebookzz.com/pameh 769833.pdf).

CAHF (2012) *Housing Finance in Africa, 2012 Year Book*. Johannesburg: Centre for Affordable Housing Finance in Africa.

Cecchetti, S. G. and E. Kharroubi (2012) "Reassessing the Impact of Finance and Growth." *BIS Working Papers*, no. 381, Basel: Bank for International Settlement, Monetary and Economic Department, July.

de la Torre, A. and A. Ize (2011) "Containing Systemic Risk: Paradigm-based Perspectives on Regulatory Reform." *World Bank Policy Research Working Paper*, no. 5523.

Detragiache, E., Tressel, T. and P. Gupta (2008) "Foreign Banks in Poor Countries: Theory and Evidence." *The Journal of Finance*, 63, 2123–60.

DTI (2010) *The New Growth Path*. Pretoria: Department of Trade and Industry.

Easterly, W., Islam, R. and J. Stiglitz (2000) "Shaken and Stirred, Explaining Growth Volatility." *Annual Bank Conference on Development Economics*. Washington, D.C.: World Bank.

Fuchs, M., Losse-Mueller, T. Strobbe, F. and M. Witte (2012a) *African Financial Sectors and the European Debt Crisis: Will Trouble Blow across the Sahara?* Washington, D.C.: The World Bank.

Fuchs, M., Losse-Mueller, T. and M. Witte (2012b) "The Reform Agenda for Financial Regulation and Supervision in Africa." In: *Financial Sector Development in Africa: Opportunities and Challenges*, edited by Beck, T. and S. M. Maimbo. Washington, D.C.: The World Bank.

Gallagher, K. P., Griffith-Jones, S. and J. A. Ocampo (2012) "Capital Account Regulations for Stability and Development: A New Approach" *Issues in Brief*, no. 22, Boston: The Frederick S. Pardee Center for the Study of the Long-Range Future.

Griffith-Jones, S., Ocampo, J. A. and A. Ortis (2009) *Building on the Counter-Cyclical Consensus: A Policy Agenda*. Paper prepared for the High-Level Roundtable in Brussels "Towards Basel 3? Regulating the Banking Sector after the Crisis". October 12.

Griffith-Jones, S., Ocampo, J. A. and J. Stiglitz (2010) *Time for a Visible Hand: Lessons from the 2008 World Financial Crisis*. New York: Oxford University Press.

Haldane, A. G. and V. Madouros (2012) *The Dog and the Frisbee*. Bank of England Speech given at the Federal Reserve Bank of Kansas City's 36th Economic Policy Symposium, "The Changing Policy Landscape". Wyoming: Jackson Hole, August 31.

Honohan, P. and T. Beck (2007) *Making Finance Work for Africa*. Washington, D.C.: The World Bank.

IMF (2012a) "Walking Hand in Hand: Fiscal Policy and Growth in Advanced Economies." *Discussion Paper*. Washington, D.C.: International Monetary Fund.

IMF (2012b) *Global Financial Stability Report: Restoring Confidence and Progressing on Reforms*. Washington, D.C.: International Monetary Fund.

IMF (2012c) "Fourth Review Under the Policy Support Instrument and Request for Modification of Assessment Criteria." *IMF Country Report*. Washington, D.C.: International Monetary Fund.

Kasekende, L. A., Bagyenda, J. and M. Brownbridge (2011) *Basel III and the Global Reform of Financial Regulation: How Should Africa Respond? A Bank Regulator's Perspective*. Washington, D.C.: New Rules for Global Finance (available online under: www.new-rules.org/storage/documents/g20-fsb-imf/kasakende.docx).

Kindleberger, C. P. (1978) *Manias, Panics, and Crashes: A History of Financial Crises*. New York: Basic Books.

Korinek, A. (2011) "Systemic Risk-Taking: Amplification Effects, Externalities, and Regulatory Responses." *Working Paper Series*, no. 1345, Frankfurt: European Central Bank.

Laeven, L. and F. Valencia (2008) "Systemic Banking Crises: A New Database." *IMF Working Paper*, no. 08/224, Washington, D.C.: International Monetary Fund.

Laeven, L. and F. Valencia (2012) "Systemic Banking Crises: An Update." *IMF Working Paper*, no. 12/163, Washington, D.C.: International Monetary Fund.

Levine, R. (2005) "Finance and Growth: Theory and Evidence." In: *Handbook of Economic Growth*, edited by Aghion, P. and S. Durlauf, vol. 1, chapter 12, 865–34. Holland: Elsevier.

Minsky, H. P. (1974) "The Modeling of Financial Instability: An Introduction." In: *Modelling and Simulation*, vol. 5, Proceedings of the Fifth Annual Pittsburgh Conference, Instruments Society of America, 267–72.

Murinde, V. (2012) *Development-Orientated Financial Regulation. New Rules for Global Finance* (available online under: www.new-rules.org/storage/documents/g20-fsb-imf/murinde-kups.pdf).

Navajas, M. C. and A. Thegeya (2013) Financial Indicators and Banking Crises. *IMF Working Paper*, 13/263. IMF Statistics Departments. December (available online under: www.imf.org/external/pubs/ft/wp/2013/wp13263.pdf).

Rajan, R. G. (2005) *Has Financial Development Made the World Riskier?* Proceedings of the 2005 Jackson Hole Conference organized by the Kansas City Fed.

Rashid H. (2011) "Credit to Private Sector, Interest Rate Spread and Volatility in Credit Flows: Do Bank Ownership and Deposits Matter?" *UN DESA Working Paper*, no. 105, May.

Sanusi, L. S. (2010) *The Nigerian Banking Industry: What Went Wrong and the Way Forward*. Convocation Lecture delivered at the Convocation Square, Bayero University, Kano, February 26.

SARB (2013) *Annual Report*. Pretoria: South African Reserve Bank.

Saurina, J. S. and R. Repullo (2011) "The Countercyclical Capital Buffer of Basel III: A Critical Assessment." *Centre for Economic Policy Research Discussion Paper*, no. DP 8304.

Sengupta, R. (2007) "Foreign Entry and Bank Competition." *Journal of Financial Economics*, 84, 502–28.

Soludo, C. (2004) *Consolidating the Nigerian Banking Industry to Meet the Development Challenges of the 21 Century*. Address delivered to the Special Meeting of the Bankers' Committee, held on July 6. Abuja: Central Bank of Nigeria.

Standard Bank (2013) *Supporting SMEs* (available online under: http://sustainability. standardbank.com/socioeconomic-development/enterprise-development/supporting-smes/).

Stiglitz, J. and J. A. Ocampo (2008) *Capital Market Liberalization and Development*. New York: Oxford University Press.

The World Bank (2013a) *Enterprise Surveys, What Businesses Experience*. Washington, D.C.: The World Bank (available online under: www.enterprisesurveys.org).

The World Bank (2013b) *World DataBank*. Washington, D.C.: The World Bank (available online under: www.databank.worldbank.org).

Tobin, J. (1984) "On the Efficiency of the Financial System." *Lloyds Bank Review*, 153, 1–15.

2 Financial regulation, stability and growth in low-income countries

A review of the evidence and agenda for research

Stephen Spratt

Introduction

> For many low income countries, especially in Africa, financial regulation policies constitute the foundation basis for the mechanisms through which financial development exerts a positive impact on economic growth and poverty reduction.
>
> (Murinde, 2012)

Without effective regulation, financial systems become unstable, potentially triggering crises with devastating effects on the real economy. The continuing impacts of the global financial crisis of 2007–8 show how large these can become. While the avoidance of crises is a necessary condition for productive economic activity to flourish, it is not sufficient. Another more positive side to regulation is one which shapes the evolution of financial structures and influences the ways in which financial actors serve the real economy. The purpose of regulation is thus twofold: to maintain financial stability and to promote inclusive economic growth. Achieving the right balance between these objectives is a delicate, but crucial task. Too great a focus on stability stifles growth, while a headlong dash for growth is very likely to sow the seeds of future crises.

The structures of low-income countries' (LICs) real and financial sectors are different to those in developed countries. Institutional capacity to implement certain kinds of financial regulation is also generally lower. Therefore, the set of regulatory instruments best able to maximise growth, while maintaining stability, should also be different.

While this has always been broadly accepted in principle – if rarely in practice – the global financial crisis highlighted a more fundamental issue. Given what we learnt about 'sophisticated' finance, it is simply no longer tenable to view the regulatory practices that evolved in the world's major financial centres as a model to which developing countries should aspire. As regulatory options continue to be re-assessed in developed economies, the time is ripe to do the same in developing countries in general, and LICs in particular.

There has been no shortage of financial sector reforms in LICs. The wave of financial liberalisation in sub-Saharan Africa in the 1980s and 1990s is a testament to the types of reforms the region has been subject to. However, these reforms clearly did not deliver the boost to growth that their advocates predicted (Nissanke and Aryeetey, 1998). Although financial systems in LICs have been relatively stable in recent years, it is difficult to argue that they have become engines of growth. Developing systems that are stable but also facilitate inclusive growth to the maximum degree possible remains an elusive goal.

It is in this context that this chapter asks the question: *How can financial regulation best support inclusive growth and financial stability in LICs?* Drawing on an extensive literature on financial systems, the chapter reviews the evidence on this question and presents the main findings.[1]

To unpack the above question, a conceptual framework was developed to capture the most important ways by which the financial sector may impact on growth and stability in LICs. The four most significant channels identified are:[2]

i) **Private sector credit from the banking sector**, which is the most developmentally important channel considered. Here we are concerned with which banking sector structures and behaviours are best suited to balancing growth with stability.

ii) **Access to finance**, a crucial foundation of inclusive growth with major implications for stability. The key question is which financial structures and behaviours are most likely to deliver affordable services that are suited to the needs of poor people.

iii) **Government interactions with the financial system** which, in LICs, are widely seen as crucial for financial stability and growth, with much of the debate focusing on the level and nature of government borrowing.

iv) **Capital markets**, which remain nascent in most LICs, but reforms to promote them have been widely recommended and implemented.

The next step is to consider how regulation mediates the impacts of financial systems on stability and growth. Two forms are identified. First, by influencing the day-to-day behaviour of financial market actors, regulation has *direct* effects – how much a bank chooses to lend to an individual or firm on a given day, for example. Second, regulation influences how the financial system evolves structurally, creating *indirect* effects – the concentration or diversity of the banking system, for example, will influence the level, terms and outreach of lending it provides.

Perhaps the most important finding of this literature review is that LIC-specific evidence on these issues is limited. Most research looks at developing countries as a group, or at high- or middle-income countries. Only a small proportion examines LICs exclusively. With this caveat, this chapter summarises the evidence that exists.[3] The remainder of the chapter examines the evidence on each of the four impact channels identified above. The next section on banking is the largest, reflecting its importance in LICs, but also the weight of evidence available. Subsequent sections examine access to finance, government borrowing, and the non-bank financial sector. The chapter concludes with a discussion of research gaps and priorities.

Bank credit to the private sector: the role of financial structure and regulation

By far the most important financial channel for both growth and stability in LICs is the level and type of credit supplied to the private sector by banks. There are two elements to this: what banking structures and what types of behaviour of financial actors are most supportive of stability and inclusive growth in LICs; and how financial regulation should be designed and implemented to support these structures and behaviours. In this section, the evidence is first assessed on the ways in which the size and structure of the banking system affects growth and stability, including whether banks are publicly or privately owned, or are branches or subsidiaries of international banking groups. Second, the role of regulation is considered.

Financial and banking sector size

Perhaps the most basic question to consider is the optimal size of the financial sector. Recent research, based on a study from 1960–2010, finds a threshold of 80–100 per cent of GDP, beyond which financial sector expansion is likely to have a negative impact upon growth (Arcand, Berkes and Panizza, 2012). The authors suggest three reasons. First, to the extent that finance tends towards crises (Minsky, 1992), the larger the financial system the greater the risk. Second, as finance grows relative to other sectors it sucks in resources – including human resources – that could be better used elsewhere (Tobin, 1984). Third, the larger the financial system the greater the risk that it becomes decoupled from the real economy and focuses on non-productive – and destabilising – 'innovation' (De la Torre, Feyen and Ize, 2013).

So how big should it be? There are two main perspectives on this question. The first is that the real economy should determine financial sector size, so that national authorities can rescue banks if necessary (Schoenmaker and Werkhoven, 2012). While this seems perfectly reasonable, it has implications for many developed countries, including those with relatively small financial systems. Bank balance sheets in France and Germany, for example, are three to four times the level of total national income. In Luxembourg, they are 20 times larger than GDP.

The second position is that banks should be as large as required by domestic companies (Krause, Brimmer and Dahl, 1975; Grosse and Goldberg, 1991). Companies prefer to use banks from their own countries, and large companies need large banks. Consequently, relatively small countries with large multi-national corporations – such as the Netherlands – should also have relatively large banking sectors (Dermine and Schoenmaker, 2010). The optimal size of the banking system will also be affected by what it does of course. A small sector serving the real economy effectively will be more beneficial than a very large sector creating esoteric financial instruments and trading them amongst itself (Schoenmaker and Werkhoven, 2012).

Unsurprisingly, the overwhelming majority of research on this question is based on developed country experience. LICs have small financial systems, so research tends to look at how they can be increased in size, not whether they are overly large. Developed country research is relevant, however, as it shows that, beyond a certain point, financial systems can become too large, and that the activities that finance undertakes will influence its ideal size.

The structure of private banking

The ideal structure of the sector – particularly the degree of concentration and competition – has been the subject of considerable research. Some find a negative relationship between banking sector concentration and income growth (Deidda and Fattouh, 2005). Others have questioned the focus on concentration in banking, arguing that it is not the same as competiveness, which is what really matters (Demirgüç-Kunt, 2006). Competition is seen as important for growth for a number of reasons: i) to enable firms and households to access financial services; ii) to ensure financial institutions seek out productive opportunities; iii) to encourage cost-efficiency; iv) to facilitate the transmission of monetary policy; v) to boost economic growth; and vi) to enhance financial stability (Amidu and Wolfe, 2011).

While the positive impact on growth is generally accepted, the relationship between competition and financial stability is not. The 'competition-fragility' perspective holds that banks operating in *non-competitive* environments hold more capital to protect themselves, enhancing stability. The 'franchise-value' hypothesis suggests that banks with monopoly power have higher franchise values, which they protect by avoiding excessive risk (Keeley, 1990). Other research finds low competition to be good for stability as banks have fewer, better quality borrowers (Boot and Thakor, 2000). Monopoly power may also enable banks to reduce information asymmetries, again enhancing stability.

There is some evidence that negative impacts of competition on stability are more likely for commercial banks than stakeholder-type institutions such as cooperatives (LopezPuertas-Lamy and Gutierrez, 2012). While some argue that fewer, larger banks are easier to monitor, which improves stability (Allen and Gale, 2000) this needs to be set against too-big-to-fail concerns, where large banks threaten stability due to excessive risk taking.

Empirically, Amidu and Wolfe (2011) report mixed findings on this question. Some researchers find that concentration is negative for stability (Uhde and Heimeshoff, 2009), while others find the opposite (Schaeck, Cihak et al., 2009). Berger and Klapper (2009) find support for both perspectives. What seems clear is that simply increasing competition will not guarantee greater stability. Rather, the impact will be determined by the structure of the existing banking sector, and the type of competition that is encouraged.

While measures to increase banking sector competitiveness are likely to have positive effects on growth, they may not resolve financing constraints in some key sectors. A recent study of 1994–2007 banking sector reform in Ethiopia, for example, found that reduced sector concentration was not enough and other measures are needed to incentivise financial institutions to lend to small and medium-sized enterprises (SMEs) (Fanta, 2012). As with competition and financial stability, the key determinant appears to be the *type* of competition. Relatively similar institutions competing for the most lucrative parts of the market, for example, will not lead to more finance for sectors such as SMEs. Rather:

> What matters most is setting up a financial sector that can serve the competitive sectors of an economy. In many poorer countries, that means focusing on activities dominated by small-scale manufacturing, farming and services firms. The size and sophistication of financial institutions and markets in the developed world are not appropriate in [LICs]. Small local banks are the best entities for providing financial services to the enterprises and households that are most important in terms of comparative advantage.
>
> (Lin, 2009)

Other research supports this approach, finding that higher shares of small, private, efficient banks are associated with higher rates of growth in both developed and developing countries (Berger et al., 2004). While all agree that small banks are important, others stress the importance of also maintaining larger banks. Due to a lack of capital buffers, for example, small banks may be too risk-averse than is optimal in LICs (Banerjee, 2009). Small banks may also lack the resources to fund corporate expansion, suggesting a diversified structure – with small, local banks serving individuals and households, and larger banks serving the entrepreneurial sector – may be ideal (Schoar, 2009; Zhuang, Gunatilake et al., 2009).

It is unlikely that financial systems will naturally evolve in this way. Liberalisation and increased competition enables large banks to grow, gaining efficiencies of scale and competitive advantages (Mugume, 2007; Hauner and Peiris, 2008). A process whereby banks become larger in size and more homogenous may be negative for stability: 'Where competition is between institutions that are very similar, it can intensify to the point where it becomes destructive' (Decker, 2012).

Because of varied funding sources, clients and returns expectations: 'financial systems with a mixed array of ownership structures, i.e. a significant proportion of SBs [stakeholder banks] competing with CBs [commercial banks], tend to be more stable' (LopezPuertas-Lamy and Gutierrez, 2012). As well as stability, diversity may also be positive for growth, as it encourages competition and innovation amongst institutions with different cost structures, approach to innovation, and strategies for meeting their customers' needs (Decker, 2012).

Public vs. private banks

Some investments, which are crucial for development, do not yield high financial returns. As a result, the private sector will invest less than is socially optimal. Similarly, providing finance to some sectors – SMEs or infrastructure, for example – produces positive spillover effects beyond the immediate investment. Again, private finance will invest less in these sectors than is ideal for society. Such externalities and other market failures[4] are often used to justify state intervention in the financial sector. Far from being anomalies, market failures are commonplace, particularly in under-developed financial systems (Stiglitz, 1993; Beck, Maimbo et al., 2011). As finance matures these problems should reduce, but they will not disappear. Many important market failures remain common in countries at all levels of development. Government intervention in agriculture, infrastructure, or SME financing is not restricted to developing countries. Canada, for example, has one of the most successful public finance institutions focused on SMEs (Rudolph, 2009).

There is, therefore, a clear case for public intervention in finance, and publicly owned banks would seem the obvious way of doing this. Given this, why are successful public banks not ubiquitous? The answer is that we also need to weigh the risks of 'government failure' (Krueger, 1991). This has proved to be a problem with government-owned banks, particularly in Africa (Caprio and Honohan, 2004; Klapper and Zaidi, 2005; Manganhele, 2010; Gutierrez and Rudolph, 2011). At a time when the reputation of public banks was very low, an influential paper appeared to show a negative relationship with growth (La Porta, Lopez-de-Silanes and Shleifer, 2002).[5] This study was extensively used to support bank privatisation in developing countries.

Following the 2007–8 financial crisis, this perception has changed. As well as triggering a re-assessment of the efficiency and effectiveness of private banks, public banks are now seen to perform a vital role in some countries, providing counter-cyclical finance when private sources freeze (Luna-Martinez and Vicente, 2012). Researchers also have begun to re-examine the econometric evidence, finding that when good measures of institutional quality are included in regressions, results on government ownership no longer hold (Andrianova, Demetriades and Shortand, 2010). Including post-crisis data, and controlling for institutional quality, one study has found that the government ownership is positively associated with growth.

Why might this be the case? The authors suggest that public banks may be less susceptible to the short-term, speculative financial practices that underpinned the 2007–8 crisis, and more likely to invest in long-term, productive enterprises in growth-supporting sectors such as SMEs and infrastructure. If these findings are correct, and the goal is to combine stability with inclusive growth, the key question today is how to create *good* government-owned banks and in particular development banks, that achieve these goals while avoiding the risks associated with governments and finance.

A number of things seem to be important. In the case of development banks, those with overly wide or vague mandates are less likely to succeed than those which address a well-defined market failure (Scott, 2007). Clear mandates also allow banks to be held to account while avoiding the danger of direct political involvement (Schapiro, 2012). Mandates also need to adjust to changing conditions, evolving dynamically over time (Thorne and Toit, 2009).

Also, how development banks are financed is important, for two reasons. First, many argue that banks need to be financially independent to avoid political interference (Yeyati, Micco and Panizza, 2007; Gutierrez and Rudolph, 2011; Luna-Martinez and Vicente, 2012). Second, the nature of the financing will influence how development banks behave. If development banks are funded purely from commercial sources, they will face the same incentives as private banks. To enable them to provide long-term 'patient' finance at reasonable cost, they need to have access to such finance themselves. How this is actually done in different countries will vary. It is the underlying principle that matters.

On the issue of the ideal size for development banks, there are advantages of scale. Sectors such as infrastructure require large, long-term investments. To act counter-cyclically, banks' balance-sheets must be large enough to impact upon aggregate demand. One suggestion from a leading development bank practitioner is that this should be at least 5 per cent of GDP.

Foreign vs. domestic banks

Until relatively recently, the consensus was that foreign banks are a stabilising presence in LICs. As well as what was seen as more 'sophisticated' risk-management procedures, such banks could potentially draw on external resources from their parent institution if financial conditions became volatile in the domestic market. Positive growth impacts were also expected via a number of channels: they would raise the efficiency of domestic banks; improve the financial services for firms and individuals; transfer knowledge and technology; enhance access to international capital; and improve host country supervision and regulation (Barth, Caprio et al., 2004).

Once again, the 2007–8 crisis altered perceptions. The difference from previous crises was that this one was based in developed countries. Rather than being a stabilising force, banks from these countries became a mechanism for transmitting the crisis, particularly where they controlled a large proportion of domestic assets. In some countries, foreign banks reduced credit more rapidly and sharply than domestic banks. This was particularly the case in Eastern Europe where foreign bank penetration is high (Vogel and Winkler, 2012). Evidence that foreign banks had stoked unsustainable booms in the pre-crisis period in Eastern Europe also emerged (Beck, 2010). The fact that banks re-allocated capital away from 'peripheral' towards 'priority' markets in the crisis is particularly concerning for LICs (Düwel and Frey, 2012).

These events have prompted a re-assessment of the benefits of foreign banks. Even before the crisis, there was evidence to suggest that foreign banks were less likely than domestic banks to lend to key sectors such as SMEs (Claessens, 2006). A growing body of research supports this, and also suggests that high levels of foreign bank penetration reduces the overall supply of credit (Detragiache, Tressel and Gupta, 2008). While some researchers dispute these findings, the evidence on financial inclusion is clear: foreign banks tend to target wealthier sections of the population, negatively affecting outreach (Beck and Peria, 2010).

For the domestic banking industry, the benefits of efficiency have to be set against the potential for foreign banks to stifle the development of the domestic banking system. A study of Tanzania, for example, finds that large foreign banks dominate the financial sector, acting as a barrier to competition from other financial players (Simpasa, 2011).

As with the structure of the domestic private banking sector, and the potential contribution of public development banks, the net benefits of foreign bank participation is likely to be the greatest when they are part of a diversified 'ecosystem' of financial institutions. In some countries foreign banks hold more than 95 per cent of banking assets. In such circumstances, the risks of foreign bank participation are likely to be maximised and the benefits minimised.

Banking sector structure and banking crises

What evidence do we have on how the structure of banking affects the probability of banking crises? An important question is whether state ownership of bank increases the risks of banking crises. Caprio and Peria (2001) find that high levels of state ownership in 1980 are associated with a greater risk of a crisis between 1980–97. Barth et al., (2001) support this finding with simple cross-country regressions. As we saw with growth, however, more recent research suggests that these results were driven by poor general institutional quality rather than the quantity of public bank ownership *per se* (Andrianova, Demetriades and Shortand, 2010).

Foreign banks, in turn, may create or reduce volatility – and thus contribute to financial instability – depending on the source of the volatility. A crisis that originates in the developed 'home' market of an international bank could trigger a crisis in the countries in which it operates, assuming market shares were large enough. In contrast, if a nascent banking crisis originates in the LIC where international banks were operating, they would be expected to have a stabilising influence.

An institutional feature of banking that is often associated with the propensity for crises is the existence and design of deposit insurance schemes. While often deemed necessary to protect depositors, such schemes create moral hazard. They have thus been associated with an increased risk of crises due to their tendency to encourage risk-taking, particularly in weak institutional environments where counter-acting forces are not effective (Demirgüç-Kunt, 2005; McCoy, 2006; Khan, 2009). While context is very important, successful deposit insurance schemes are designed to fit country conditions, are funded by banks themselves, and have a cap on deposits covered. Effective political accountability is strongly associated with successful schemes (Kane, 2000). When weighing risks and potential benefits, factors such as these will determine whether adopting a deposit insurance scheme is a good idea in a particular country.

Bank sector structure: the role of regulation

If more competition in banking is positive for growth, how can regulation and policy affect this? Clearly, relatively low regulatory barriers to entry are important

(Claessens, 2009), though this needs to be balanced by the need to ensure new entrants are stable.

Fostering and maintaining a diverse financial system requires regulation to suit different types of institutions. Regulation of microfinance institutions (MFIs) affects the way these evolve; the more regulation mirrors that for commercial banks, the more MFIs will act like such banks. Applying the full weight of prudential banking regulation to MFIs will drive consolidation in the sector, as only larger institutions will be able to comply. If the goal is to encourage a diverse mix of large and small institutions serving their customers in a variety of ways, a 'bespoke regulation, tailored to different circumstances, is needed' (UNCTAD, 2015). The same is true for stakeholder institutions such as Savings and Credit Co-operative Associations (SACCOs). The mechanical application of commercial bank regulation is likely to be too onerous, and also to restrict these institutions from certain forms of valuable activity (Muthuma, 2011). Regulation should facilitate the diverse objectives of MFIs, SACCOs and other institutions focused on sectors such as agriculture or SMEs, not stifle them.

As regards the regulation of development banks, an issue is whether these banks should be subject to the same regulation and supervision as the private sector. As we have seen, public banks should have development objectives that are distinct from those of commercial banks. Given this, there is also a case for designing regulatory and supervisory approaches to support these objectives. The application of Basel II guidelines to public banks, for example, could prevent them from operating in a counter-cyclical way (Gottschalk and Sen, 2006).

The regulation and supervision of foreign banks also raises important issues,[7] at the heart of which is the issue of 'home' versus 'host' country supervision. The question is whether banks operating in LICs are branches or subsidiaries. The former are legally and financially part of the parent bank, while the latter are independent legal entities. Broadly, the parent bank is responsible for the solvency of its branches, but not its subsidiaries. Host country supervisors thus have more control over subsidiaries than the branches of international banks. They are also insulated from any problems the parent bank may encounter.

Generally speaking, therefore, subsidiaries are preferable to branches in LICs. Financial regulation and supervision has more capacity to balance inclusive growth with stability if authorities can influence the banks operating in their jurisdictions. Maintaining a balance between stability and growth requires different approaches at different times. Regulation and supervision thus needs to adjust dynamically.

Micro- and macroprudential regulation in LICs

For microprudential regulation in LICs, there are three questions to address: *who* should regulate/supervise; *what* should they regulate/supervise; and *how* should they do this?

For who should supervise, we first need to consider if a single agency should be responsible for financial supervision, or should this be apportioned to different agencies?

Both single and multiple agency approaches have strengths and weaknesses. The UK is often cited as a good example of the former and the US the latter – both were at the heart of the 2007–8 crises, despite the difference in approach. In LICs financial systems are less complex, but there are also other important differences. First, non-banking sectors are small, weakening arguments for multiple supervisors relative to more diversified financial systems. Second, available supervisory capacity is more limited. This suggests that a unified approach – where limited capacity is concentrated in a single agency – may be preferable in an LIC context (Beck, Maimbo et al., 2011).

The next question is which institution(s) should undertake this function? The central bank is the most respected financial institution in most LICs, and also often is where expertise and capacity are concentrated. Therefore, it makes sense for the supervisory authority to be concentrated in the central bank (Quintyn and Taylor, 2007). This is supported by research, which finds central bank involvement in supervision to be positively associated with financial sector development (Cuadro, Gallego et al., 2003) and bank profitability (Abdennour and Khediri, 2010).

For the question of *what* should be regulated and supervised, the answer is: everything, but not in the same way. As described above, regulation should ideally fit the size, complexity, and systemic risk of institutions, but also encourage innovative business models and support specific development-oriented sectors.

The question of *how* to regulate and supervise has both a general and a specific answer. In general terms, the issue is whether to adopt 'rules' or 'principles-based' approaches.[8] Historically, rules-based regulation has been the norm. Principles-based approaches have emerged in response to the increasing complexity of finance, where it may not be possible to specify with precise rules what is acceptable behaviour in any given circumstance, and fixed rules create easy targets for 'gaming the system'. A nuanced application of principles has the potential to avoid these problems. Others contend that the capacity requirements for principles-based supervision may be too high. As financial complexity is not an issue in LICs, and principles-based approaches rely on a high level of supervisory capacity, which may not hold, rules-based approaches are likely to remain appropriate (Ping, 2011).

What about more specific tools and instruments of regulation and supervision? The principal tool employed in recent decades is regulatory capital, held as a buffer against risk.[9] It is often argued that banks in developing countries need higher capital buffers because of greater risks: economic shocks have been more frequent and severe; bank portfolios in LICs reflect their economies, and thus tend to be concentrated in a narrow range of sectors, increasing the likelihood of correlated default (Rabanal, Narain et al., 2003); key sectors in LICs – such as natural resources – are also volatile (Kasekende, Bagyenda and Brownbridge, 2012).

While regulatory capital remains a crucial policy tool, many developing countries have also retained a wider 'tool-kit' of regulatory instruments than is common in developed countries:

For example, many African countries impose restrictions on banks' large loan concentrations, foreign exchange exposures and business activities which fall outside of traditional commercial banking. They also impose minimum liquid asset requirements and more stringent loan loss provisioning requirements than is the case in advanced economies. As a consequence, one can argue that African bank regulation is more robust than that which prevails in the advanced economies in that the former relies less exclusively on just one regulatory instrument, the capital adequacy requirement, which in the advanced economies proved very vulnerable to "gaming" by banks to lower the amount of capital they had to hold.

(Kasekende, Bagyenda and Brownbridge, 2012)

In developed economies, direct restrictions on the concentration of portfolios, foreign borrowing levels, or 'non-traditional' banking activities came to be seen as 'crude' and unnecessary. Similarly, the requirement to hold reserves in the central bank was also largely phased out. As noted in the quote above, however, there is a good case for retaining a range of instruments to respond to different situations, and reduce the risk of market actors 'gaming' a single instrument.

The discussion of regulatory capital leads us to the Basel Capital Accords. Despite the fact that the Accords were designed for internationally active banks in developed countries, they soon became the global standard in all countries. It is outside the scope of this chapter to recount the long development of Basel II, and its more recent evolution into Basel III. In brief, Basel II gave far more weight to the internal risk assessments of banks when setting capital requirements. In the light of the 2007–8 crisis, however, it was realised that: a) banks had been insufficiently capitalised; b) banks' assessments of risk were deeply flawed; and c) some significant risks had not been understood. In response, Basel III brought important restrictions on leverage, the introduction of liquidity coverage ratios (LCRs),[10] and counter-cyclical capital buffers.

While Basel is an important global process, its applicability to LICs is questionable. Some have suggested that implementation could reduce growth in developing countries (Abdel-Baki, 2012). Others question the general applicability of Basel approaches to LICs (Salami, 2012). Pointing out that most African countries have capital requirements well in excess of the Basel 8 per cent minimum, African regulators argue that, in Africa, a much broader approach than that of Basel III is required for a more resilient banking system, including stronger supervision to ensure enforcement and an effective macroprudential tool-kit (Bagyenda et al., 2011).

The issue of macroprudential regulation has become prominent since the 2007–8 crisis. It is concerned with system-wide risk, which the FSB (2011) breaks down into two categories: the evolution of risk *over time*; and the distribution of risk at *a point in time*. The first concerns the tendency of financial systems to procyclicality – or 'booms and busts'; the second, the degree of concentration and correlation in the exposures of different financial institutions (i.e. 'herding'). We now have considerable evidence that: a) banks are prone to procyclical behaviour and herding; b) they fail to make sufficient provisioning for future losses (Laeven and Majnoni, 2003); and c) macroprudential tools[11] can effectively smooth booms and busts (Levieuge, 2010).

While LIC financial systems are less complex, this does not mean that macroprudential considerations are not important. Both procyclicality and herding are significant issues, and cycles of boom and bust have long been a feature of developing and emerging economies.

Perhaps the most important difference between developing and developed countries is the potentially destabilising effects of capital inflows. Given the small size of their economies relative to international finance, LICs are particularly vulnerable to procyclical behaviour and herding. While the focus of this review is on the regulation of domestic finance to balance growth and stability, it is impossible to ignore the potential impact of external inflows on these outcomes. A country could have a perfect system of micro- and macroprudential regulation, and still be undermined by unsustainable capital flows into key sectors (Kasekende, Brixova and Ndikumana, 2010).

This suggests that external mechanisms are needed to complement domestic efforts. A number of proposals have been made, including a variety of capital controls that may be used strategically to manage inflows over time (Ocampo, 2003; Akyüz, 2008). This is no longer controversial. Since the 2007–8 crisis, the IMF has reversed its long-standing opposition, and accepted that capital controls are necessary under certain conditions (see the next chapter in this book).

Access to finance: the role of financial structure and regulation

As with the review on banking in LICs, this section first assesses how financial structures affect access to finance and thus inclusive growth and stability. It also examines how financial regulation can influence these structures as well as the behaviour of financial actors.

The challenge is how to provide accessible and affordable financial services that are suited to the needs of poor people.[12] As was shown all too clearly by the sub-prime mortgage market in the US, providing financial services that are unaffordable can have serious implications for financial stability.

Accessibility, affordability, growth, and stability

On the question of accessibility, financial exclusion in LICs remains the norm: only 24 per cent of adults in sub-Saharan Africa have an account at a formal institution, compared with 33 per cent in South Asia. While the developing country average is 41 per cent, the figure for those living on less than $1 per day is 23 per cent (Demirgüç-Kunt and Klapper, 2012). Similarly, the costs of financial services remain much higher in developing than developed countries, and the gap is particularly pronounced in sub-Saharan Africa (Beck, Maimbo et al., 2011).

While there has been some progress on understanding the types of financial services the poor need, there is little evidence of such services being provided at scale by commercial banks or MFIs (IFPRI, 2002; Juanah, 2005). An exception to this trend may be mobile banking, the exponential growth of which suggests strongly that it is offering valuable service. We therefore have a situation where financial services are often not available to people in LICs, or are excessively expensive, and are not tailored to the needs of the poor. While microfinance has increased the supply of financial services, it has also led to problems of over-indebtedness. Mobile banking seems to be an exception to these trends.

Some of these problems are inherent to LICs. Providing physical access in rural areas with widely dispersed populations is expensive. Small loan sizes exacerbate this by creating high transaction costs per loan. Relatively small national markets limit opportunities to lower costs through economies of scale (Lyons, 2010), while asymmetric information on creditworthiness raises borrowing costs and leads to credit rationing (Akerlof, 1970; Stiglitz and Weiss, 1981). Finally, few borrowers can mitigate these issues with collateral. The question is whether high finance costs simply reflect these characteristics, or could in fact be lower. While we are focused on individuals and households in this section, this is also a crucially important issue for businesses in LICs.

The problems described appear to be made considerably worse by bank ineffi-ciency and a lack of competition. A study of sub-Saharan African countries, for example, found that banks could save 20–30 per cent of total costs if they were operating efficiently (Chen, 2009). Limited competition is the most important problem cited in comparative research on banking (Demirgüç-Kunt and Huizinga, 1999; Beck, Maimbo et al., 2011), as well as country case studies (Chirwa, 2001).

What has been done to address these problems? Mobile banking has prospered, to a significant extent, because of its ability to lower transaction costs (Beck, Maimbo et al., 2011). Another promising way of reducing transaction costs is through 'branchless banking', where financial services are provided through retail outlets in rural areas. This has proved highly successful in Latin America, and provides an interesting example for African countries (Alexandre, Mas et al., 2011). Microfinance has expanded strongly in recent years, and this is also partly due to relatively low transaction costs, as well as the peer-lending model, which reduces uncertainties over credit risk. A more systematic approach to problems of asymmetric information is to establish third party credit bureaux to collate and provide information.

Although the empirical evidence linking credit bureaux coverage to financial sector development is clear (McDonald and Schumacher, 2007), only four countries in sub-Saharan Africa have coverage at half the adult population or more, and all of these are served by private credit bureaux from the adjacent South Africa. Outside this group, coverage falls to single digits, or to zero for 39 sub-Saharan African countries.[13]

Banking sector structure and financial access

What do we know about how the size and structure of the financial sector could affect access to finance positively? While the simplest option would be to focus on increasing the size of the sector, and assume this will address financial inclusion, this is unlikely to be sufficient. Although a deep financial system is likely to also be broad, this does not automatically follow, particularly at early stages of financial development (Beck, 2008).

The next question is whether large or small banks are better? Some propose that larger banks, which have developed the economies of scale needed to deliver affordable financial services, should be primarily encouraged. Others argue the opposite, suggesting that small banks, rooted in local communities, are better for inclusion (Lin, 2009; Zhuang, Gunatilake et al., 2009).

Other research stresses the importance of sector-focused institutions, such as rural banks, for inclusion (Addo and Kwarteng, 2012). In the light of the success of mobile banking – particularly M-Pesa in Kenya – the potential of technology to promote financial inclusion is the subject of a large and growing literature (Kpodar and Andrianaivo, 2011; Caballero, 2012). A more specific area of research positively links the use of ICT to the inclusion impact of rural and agricultural development banks (Kloeppinger-Todd and Sharma, 2010).

An overview of this research leads to a number of conclusions. First, while competition is important, not all forms will promote financial inclusion. Competition between banks can focus on gaining market share in the most lucrative parts of the market, which is unlikely to be expanding financial access in rural areas. What appears to be needed is diversity, with different types of institutions focusing on different market segments.

Indeed, a diverse system that includes different types of institutions including SACCOs, is likely to be most positive for growth and stability-supporting financial access. Plurality of mandate and geography should extend physical access, while competition holds down costs and encourages innovation. A diverse system should also be more stable and, by producing a greater range of products to serve the interests of different groups, positive for inclusive growth (Cuevas and Fisher, 2006).

Access to finance: the role of regulation

What can regulation and policy do to address these issues? The most direct solution to overly expensive credit is interest rate caps or limits on spreads. The former has been hotly debated in the microfinance sector. Those focused on impact and outreach see very high interest rates as developmentally damaging. For interest rate spreads, one study finds that ceilings raise intermediation costs, but protect lenders and borrowers from macroeconomic disturbances, and are therefore desirable in developing countries with volatile macro environments (Özyıldırım, 2010).

Increasing competition requires new market entrants, but this needs to be balanced with financial stability concerns. Regulatory hurdles thus need to be high enough to encourage stable and sustainable financial institutions, but not so high that it is impossible to enter the market. This is no different for MFIs than for commercial banks (Meagher, 2010).

A further point is the cost of regulatory compliance, which in many African countries is seen as excessive (Beck, Maimbo et al., 2011). The distinction made between commercial banking and MFIs in the previous section is also relevant for financial access. While there is consensus that MFIs need to be brought into the regulatory framework, the question is whether this should be on the same terms as commercial banks? The task is to ensure a 'level playing field', particularly for deposit taking institutions, while avoiding making the regulatory unnecessarily burdensome for small MFIs (Beck et al., 2010).

Government borrowing

In what ways could government borrowing from the financial sector affect growth and stability? In both cases, borrowing has potentially positive effects. Establishing a yield curve creates a benchmark to price corporate bonds. Second, government borrowing provides instruments for financial institutions to buy and trade, facilitating financial sector development. Third, borrowing enables the government to invest in sectors such as economic and social infrastructure that the private sector does not reach, and to smooth and manage expenditures over time.

Too much borrowing, however, can negatively affect growth by 'crowding out' domestic investment and increase debt service costs to unsustainable levels. Debt sustainability is generally measured in terms of total debt as a proportion of a country's GDP. The threshold is debatable. According to Rogoff and Reinhart (2010) it may be 90 per cent, while other researchers found it actually might be higher than that (Herndon, Ash and Pollin, 2014). An important point is that these thresholds are based on the experience of developed rather than developing countries. We cannot assume that what held in a set of developed countries, on average, over the post-war period holds in LICs today.

In any case, given that debt sustainability depends a great deal on the size of GDP and how it evolves over time, the ability to generate high and sustained growth is a major influence on the sustainability of debt. Of course, the limits to borrowing are not just in terms of debt sustainability, but also due to possible private sector crowding out. Crowding out concerns could be addressed by limiting the amount of government debt that private financial institutions are allowed to hold. The level could vary depending on the asset-liability structures of institutions, but within an overall cap such that financial sector development was encouraged but crowding out avoided.

Capital markets

Capital markets in LICs remain small. Of 36 LICs, nine have functioning stock markets, most with low levels of market capitalisation and turnover. Corporate bond markets are even less developed, with only a handful of countries having any meaningful activity. Despite this, considerable effort has gone into promoting capital markets in LICs, seen by the Bretton Woods institutions and others as crucial for long-term growth. This section reviews the evidence and considers which elements of capital market development should be prioritised.

Stock markets

For Singh (2008), stock market development has been promoted in LICs for two reasons. First, to provide an alternative source of capital – and more efficient capital allocation – to public finance institutions such as development banks. Second, the development of stock markets was seen as a 'natural progression' as countries develop and become more complex: developed countries have stock markets, so developing countries should naturally aspire to the same. A third rationale is that developing country stock markets offer the opportunity for developed country investors to obtain higher returns than are available in their markets, providing additional finance in capital-scarce LICs (Reisen, 1994).

These arguments proved persuasive in the 1990s, when many LIC stock exchanges were established. To consider the results, Table 2.1 gives data on stock market capitalisation and turnover for some LICs. Three middle-income and two high-income countries are included for comparison.

Looking at capitalisation, Uganda, Kenya, and Malawi appear quite large. When we consider turnover, however, we see that Uganda is highly illiquid, with turnover of just 0.09 per cent of GDP. At 2.6 per cent of GDP, turnover on the Kenyan Stock Exchange is the highest in the region. These figures compare with 23 per cent in Chile, 67 per cent in Thailand, and 121 per cent in the UK. In terms of size and turnover, there is a very large gap, even compared with middle-income countries.

If LIC stock markets do not have sufficient liquidity to attract international investors, one of the main arguments in favour of creating stock exchanges is undermined.[14] Without this, they are limited to 'scarce' domestic investment,

Table 2.1 Stock exchanges in some LICs, MICs, and HICs, 2011

Market cap. (% of GDP)		Stocks traded (% of GDP)	
Kyrgyz Republic	2.66	Kyrgyz Republic	0.05
Latvia	3.81	Uganda	0.09
Tanzania	6.45	Tanzania	0.14
Nigeria	16.10	Latvia	0.18
Nepal	20.38	Nepal	0.42
Malawi	24.63	Malawi	0.95
Kenya	30.35	Nigeria	1.70
Uganda	45.97	Kenya	2.61
Brazil	49.62	Chile	22.89
France	56.57	Brazil	38.81
Thailand	77.67	France	53.16
Chile	108.73	Thailand	67.24
United Kingdom	118.72	United Kingdom	121.53

Source: WDI.

while large domestic companies are likely to list on major international stock exchanges if they can (Gugler, Mueller and Yurtoglu, 2004).

Stock markets can only allocate capital efficiently if prices reflect underlying fundamentals, providing accurate signals to investors. There is evidence that this is generally not the case in LICs, where share prices often move up and down together depending on market sentiment (Durnev, Li, Mork and Yeung, 2004; Agu and Chukwuma-Agu, 2010; Afego, 2012). Rather than boost growth by increasing the efficiency with which capital is allocated, therefore, LIC stock markets may be more likely to undermine stability by amplifying boom and bust cycles.

These factors suggest that the growth benefits of stock market development are less likely to be felt in LICs than the risks to financial stability. While stock markets are an important part of financial systems in more developed economies, there is a good case for LIC policy-makers to focus their efforts elsewhere.

Bond markets

Corporate bond market development faces similar problems to stock markets in LICs, particularly the difficulty in attracting foreign investors (Edo, 2011). As well as liquidity concerns, a major obstacle is the currency risk attached to local currency bonds. This can be avoided by borrowing in an international currency, but this just transfers risk to the borrower. As well as constraints on market size and liquidity, there may be other obstacles to developing local currency bond markets in LICs. Some research suggests, for example, that banks in developing countries will tend to oppose this form of financial sector development, as it offers an alternative form of debt, threatening market share. Where the banking sector is concentrated, the ability of banks to retard bond market development is likely to be higher (Dickie and Fan, 2005).

Given the issues of market size and liquidity, it is unlikely that either stock or bond market development will have a significant impact on growth prospects in LICs, though offering an alternative source of debt to the banking sector would be a positive development. The situation with stability is different. While stock market development in LICs could potentially undermine stability, the opposite is true for *domestic currency* corporate bonds markets. These would reduce the potential for currency mismatches in the corporate sector, which is supportive of stability, and could be particularly important as larger firms seek to expand. When considering where to prioritise efforts, therefore, this suggests that LIC governments should devote more resources and strategic effort to bond than stock market development.

Research gaps and concluding remarks

Clearly there is not enough finance to support inclusive growth in LICs. It is not just the quantity of finance that matters though, but what might be called its *quality*. By that, this chapter means the types of finance and the terms on which they are available. Maturity is important, but so is the cost of finance, and the extent to which it generates instability and risk, and for whom.

The quantity *and* the quality of finance in LICs are both problematic. There is insufficient finance, and that which is available is short term, expensive, and not well suited to the needs of borrowers. This is broadly true for individuals, households, firms, and also governments.

The cost of finance remains prohibitively high in many LICs, which restrains growth and fosters financial instability. While the causes are relatively well-known, solutions have proved elusive. Numerous reforms to increase competitive pressure and efficiency in the banking sector have had little impact upon spreads (see the country chapters in this book). The cost of financial services for the poor, including from microfinance institutions, can also be excessive, creating concerns about sustainability and, ultimately, stability. Identifying and addressing the 'binding constraints' to reducing the cost of finance for individuals and firms in LICs is a crucial area of research.

The structure of the banking sector is an important part of this. The evidence suggests that a diverse set of banking institutions would improve both the quantity and quality of finance, and thus have positive impacts on inclusive growth and stability. We know little about what the ideal composition of this 'ecosystem' should be in LICs, however, particularly the balance between public and private banks, large and small institutions, and between commercial banks, MFIs, SACCOs, and banks focused on particular sectors such as SMEs.

The potential for development banks to foster inclusive growth in LICs is significant, even though there might be risks as well. The need for development banks is certainly not new, but the challenges and context of the 21st century are, and what we have learned about what successful development banks need, makes this a new area of research in development finance. Focusing on LICs, where the need for development banks is greatest is a particularly important area of research.

Regulation is fundamental to all of these aspects of finance and development. If we know more about the types of financial institutions that are best suited to balancing inclusive growth and stability in LICs, the next question is what regulatory frameworks would support the emergence of these institutions. A second question is how different types of institutions should be regulated and supervised. The benefit of a diverse set of financial institutions is that they compete to offer different services to different groups of customers. This diversity is based upon different funding models, strategies, and mandates. To avoid a process whereby regulation encourages increasing uniformity, it is important that it is designed to support – rather than stifle – the aims of different financial institutions. While there are some lessons to draw from the microfinance sector, significant research is required to build upon this.

As well as these microprudential issues, we also need to consider how regulation affects the financial 'ecosystem' as a whole. Finance tends towards large scale, relatively homogeneous institutions. A diverse mix of large, small, and heterogeneous institutions is very unlikely to evolve naturally, or to survive if it does so. Understanding how regulation can help support and maintain this process in LICs is a new area of research. For macroprudential regulation more generally, we need to understand better how domestic regulation interacts with the external environment in a LIC setting, including which tools are most appropriate to manage this interaction such that stable, inclusive growth is supported.

At both the micro and macro level, simply importing frameworks from developed countries, such as Basel II–III, is not the solution. If LICs are to use financial regulation to help strike the right balance between growth and stability, this will need to be designed explicitly for the circumstances of LICs. Again, this is an under-explored area.

The evidence on capital market development suggests that LIC governments should prioritise local currency bond market development over stock markets. How to overcome the formidable problems to doing this, however, is little understood, including the role that regional cooperation could potentially play.

To conclude, although a large quantity of research has been reviewed, many of the most important questions remain unanswered. We know that financial sector development is crucial for inclusive growth in LICs. We also know that financial instability can have devastating consequences. How finance can help achieve the optimal balance between growth and stability in LICs, and the role that regulation should play in this, is among the most pressing development questions we face, and will remain so for many years to come.

Notes

1 From an initial set of 14,000 titles and abstracts, a little over a thousand papers were considered potentially relevant and of sufficient quality to be downloaded in full.
2 For details of the impact channels considered and the rationale for selecting the four identified here, see Spratt (2013).
3 For the full study on which this chapter is based, see Spratt (2013).
4 As well as presence of externalities, three other market failures are generally used to justify government intervention: monopoly power; imperfect information; and contract enforcement problems (Scott, 2007). Where finance is characterised by one or more of these problems, the allocation of resources will be suboptimal, and there is the potential to improve welfare outcomes by public intervention.
5 The study predicted a 0.23 percentage point increase in the long run growth rate for each 10 percentage point reduction in government bank ownership.
6 The Brazilian Development Bank (BNDES), for example, receives a significant proportion of its funding from a small levy on the Worker's Pension Fund, for which it pays a 5 per cent return.
7 For example, Song (2004) identifies the following: (i) selecting a licensing policy and fitness test for managers and owners of a complex institution; (ii) monitoring local establishment of international banks; (iii) upgrading supervisory capacity to oversee complex financial products; (iv) agreeing and organising parent bank support in case of difficulties of a branch or subsidiary; (v) exchanging information with home supervisors; and (vi) dealing with increasing penetration by foreign banks.
8 In rules-based systems, detailed rules are prescribed, with the job of supervision being to see that such rules are adhered to. In principles-based systems, a smaller number of high-level principles are stipulated, with the job of supervisors being to ensure that financial institutions adhere to the spirit of these. Principles-based approaches thus entail considerably more discretion for supervisors.

9   Following the first Basel Accord in 1988, and its successors, an international standard of 8 per cent of regulatory capital to risk-weighted assets became the international standard.

10

The LCR is one of the Basel Committee's key reforms to strengthen global capital and liquidity regulations with the goal of promoting a more resilient banking sector. The LCR promotes the short-term resilience of a bank's liquidity risk profile. It does this by ensuring that a bank has an adequate stock of unencumbered high-quality liquid assets (HQLA) that can be converted into cash easily and immediately in private markets to meet its liquidity needs for a 30 calendar day liquidity stress scenario. It will improve the banking sector's ability to absorb shocks arising from financial and economic stress, whatever the source, thus reducing the risk of spillover from the financial sector to the real economy.

(BIS, 2013)

11   The FSB (2011) describes various macroprudential tools. Some, such as counter-cyclical capital buffers or margin requirements build up risk cushions in 'booms' to increase resilience to shocks. Others, such as direct control over lending – e.g. limits on new lending after specified thresholds of loan growth are breached – aim to prevent bubbles forming in the first place.

12   'Accessible' simply refers to whether financial services are available to people. 'Affordability' has two aspects: first, whether the cost of financial services accurately reflects creditworthiness; second, whether the total level of debt taken on by individuals and households is sustainable.

13   Data from the World Bank's World Development Indicators (WDI). Accessed August 2013.

14   For some, this supports the idea of regional stock exchanges in LICs. For example, see Moulonguet and Rocher (2012). Others argue that, while this is sensible in principle, different legal, political, and cultural traditions make it very difficult in practice (Singh, 2008).

References

Abdel-Baki, M. A. (2012) "The Impact of Basel III on Emerging Economies." *Global Economy Journal*, 12(2): 1–33.

Abdennour, F. and K. B. Khediri (2010) "Bank Supervision and Bank Profitability: The Case of MENA Countries." *International Journal of Monetary Economics and Finance*, 3(4): 316–329.

Addo, A. and K. Kwarteng (2012) "The Impact of Rural Banks on Poverty Alleviation in Ghana: A Case of Bosomtwe and Atwima Rural Banks Limited." *ijsst.com*.

Afego, P. (2012) "Weak Form Efficiency of the Nigerian Stock Market: An Empirical Analysis (1984–2009)." *International Journal of Economics and Financial Issues*, 2(3): 340–347.

Agu, C. and C. Chukwuma-Agu (2010) "Shaky Pillars: Are Micro and Macroeconomic Fundamentals Enough to Explain the Strength of the Nigeria Stock Exchange?" *International Research Journal of Finance and Economics*, (40): 74–86.

Akerlof, G. A. (1970) "The Market for 'Lemons': Quality Uncertainty and the Market Mechanism." *The Quarterly Journal of Economics*, 84(3): 488–500.

Akyüz, Y. (2008) "Financial Instability and Countercyclical Policy." *UNDESA*. Background Paper to World Economic Social Survey 2008.

Alexandre, C., I. Mas and D. Radcliffe (2011) "Regulating New Banking Models to Bring Financial Services to All." *Challenge*, 54(3): 116–134.

Allen, F. and D. Gale (2000) "Bubbles and Crises." *The Economic Journal*, 110(460): 236–255.

Amidu, M. and S. Wolfe (2011) "Credit Market Competition, Diversification and Stability." *papers.ssrn.com*.

Andrianova, S., P. Demetriades and A. Shortand (2010) "Is Government Ownership of Banks Really Harmful to Growth?" Discussion Papers of DIW Berlin, No 987. German Institute for Economic Research (DIW), Berlin.

Arcand, J.-L., E. Berkes and U. Panizza (2012) *Too much finance?*, IMF Working Paper 12/161. International Monetary Fund.

Bagyenda, J., M. Brownbridge and L. Kasekende (2011) "Basel III and the Global Reform of Financial Regulation: How Should Africa Respond? A Bank Regulator's Perspective." Paper prepared for AERC input to Connect-USA project on global financial reform, February, Bank of Uganda.

Banerjee, A. (2009) "Lin Roundtable: Difficult Trade-offs." Free Exchange, Economist. com blogs.

Barth, J. R., G. Caprio and D. Nolle (2004) *Comparative International Characteristics of Banking*. Available at SSRN: http://ssrn.com/abstract=2318118 or http://dx.doi.org/10.2139/ssrn.2318118

Barth, J. R., G. Caprio, Jr and R. Levine (2001) "Banking Systems Around the Globe: Do Regulation and Ownership Affect Performance and Stability?" In: Mishkin, F. (ed.), *Prudential Supervision: What Works and What Doesn't*. National Bureau of Economic Research. Chicago: University of Chicago Press.

Beck, T. (2008) "2. Policy Choices for an Efficient and Inclusive Financial System." In: Dahan, F. and Simpson, J. (eds), *Secured Transactions Reform and Access To Credit*. Cheltenham: Edward Elgar, chapter 2.

Beck, T. (2010) "The Role of Cross-Border Banks in the Current Crisis: A Mitigating or Exacerbating Impact?" *Presentation of a Draft Chapter of a Forthcoming Policy*. Unpublished. Available at: www.researchgate.net/publication/265323982

Beck, T. and M. S. M. Peria (2010) "Foreign Bank Participation and Outreach: Evidence from Mexico." *Journal of Financial Intermediation*, 19(1): 52–73.

Beck, T. et al. (2010) "Banking Sector Stability, Efficiency, and Outreach in Kenya." Policy Research Working Paper 5442, World Bank, October.

Beck, T., S. M. Maimbo, I. Faye and T. Triki (2011) "Financing Africa: Through the Crisis and Beyond." The World Bank. ISBN: 978-0-8213-8797-9. Washington DC.

Berger, A., I. Hasan and L. Klapper (2004) "Further Evidence on the Link between Finance and Growth: An International Analysis of Community Banking and Economic Performance." *Journal of Financial Services Research*, 25(2): 169–202.

Berger, A. N. and L. F. Klapper (2009) "Bank Competition and Financial Stability." *Journal of Financial Services Research*, 35(2): 99–118.

BIS (2013) Basel III: The Liquidity Coverage Ratio and Liquidity Risk Monitoring Tools. www.bis.org/publ/bcbs238.htm

Boot, A. W. and A. V. Thakor (2000) "Can Relationship Banking Survive Competition?" *The Journal of Finance*, 55(2): 679–713.

Caballero, L. (2012) "Strategic Analysis of Mobile Money Ventures in Developing Countries." Master thesis submitted to the MIT Sloan School of Management, June. Unpublished.

Caprio, G. and P. Honohan (2004) "Can the Unsophisticated Market Provide Discipline?" *World Bank Policy Research Working Paper* (3364).

Caprio, G. and M. S. M. Peria (2001) "Avoiding Disaster: Policies to Reduce the Risk of Banking Crises." In: Mishkin, F. (ed.), *Monetary Policy and Exchange Rate Regimes: Options for the Middle East*. Chicago: University of Chicago Press, 193–230.

Chen, C. (2009) "Bank Efficiency in Sub-Saharan African Middle Income Countries." IMF Staff Papers 1–32, International Monetary Fund, Washington DC.

Chirwa, E. W. (2001) "Market Structure, Liberalization, and Performance in the Malawian Banking Industry." African Economic Research Consortium.

Claessens, S. (2006) "Competitive Implications of Cross-Border Banking." *World Bank Policy Research Working Paper*.

Claessens, S. (2009) "Lessons from the Recent Financial Crisis for Reforming National and International Financial Systems." *A Keynote paper Presented at the Annual World Bank*.

Cuadro, L., S. Gallego and A. G. Herrero (2003) *Why Do Countries Develop More Financially than Others? The Role of the Central Bank and Banking Supervision*. Unpublished. Banco de Espana. Available at: http://econwpa.repec.org/eps/fin/papers/0304/0304006.pdf

Cuevas, C. and K. Fisher (2006) "Cooperative Financial Institutions: Issues in Governance, Regulation, and Supervision." *World Bank Working Paper*, No. 82.

De la Torre, A., E. Feyen and A. Ize (2013) "Financial Development: Structure and Dynamics." *The World Bank Economic Review*: lht005.

Decker, O. (2012) "Structural Change and Competition in the Sierra Leone Banking Sector: An Empirical Investigation." Economic Challenges and Policy Issues in Early 21st Century Sierra Leone.

Deidda, L. and B. Fattouh (2005) "Concentration in the Banking Industry and Economic Growth." *Macroeconomic Dynamics*, 9(2): 198–219.

Demirgüç-Kunt, A. (2005) "Deposit Insurance Around the World: A Comprehensive Database." *World Bank Policy Research Working Paper*.

Demirgüç-Kunt, A. (2006) "Finance and Economic Development: Policy Choices for Developing Countries." *World Bank Policy Research Working Paper*.

Demirgüç-Kunt, A. and H. Huizinga (1999) "Determinants of Commercial Bank Interest Margins and Profitability: Some International Evidence." *The World Bank Economic Review*, 13(2): 379–408.

Demirgüç-Kunt, A. and L. Klapper (2012) "Measuring Financial Inclusion: The Global Findex Database." The Global Findex Database. *World Bank Policy Research Working Paper* (6025).

Dermine, J. and D. Schoenmaker (2010) "In Banking, is Small Beautiful?" *Financial Markets, Institutions & Instruments*, 19(1): 1–19.

Detragiache, E., T. Tressel and P. Gupta (2008) "Foreign Banks in Poor Countries: Theory and Evidence." *Journal of Finance*, 63(5): 2123–2160.

Dickie, P. M. and E. X. Fan (2005) *Banks and Corporate Debt Market Development*. Asian Development Bank.

Durnev, A., K. Li, R. Mork and B. Yeung (2004) "Capital Markets and Capital Allocation: Implications for Economies in Transition." *Economics of Transition*, 12(4): 593–634.

Düwel, C. and R. Frey (2012) "The Funding of Multinational Banks and Foreign Affiliate Lending in the Crisis", *eea-esem.com*.

Edo, S. E. (2011) "Capital Market Development in an Emerging Economy and the Challenge of Fostering Foreign Participation." *International Journal of Monetary Economics and Finance*, 4(2): 195–215.

Fanta, A. B. (2012) "Banking Reform and SME Financing in Ethiopia: Evidence from the Manufacturing Sector." *African Journal of Business Management*, 6(19): 6057–6069. Available at: www.academicjournals.org/AJBM

FSB (2011) "Macroprudential Policy Tools and Frameworks: Update for G20 Finance Ministers and Central Bank Governors." Unpublished (February 2011).

Gottschalk, R. and S. Sen (2006) *Prudential Norms for the Financial Sector: Is Development a Missing Dimension? The Cases of Brazil and India.* Brighton: Institute of Development Studies.

Grosse, R. and L. G. Goldberg (1991) "Foreign Bank Activity in the United States: An Analysis by Country of Origin." *Journal of Banking & Finance*, 15(6): 1093–1112.

Gugler, K., D. C. Mueller and B. Yurtoglu (2004) "Corporate Governance and Globalization." *Oxford Review of Economic Policy*, 20(1): 129–156.

Gutierrez, E. and H. Rudolph (2011) "Development Banks: Role and Mechanisms to Increase their Efficiency." *World Bank Policy Research Working Paper*.

Hauner, D. and S. J. Peiris (2008) "Banking Efficiency and Competition in Low Income Countries: The Case of Uganda." *Applied Economics*, 40(19–21): 2703–2720.

Herndon, T., M. Ash and R. Pollin (2014) "Does High Public Debt Consistently Stifle Economic Growth? A Critique of Reinhart and Rogoff." *Cambridge Journal of Economics*, 38(2): 257–279.

IFPRI (2002) "Banking on the Poor: Unleashing the Benefits of Microfinance." Issue Brief 12, International Food Research Policy Institute, Washington DC.

Juanah, M. (2005) "The Role of Micro-financing in Rural Poverty Reduction in Developing Countries." No. 18. Wismarer Discussions papiere.

Kane, E. (2000) "Designing Financial Safety Nets to Fit Country Circumstances." *World Bank Policy Research Working Paper*.

Kasekende, L., J. Bagyenda and M. Brownbridge (2012) "Basel III and the Global Reform of Financial Regulation: How Should Africa Respond? A Bank Regulator's Perspective." *fsbwatch.org*.

Kasekende, L., Z. Brixova and L. Ndikumana (2010) "Africa: Africa's Counter-Cyclical Policy Responses to the Crisis." *Journal of Globalisation and Development*, 1(1): Article 16.

Keeley, M. C. (1990) "Deposit Insurance, Risk and Market Power in Banking." *American Economic Review*, December.

Khan, M. A. H. (2009) "Essays on Banking Crises." PhD Dissertation. Kansantaloustieteen laitoksen tutkimuksia, No. 116:2009.

Klapper, L. and R. Zaidi (2005) "A Survey of Government Regulation and Intervention in Financial Markets." Background paper for the World Development Report, 2005.

Kloeppinger-Todd, R. and M. Sharma (2010) "Innovations in Rural and Agriculture Finance." *Intl Food Policy Res Inst*, 18.

Kpodar, K. and M. Andrianaivo (2011) "ICT, Financial Inclusion, and Growth Evidence from African Countries." IMF Working Paper WP/11/73, International Monetary Fund, Washington DC.

Krause, L., A. F. Brimmer and F. Dahl (1975) "Growth of American International Banking: Implications for Public Policy." *The Journal of Finance*, 30(2): 341–363.

Krueger, A. O. (1991) "Government Failures in Development." National Bureau of Economic Research.

La Porta, R., F. Lopez-de-Silanes and A. Shleifer (2002) "Government Ownership of Banks." *The Journal of Finance*, 57(1): 265–301.

Laeven, L. and G. Majnoni (2003) "Loan Loss Provisioning and Economic Slowdowns: Too Much Too Late? *Journal of Financial Intermediation*, 12(2): 178–197.

Levieuge, G. (2010) "The Bank Capital Channel and Counter-Cyclical Prudential Regulation in a DSGE Model." *Recherches économiques de Louvain*, 75(4): 425–460.

Lin, J. (2009) "Walk, Don't Run." *The Economist*, July.

LopezPuertas-Lamy, M. and O. Gutierrez (2012) "The Effect of Ownership Structure on Financial Stability: An Empirical Investigation." Available at SSRN 2085758.

Luna-Martinez, D. and C. L. Vicente (2012) "Global Survey of Development Banks." *World Bank Policy Research Working Paper* (5969).

Lyons, P. (2010) "A Financial Analysis of Mobile Money Services." *Communications and Strategies*, (79): 29–40.

McCoy, P. A. (2006) "The Moral Hazard Implications of Deposit Insurance: Theory and Evidence." In International Monetary Fund, Seminar on Current Developments in Monetary and Financial Law.

McDonald, C. and L. Schumucher (2007) *Financial Deepening in Sub-Saharan Africa: Empirical Evidence on the Role of Creditor Rights Protection and Information Sharing.* Washington DC: International Monetary Fund.

Manganhele, A. T. (2010) "Why did the People's Development Bank of Mozambique Fail? Lessons from Successful Government Development Banks from Asia and Africa." In 2010 AAAE Third Conference/AEASA 48th Conference, 19–23 September, 2010, Cape Town, South Africa (No. 96811). African Association of Agricultural Economists (AAAE) & Agricultural Economics Association of South Africa (AEASA).

Meagher, P. (2010) "Constant Gardening: A Study of Malawi's Enabling Environment for Microfinance." Financial Services Assessment, IRIS Center, University of Maryland.

Minsky, H. P. (1992) "The Financial Instability Hypothesis." *The Jerome Levy Economics Institute Working Paper* (74).

Moulonguet, J. and E. Rocher (2012) "Financial Market in the CFA Franc Zone: Recent Developments." *Techniques financières et développement*, 107.

Mugume, A. (2007) "Market Structure and Performance in Uganda's Banking Industry." African Econometrics Society. Unpublished, Makerere University, Kampala, Uganda.

Murinde, V. (2012) "Financial Development and Economic Growth: Global and African Evidence." *Journal of African Economies*, 21: 110–156.

Muthuma, E. W. (2011) "Economic Cooperation in Kenyan Credit Cooperatives: Exploring the Role of Social Capital and Institutions." Doctoral dissertation, University of the Witwatersrand, Johannesburg.

Nissanke, M. and E. Aryeetey (1998) "Financial Integration and Development: Liberalization and Reform in Sub-Saharan Africa", *Studies in Development Economics*, vol. 11. London and New York: Routledge.

Ocampo, J. A. (2003) "Capital-Account and Counter-Cyclical Prudential Regulations in Developing Countries." *CEPAL Review.*

Özyıldırım, S. (2010) "Intermediation Spread, Bank Supervision, and Financial Stability." *Review of Pacific Basin Financial Markets and Policies*, 13(4): 517–537.

Ping, L. (2011) "The Current State of the Financial Sector and the Regulatory Framework in Asian Economies: The Case of the People's Republik of China." ADBI working paper series 310. Asian Development Bank Institute.

Quintyn, M. and M. Taylor (2007) "Building Supervisory Structures in Sub-Saharan Africa – An Analytical Framework." (No. 7–18). International Monetary Fund, Washington DC.

Rabanal, P., A. Narain and S. Byskov (2003) *Prudential Issues in Less Diversified Economies.* IMF Working Papers WP/03/198, International Monetary Fund, Washington DC.

Reisen, H. (1994) "On the Wealth of Nations and Retirees". In: O'Brien, R. (ed.), *Finance and the International Economy*, 8, The Amex Bank Review Prize Essays, Oxford, Oxford University Press: 86–107.

Rogoff, K. S. and C. M. Reinhart (2010) "Growth in a Time of Debt." *American Economic Review*, 100(2): 573–578.

Rudolph, H. P. (2009) "State Financial Institutions: Mandates, Governance, and Beyond." World Bank Policy Research Working Paper Series, No. 5141.

Salami, I. (2012) "International Financial Standards and the Application of Basel III in Emerging and Frontier Markets." *Law and Financial Markets Review*, 6(5).

Schaeck, K., M. Cihak and A. Wolfe (2009) "Are Competitive Banking Systems More Stable?" *Journal of Money, Credit and Banking*, 41(4): 711–734.

Schapiro, M. (2012) *Making the Developmental State Work: How Does a Mandate Matter for the Brazilian Development Bank?* Paper presented in the workshop "Autopsias Institucionais" at Direito GV, March; and at the Harvard-Stanford Young Faculty Forum at Stanford Law School, Stanford, California, October.

Schoar, A. (2009) "Lin Roundtable: Difficult Trade-offs. Free Exchange." *Economist.com blogs*.

Schoenmaker, D. and D. Werkhoven (2012) "What is the Appropriate Size of the Banking System?" *Duisenberg School of Finance*, Policy Paper No. 28. Available at: http://ssrn.com/abstract=2158606 or http://dx.doi.org/10.2139/ssrn.2158606

Scott, D. H. (2007) "Strengthening the Governance and Performance of State-Owned Financial Institutions." *World Bank Policy Research Working Paper* (4321).

Simpasa, A. M. (2011) "Competitive Conditions in the Tanzanian Commercial Banking Industry." *African Development Review/Revue Africaine de Developpement*, 23(1): 88–98.

Singh, A. (2008) "Stock Markets in Low and Middle Income Countries." *Centre for Business Research, University of Cambridge Working Paper No. 377*.

Song, I. (2004) "Foreign Bank Superision and Challenges to Emerging Market Supervisors." *IMF Working Paper WP/04/82*. Washington DC: International Monetary Fund, May.

Spratt, S. (2013) *Balancing Growth with Stability in Low-Income Countries: A Conceptual Framework on the Impact of Financial Sector Structure and Financial Regulation*. Brighton UK, Institute of Development Studies. Unpublished.

Stiglitz, J. E. (1993) *The Role of the State in Financial Markets*. Proceedings of the World Bank Annual Conference on Development Economics, World Bank, Washington DC.

Stiglitz, J. E. and A. Weiss (1981) "Credit Rationing in Markets with Imperfect Information." *The American Economic Review*, 71(3): 393–410.

Thorne, J. and C. d. Toit (2009) "A Macro-Framework for Successful Development Banks." *Development Southern Africa*, 26(5): 677–694.

Tobin, J. (1984) "On the Efficiency of the Financial-System." *Lloyds Bank Annual Review*, 153: 1–15.

Uhde, A. and U. Heimeshoff (2009) "Consolidation in Banking and Financial Stability in Europe: Empirical Evidence." *Journal of Banking & Finance*, 33(7): 1299–1311.

UNCTAD (2015) "Making the International Financial Architecture Work for Development." Trade and Development Report, Chapter 4. United Nations. New York and Geneva. 187 pages.

Vogel, U. and A. Winkler (2012) "Do Foreign Banks Stabilize Cross-Border Bank Flows and Domestic Lending in Emerging Markets? Evidence from the Global Financial Crisis." *Comparative Economic Studies*, 54(3): 507–530.

Yeyati, E. L., A. Micco and U. Panizza (2007) "A Reappraisal of State-Owned Banks." *Economia*.

Zhuang, J., H. Gunatilake, et al. (2009) "Financial Sector Development, Economic Growth, and Poverty Reduction: A Literature Review." ADB Economics Working Paper Series No. 173, Asian Development Bank, Manila.

3 Literature survey on capital account management in low-income countries

Isabella Massa[1]

Introduction

Over the last few years, the debate on private capital flows and their management has regained momentum. This is due to the fact that since the 1990s the trend and composition of private capital flows directed to low-income countries (LICs) have changed quickly and significantly. Private capital flows, indeed, experienced a number of surges as well as declines, reversals or even sudden stops in times of crisis. Moreover, foreign direct investment (FDI) and portfolio investment (equity and bond flows) became dominant compared to bank lending. As a result, new opportunities and challenges have arisen for LICs.

This chapter reviews the literature on the growth benefits and risks of private capital flows as well as on capital account management, with a focus on LICs. Source papers include professional journal articles, refereed research studies, empirical reports, and policy briefs. Since the literature relating to private capital flows and capital account management is voluminous, a number of decision rules in choosing articles are used. First, given the focus on LICs, we include mostly papers dealing with LICs specifically within the sub-Saharan African (SSA) region where the majority of LICs are located. Where information is scarce or not available at all with respect to those countries, evidence is drawn from the experience of emerging economies. Second, because private capital flows and capital account management tools are changing fast in today's environment, we use mostly sources published over the last decade, except where articles are needed specifically for their historical relevance and perspective on broad issues relating to private capital flows and capital account management.

The chapter is structured as follows. The second section analyses the growth benefits and the risks associated with private capital flows to LICs or SSA economies. The third section provides an overview of the existing capital account management tools highlighting their main advantages and disadvantages. Examples of LICs where the different capital account management tools have been implemented are reported to the possible extent. In this section, the effectiveness of capital account management tools is also discussed. The final section concludes.

Private capital flows: benefits versus risks

Growth benefits of private capital flows

The empirical literature on the effects of private capital flows on economic growth in LICs is rather scant, and has been unable to provide conclusive evidence about the positive impact of private capital flows on growth. Indeed, some papers show that private capital flows enhance economic growth, while others report that there is no direct evidence of such a relationship. Some papers also find that private capital inflows have a negative impact on economic growth.

The literature on the growth benefits of private capital flows in LICs can be divided into two strands. The first investigates individually the growth impacts of specific types of private capital flows. The second, instead, looks jointly at the effects on growth of different private capital flows (i.e. FDI, portfolio equity flows, bond flows, cross-border bank lending) in a common framework.

Much of the research studies assessing the impacts on growth of individual types of private capital flows in LICs focus on FDI. Most of the studies find a positive relationship between FDI inflows and growth, although there are a few exceptions. The main channels through which FDI may affect growth are capital formation, technology transfer and spillover, human capital enhancement, and increased competition.

The papers assessing the relationship between FDI and economic growth use mainly three methodologies: cross-country analysis, panel data analysis, and time series analysis. Cross-country studies generally find evidence of a positive impact of FDI on economic growth in LICs (e.g. Seetanah and Khadaroo, 2007, and Deléchat et al., 2009, on samples of SSA countries).

Findings on the relationship between FDI and growth are more mixed in panel studies. Indeed, several works find that FDI is growth conducive in LICs (e.g. see Toulaboe et al., 2009, on a sample of 14 LICs, or Adefabi, 2011, and Ndambendia and Njoupouognigni, 2010, on samples of selected SSA countries). Interestingly, FDI inflows are found to lead to higher growth benefits in countries with higher levels of financial sector development, more diversified economic structures, better infrastructure, stronger institutions, and greater macroeconomic stability (Dabla-Norris et al., 2010; Lumbila, 2005). Nevertheless, there are also studies that find no effect of FDI on growth in both LICs (Dabla-Norris et al., 2010) and SSA countries (Sukar et al., 2007; Adams, 2009).

Most of the studies using time series analysis find a positive long-run relationship between economic growth and FDI (see Obwona, 2001, in the case of Uganda; Lamine and Yang, 2010, in the case of Guinea; and Adnan, 2011, in the case of Liberia, among others). However, no relationship is found by Esso (2010) in the case of Congo as well as by Rusuhuzwa and Baricako (2009) in the case of Burundi and Rwanda, while a negative impact of FDI on growth is found by Ahmed et al. (2011) in Kenya. Evidence on the direction of causality is also rather mixed. Tekin (2012), for example, shows that FDI Granger-causes GDP in Benin and Togo, while GDP Granger-causes FDI in Burkina Faso, Gambia, Madagascar, and Malawi.

Differently from the studies focusing on the growth impact of FDI, the literature examining the effects of other types of private capital flows on economic growth in LICs does not focus on portfolio equity flows or debt flows individually, but rather investigates simultaneously the growth impact of different types of flows. The evidence is mixed. Focusing on selected samples of LICs, Choong et al. (2010) and Shen et al. (2010) find that portfolio investment has a negative effect on growth. De Vita and Kyaw (2009), instead, find that the growth impact of portfolio investment in LICs is not significant. In SSA countries, portfolio equity flows and bonds flows have been found to have no growth impact by Brambila-Macias and Massa (2010). Cross-border bank lending, instead, appears to exert a significant and positive impact on growth when the whole sample of SSA countries is considered, but interestingly this effect becomes negative and significant when the sub-sample of natural resource economies is considered (Brambila-Macias et al., 2011). This may be explained by the fact that oil producer countries are characterized by relatively weak institutions (resource curse) and have less incentive to invest in financial sector reforms and regulation than non-oil countries. In the long-run, these factors might expose resource rich countries to international banking risks, including potential additional transmission channels of systemic risk across countries, and so they are likely to have a negative impact on economic growth.

Risks of private capital flows

Private capital flows are a double edged sword. As discussed above, under certain conditions and depending on the type of flows, they may contribute to foster economic growth in LICs. However, sudden increases or drops in private capital flows may also create upheavals in recipient economies, especially in the most fragile LICs.

Kawai and Takagi (2008) argue that the risks stemming from private capital flows can be classified into three categories: i) macroeconomic risks; ii) financial stability risks; and iii) risk of capital flow reversal/sudden stop. The macroeconomic risks are associated with sudden surges in capital inflows, which can lead to appreciation and volatility of real exchange rates as well as to inflation, thus affecting domestic policy objectives such as export promotion, exchange rate stability, and national price stability. By looking at a sample of selected LICs over the period 1980–2008, Reinhart and Reinhart (2008) show that there is a cumulative exchange rate appreciation up to the last year of capital flow bonanza and a sharp depreciation afterwards. In turn, inflation tends to decline before the surge of capital inflows and then to increase. Moreover, the authors argue that low- (and middle-) income countries record the highest increase in probabilities of currency and inflation crises around periods of capital inflows bonanza. By focusing on SSA, Lartey (2008) shows that increases in FDI inflows lead to real appreciation, while changes in 'other capital inflows' do not appear to affect the real exchange rate. The 2008 IMF Sub-Saharan Africa Regional Economic Outlook (IMF, 2008) also reports that surges of capital inflows in Uganda, Tanzania, and Zambia have caused appreciation pressures on their currencies.

Financial stability risks refer to the adverse impacts that surges in capital inflows may have on asset prices and credit. To our knowledge, the issue of financial stability risks in LICs stemming from capital inflows is still relatively unexplored by the empirical economic literature. However, stylized facts reported by Reinhart and Calvo (1999) show that capital inflow surges have led to stock market booms in South Africa, Zimbabwe, and Nigeria in the 1990s. Moreover, there are a few studies focusing on developing countries, including some LICs and emerging markets, from which lessons can be drawn. These studies show that stock prices tend to boom in bonanza periods thus leading to a higher incidence of financial crises (Reinhart and Reinhart, 2008). Caballero (2012) also finds that the incidence of banking crises is higher in the case of surges in portfolio flows. Furthermore, capital inflow shocks tend to lead to credit expansion (Furceri et al., 2011; Magud et al., 2012; Calderón and Kubota, 2012; Ostry et al., 2011).

Finally, the risk of a sudden capital flow reversal could lead to depletion of reserves and sharp currency depreciations; it could also cause a currency crisis that may be linked to a banking crisis (Reinhart and Rogoff, 2008). The likelihood that a country experiences a capital flow reversal or a sudden stop depends on the composition of its capital flows. The implicit assumption is that different types of capital flows are characterized by different levels of volatility, and that highly volatile ('hot') capital flows have a high potential for reversal or sudden stop in a crisis. Conventional wisdom says that short-term flows are generally more volatile than long-term ones, and that FDI is the least volatile flow especially compared to short-term loans and portfolio investment. A number of stylized facts seem to confirm these views with respect to LICs. A recent UNDP (2011) study, indeed, reports that between 1995 and 2008 in LICs, the volatility of portfolio investment was significantly higher than that of FDI. Moreover, during the 2007–08 global financial crisis, short-term loans and portfolio investment appear to have been highly volatile and subject to sudden reversals or stops. Bhinda and Martin (2009), for example, report that portfolio equity flows in Africa turned sharply negative in 2008, and argue that historical greater volatility of loans compared to other financing has been confirmed in the global financial crisis. In a similar way, te Velde et al. (2009) note that in 2008 low-income economies such as Bangladesh, Kenya, and Uganda experienced significant portfolio investment flow reversals, while FDI inflows have been less volatile. During the global financial crisis, the IMF (2009) found evidence of portfolio inflow reversals even in LICs with capital restrictions (e.g. Kenya and Tanzania). Bond issuance has also suddenly stopped in SSA countries such as Tanzania, Kenya, and Uganda (see Griffith-Jones and Ocampo, 2009; te Velde et al., 2009; Brambila-Macias and Massa, 2010; among others).

Managing capital flows

Capital account management tools

Three measures can be used to manage surges in capital inflows: i) capital controls; ii) macroeconomic measures; and iii) structural measures.

Capital controls are restrictions on the level or composition of foreign capital into or out of a country. According to Magud and Reinhart (2006), there are four reasons that drive countries to adopt capital controls: fear of appreciation; fear of 'hot money'; fear of large inflows; and fear of loss of monetary autonomy (the so-called 'trilemma'). Several other arguments have been advanced to justify capital controls. For example, the need to compensate for financial market imperfections resulting from asymmetric information problems and herding behaviour, to protect a fixed exchange rate regime, or to support policies of financial repression to provide cheap financing for government budgets and priority sectors (Johnston and Tamirisa, 1998). Korinek (2011) also reports that capital controls can be used for prudential reasons. A number of other key political and structural determinants of capital controls are discussed by Grilli and Milesi-Ferretti (1995). A drawback of capital controls is represented by the fact that a number of mechanisms may be developed for circumvention of these regulations. Such circumvention can be reduced or almost eliminated if costs of avoiding capital controls are increased by policy actions, and are higher than the profits generated by the avoidance (Spiegel, 2012).

Capital controls can be placed on both capital inflows and outflows. Ariyoshi et al. (2000) argue that controls on inflows are typically introduced to counteract the macroeconomic implications of large and volatile capital inflows. Controls on outflows are mainly applied to short-term capital transactions to avoid that speculative flows undermine the stability of the exchange rate and deplete foreign exchange reserves. Data reported by the IMF (2012a) show that among the different country-income groups, LICs account for the highest shares of capital inflows and outflows subject to controls. Moreover, in LICs the use of capital controls on outflows is more widespread than that on inflows. Until the mid-2000s the use of capital controls in LICs had slightly declined, but this process of modest liberalization has stopped following the 2008–09 global financial crisis, which marked a revival in the use of capital controls. For example, during the crisis Tanzania and Zambia tightened capital controls in order to discourage speculative inflows (IMF, 2011).

Capital controls can be of two types: i) quantity-based; and ii) price-based. The former aims to affect directly the volume of capital transactions by imposing quantitative limits (rule-based or discretionary), approval procedures or by completely prohibiting cross-border flows. Price-based capital controls, instead, aim to discourage cross-border flows by making them more costly to undertake through dual or multiple exchange rate systems, explicit or implicit taxation, or through other indirect regulatory controls (e.g. asymmetric open limit positions, or reporting requirements). Price-based capital controls may affect both the price and the volume of capital flows, and they are usually mixed with some quantity-based measures. A widely used measure is the so-called unremunerated reserve requirement (URR). In SSA, price-based capital controls have been designed in Ghana (Chea, 2011). Moreover, the IMF (2008) and Murinde (2009) highlight that in the region there are still administrative or bureaucratic procedures in place that limit capital flows. For example, there are significant restrictions in Mozambique, Cameroon, and Tanzania, and just partial opening in Nigeria and South Africa. In Zambia and Uganda, instead, there are no capital controls.

In the face of surges in capital inflows, three *macroeconomic measures* can be used: i) official foreign exchange intervention; ii) exchange rate intervention; and iii) fiscal policy. Official foreign exchange interventions are widely used to prevent exchange rate appreciation, and may be sterilized (sterilization) or unsterilized. Historically, sterilization has been often used by countries as a first response to capital flow surges. For example, the governments in Uganda and Tanzania used sterilization as an initial response to the surges in private capital inflows in 2004 and 2007, respectively (IMF, 2008). Sterilization can be realized through open market operations, increasing bank reserve requirements, or transferring government deposits from the banking system to the central bank.

Sterilization via open market operations takes place through the central bank sale of either government securities or central bank sterilization bonds. Open-market operations were implemented in Uganda in 1993–94, Kenya in 1993, Uganda and Tanzania in 2007 (Deléchat et al., 2008; Adam, 2009). Other SSA countries such as Zambia and Ghana were active in sterilization operations, primarily through open market operations, after the 2008–09 global financial crisis (IMF, 2011). The main advantage associated with this policy measure is that it neutralizes the liquidity impact of capital inflows. Moreover, it has the beneficial side effect of building reserve buffers which may be useful in the case of a sudden reversal of flows. However, one drawback is that by increasing the outstanding stock of domestic debt, it ends up increasing domestic interest rates. As a consequence, open-market operations may induce further capital flows, alter the composition of capital flows by increasing the share of short-term and portfolio flows, and raise quasi-fiscal costs by widening the domestic and foreign interest rate spread (Lopez-Mejia, 1999). For these reasons, sterilization works at best in the short term (except when interest rates are kept low as in the case of China).

An increase in bank reserve requirements allows controlling liquidity conditions in periods of capital inflows by reducing the money multiplier and neutralizing the monetary expansion associated with central bank purchases of foreign exchange. However, this policy measure is associated with a number of drawbacks as reported by Calvo et al. (1996) and Lopez-Mejia (1999), among others. First, it may discourage financial intermediation in countries that are trying to liberalize their financial markets. Second, in the long-run it may lead to disintermediation, as new institutions may develop to circumvent these regulations. Third and similarly to open-market operations, it may encourage further capital inflows by inducing borrowing from abroad. Moreover, Gupta et al. (2006) highlight that the impact of this policy may be limited in a country where there are some banks which already have reserve assets in excess of requirements. Notwithstanding these shortcomings, this type of sterilization policy has been used extensively in the 1990s by LICs in Africa such as Kenya in 1992–93 (Reinhart and Reinhart, 1999; Lopez-Mejia, 1999) and Tanzania in 1993–94 (Reinhart and Calvo, 1999).

Compared with the other two types of sterilization policy, the transfer of public sector deposits from commercial banks to central bank accounts has the advantage of entailing fewer fiscal or quasi-fiscal costs and of not shifting costs to the banking system. Nevertheless, its main drawback is that there is often limited scope for such operations due to the scarce availability of eligible funds (Lopez-Mejia, 1999). For example, Gupta et al. (2006) report that, on average, in SSA central government, deposits in commercial banks amount to just about 2 per cent of GDP. In addition to this, large and frequent changes in bank deposits may also inhibit the optimal management of commercial bank portfolios.

Unsterilized intervention is a more passive approach to exchange rate fluctuations in the case of capital inflow surges, which does not correct for the effect on the monetary base. Differently from sterilization, unsterilized interventions have the advantage of lowering domestic interest rates, thus allowing capital inflows to slow down and the fiscal cost of the outstanding domestic credit to be reduced (Calvo et al., 1994). Nevertheless, they may contribute to the vulnerability of the financial system due to a possible build-up of a financial bubble.

Another option for a country experiencing a large influx of private capital flows and characterized by a de facto peg or a tightly managed float, is to allow greater exchange rate flexibility. This does not mean to switch to a floating exchange rate system, but rather to allow greater variability of the nominal exchange rate (through flexibly managed exchange rate systems) or introduce a wider band of fluctuation of the nominal exchange rate. In 2007, greater exchange rate flexibility was allowed in Nigeria and Uganda to respond to surges in capital inflows (IMF, 2008). Before the 2008–09 global financial crisis, Kenya, Zambia, South Africa, and Mauritius, which had a 'de jure' floating or managed floating exchange rate regime but were found to be a 'de facto' soft peg (Slavov, 2011), allowed upward movements in their exchange rates to respond to rising capital inflows (IMF, 2010). An advantage of greater flexibility is that it may discourage speculative short-term capital inflows by introducing higher uncertainty (Calvo et al., 1994). Nevertheless, in the presence of large capital inflows it implies both nominal and real appreciation of the domestic currency, and the latter may hurt strategic sectors of the economy and reduce competiveness of tradables, which can lead to increasing current account deficits (Lopez-Mejia, 1999).

The last macroeconomic measure discussed here that a country may adopt to react to surges in private capital inflows is fiscal tightening, usually through cuts in public expenditures. According to the literature, this policy measure allows countering the adverse effects of capital inflows on aggregate demand and inflation. By lowering aggregate demand, fiscal consolidation lowers interest rates and therefore discourages capital inflows. Furthermore, given that government expenditure is often directed to non-tradable goods, fiscal tightening limits the appreciation of the real exchange rate. A number of drawbacks, however, are associated with this policy measure. First, fiscal tightening requires changes in the legislation and policy actions that are difficult to be undertaken on short notice. Second, this macroeconomic measure may be difficult to implement if it is at odds with long-term goals related to taxes and expenditures. In LICs, fiscal tightening may also be particularly difficult to implement because of their needs for social and infrastructure spending (Deléchat et al., 2008; IMF, 2011). Because of these limitations, only few countries have used fiscal tightening in inflow periods, such as Zambia in the 1990s (Deléchat et al., 2008).

Moving to *structural measures*, it is worth mentioning financial sector reforms and easing restrictions on capital flows. Financial sector reforms (e.g. prudential regulation and supervision) aim to influence indirectly capital inflows or outflows with the objective of reducing the vulnerability of an economy to systemic financial crises. Particularly relevant in this context are regulations on currency mismatches in the balance sheets of financial and non-financial agents. A number of empirical studies show that strong prudential regulation and supervision help to avoid or reduce the impacts of financial crises (Lindgren et al., 1996; Williamson and Mahar, 1998). A possible limitation of financial sector reforms in managing capital flows is, however, the fact that reform processes take time thus constraining prompt and timely solutions (Kawai and Takagi, 2008). Ostry et al. (2012) also shed light on a number of other costs associated with the use of prudential regulation.

Among LICs, many countries have adopted regulatory reforms, especially with respect to banks, in the 1980s and early 1990s (see the paper by Brownbridge and Kirkpatrick (2000) which focuses on LDCs most of which are LICs). Efforts to improve the supervision and regulatory framework have also been made by some low-income economies more recently (see Chapter 4 in this book). Furthermore, in response to the 2008–09 global financial crisis, Mozambique and Zimbabwe made efforts to improve their banking supervision and regulatory framework (IMF, 2011). Note also that, in Africa, there exist tight regulatory limits on open positions which limit significantly the exposure of the banking systems to currency mismatches (O'Connell et al., 2007). A study by Čihák and Podpiera (2005) also shows that in East African countries such as Kenya, Tanzania, and Uganda, banks tend to be reluctant to lend in foreign exchange against domestic currency revenues thus limiting significantly the exposure of private firms to currency mismatches.

The liberalization of outflows may also be used as a tool to limit surges in net capital inflows. The easing of restrictions on outflows may be problematic, though, and deserves further study in countries such as several African countries where there are significant concerns on capital flight (Murinde, 2009). In the past, restrictions on capital outflows have been eased in several developed and emerging economies, including South Africa (since 1994) (Gottschalk and Azevedo Sodre, 2008).

Effectiveness of external financial regulation

The debate on the *effectiveness of capital controls* regained momentum in the aftermath of the 2008–09 global financial crisis, but it is far from settled. Opponents to capital controls argue that their use could lead to local and global misallocation of resources, thus perpetuating global imbalances by allowing countries to maintain undervalued real exchange rates. Supporters, in their turn, see capital controls as an important tool to prevent the build-up of financial sector risks, as well as to reduce the damages associated with capital flow sudden reversals (Aizenman and Pasricha, 2013).

From an international organization perspective, the International Monetary Fund (IMF) until not long ago had a position broadly against capital controls, and favoured capital account liberalization. However, in the aftermath of the 2008–09 global financial crisis, the IMF made a U-turn and decided to endorse the use of capital controls under certain circumstances. According to the new IMF official position, capital controls could be used when countries have little room for economic policies such as lowering interest rates or when sudden increases of capital inflows threaten financial stability. However, the IMF stressed that capital controls should be targeted, temporary and take care of not discriminating between residents and non-residents (IMF, 2012b). The IMF draws on the work done by Ostry et al. (2010), according to which the economy should be running near its potential, the level of reserves should be adequate, and the exchange rate should not be undervalued.

However, country-based evidence challenges the IMF position that capital controls should be deployed only under certain conditions, by showing that controls are most effective when used as part of a permanent framework and with flexibility to target specific flows and financial actors (UNCTAD, 2013). Flexibility is seen as important in part because it allows for the use of capital control tools in response to cyclical needs; and when the tools are part of a permanent framework, a response to changing circumstances is made easier (Eichengreen and Rose, 2014).

The literature on the effectiveness of capital controls is vast, but very few studies have focused on LICs. Among these, Binici et al. (2010) estimate the effects of capital inflow and outflow controls on equity, FDI and debt flows, distinguishing across country income groups. Their findings show that in the low-income group, outflow controls are effective in reducing FDI and equity outflow but not debt flows. Controls on capital inflows, in turn, are not effective in reducing capital inflows for whichever asset class. Given the paucity of studies on the effectiveness of capital controls to help avoid financial instability, generalizations should be taken with extreme caution.

Among all the *macroeconomic measures* used to respond to surges in capital inflows, there seems to be consensus that fiscal tightening might be a most effective policy tool, although it is difficult to implement and the costs it incurs in terms of reduction in social and infrastructure spending might be painful and counterproductive in the long term. The empirical work on the effects of fiscal restraint in episodes of large capital inflows is rather limited, probably due to the fact that few governments adopted this policy measure to respond to large capital inflows (Kaminsky et al., 2004). Looking at LICs, Deléchat et al. (2008) report that in Zambia, expenditure restraint helped to respond to the 2007 capital inflows surge, mitigating pressures on aggregate demand and the exchange rate.

As regards the *effectiveness of structural measures*, episodic evidence (in developed and emerging economies) suggests that the easing of restrictions on capital outflows is ineffective in responding to the adverse effects of surges in capital inflows since it actually stimulates further net inward flows. In order to explain these phenomena, Laban and Larrain (1997) argue that the removal of outflow controls reduce the degree of irreversibility of the decision to invest in a given country. This, in turn, makes investors more willing to invest in that country since it is easier to get their capital out in the future. As a consequence, net capital inflows are likely to increase. In addition to this, Bartolini and Drazen (1997) highlight that the removal of outflow controls not only provides greater flexibility for current allocation of capital, but it also signals that imposition of controls is less likely to occur in the future thus making the countries more attractive to forward-looking investors.

Conclusions

Over the last few years, the debate on private capital flows and their management has regained momentum. This chapter surveys the literature on the following private capital flows-related issues, with a focus on LICs: i) impact on growth; ii) risks; iii) capital account management tools; and iv) effectiveness of different policy measures. Overall, the analysis confirms conventional wisdom according to which private capital flows (i.e. FDI, portfolio investment, cross-border bank lending), in some cases and under certain conditions, may carry important opportunities, but they are also a significant source of risks. Therefore, it is important to develop adequate and effective capital account management policy tools.

Looking in detail at the key findings of the literature survey in each of the four categories of issues mentioned above, it is worth highlighting that there are some studies on the growth impacts of FDI flows in LICs (in particular cointegration and causality analyses), but much less work has been done on the growth benefits of other types of private capital flows, especially bond flows and international bank lending. This is particularly worrying since bond flows are becoming an increasingly important part of private capital flows in a number of SSA low-income economies. Moreover, given that portfolio investment has been found to be much more volatile than FDI in LICs, it is important to identify the threshold beyond which the risks associated to high volatility of portfolio investment flows offset the growth benefits.

Second, most of the analyses on risks of private capital flows in LICs are based on sporadic episodic evidence and stylized facts, while empirical studies are extremely scarce or even non-existent. This is particularly true with respect to financial stability risks and risks of capital flow reversal/sudden stop. In light of the recent financial crisis that has led to significant portfolio investment flow reversals in some LICs (e.g. Kenya and Uganda), it becomes imperative to conduct more quantitative studies on these issues, as well as to monitor regularly the composition and volatility of private capital flows at the country level.

Third, the evidence on the types of capital account management tools that have been used in LICs over time is extremely limited and in many cases out of date. Therefore, much more detailed information on the use of the different types of capital account management policy measures in LICs is needed. Moreover, it is important to analyse in depth the issues that might arise in implementing specific capital account management tools in LICs. Indeed, the conducted survey highlights that in SSA there is limited availability of eligible funds for implementing transfers of public sector deposits from commercial to central banks; fiscal tightening is problematic in the presence of huge needs for social and infrastructure spending; the implementation of prudential regulation and supervision may be challenging due to a lack of financial information and limited skilled personnel; and the easing of restrictions on capital outflows is equally challenging in the presence of significant concerns on capital flight.

Finally, the evidence on the effectiveness of capital account management tools in LICs is extremely limited. Further investigation is needed (also in light of the new guidelines of the IMF). Therefore, future studies should look at the effects in LICs of capital controls (at both the aggregate and country level) on the volume, composition, and volatility of various types of private capital flows. Moreover, given that the global financial crisis has raised some doubts on the effectiveness of the sophisticated prudential regulation and supervision used in the developed world to promote financial stability, further investigation is needed on which regulatory and supervisory policies may work best in LICs taking into account their country-specific characteristics. In particular, it is important to examine whether regulatory measures should be done via domestic prudential policies (e.g. regulating currency mismatches in the balance sheets of banks) or through capital controls by analysing their respective advantages and disadvantages.

Note

1 The author is grateful to Stephany Griffith-Jones and participants at the ESRC/DFID Project Workshop on "Financial Regulation in Low-Income Countries: Balancing Inclusive Growth with Financial Stability", held in Accra (Ghana) on 10–11 September 2013, for valuable comments and suggestions received. The views presented are those of the author and do not necessarily represent the views of ODI or DFID/ESRC.

References

Adam, C. (2009) The conduct of monetary policy in Uganda: An assessment, EPRC Research Series No. 65. Available at: http://ageconsearch.umn.edu/bitstream/101712/2/series65.pdf.

Adams, S. (2009) "Foreign direct investment, domestic investment, and economic growth in sub-Saharan Africa." *Journal of Policy Modeling*, 31, pp. 939–949.

Adefabi, R. A. (2011) "Effects of FDI and human capital on economic growth in Sub-Saharan Africa." *Pakistan Journal of Social Sciences*, 8(1), pp. 32–38.

Adnan, R. R. (2011) Foreign direct investment and economic growth: Evidence from Liberia, Thesis submitted to the Department of Economics of the Faculty of Social

Sciences, University of Cape Coast, August 2011. Available at: http://ir.ucc.edu.gh/dspace/bitstream/123456789/1137/1/ADNAN%202011.pdf.

Ahmed, A. D., Cheng, E., and G. Messinis (2011) "The role of exports, FDI and imports in development: evidence from Sub-Saharan African countries." *Applied Economics*, 43(26), pp. 3719–3731.

Aizenman, J. and G. K. Pasricha (2013) Why do emerging markets liberalize capital outflow controls? Fiscal versus net capital flow concerns, NBER Working Paper No. 18879. Massachusetts: National Bureau of Economic Research.

Ariyoshi, A., Habermeier, K., Laurens, B., Otker-Robe, I., Canales-Kriljenko, and A. Kirilenko (2000) Capital controls: Country experiences with their use and liberalization, IMF Occasional Paper 190. Washington DC: International Monetary Fund.

Bartolini, L. and A. Drazen (1997) "Capital-account liberalization as a signal." *The American Economic Review*, 87(1), pp. 138–154.

Bhinda, N. and M. Martin (2009) Private capital flows to low-income countries: Dealing with boom and bust, FPC CBP Series No. 2, November 2009. Foreign Private Capital Capacity Building Programme (FPC CBP).

Binici, M., Hutchison, M., and M. Schindler (2010) "Controlling capital? Legal restrictions and the asset composition of international financial flows." *Journal of International Money and Finance*, 29(4), pp. 666–684.

Brambila-Macias, J. and I. Massa (2010) "The global financial crisis and sub-Saharan Africa. The effects of slowing private capital flows on growth." *African Development Review*, 22(3), pp. 366–377.

Brambila-Macias, J., Massa, I., and V. Murinde (2011) "Cross-border bank lending versus FDI in Africa's growth story". *Applied Financial Economics*, 21(16), pp. 1205–1213.

Brownbridge, M. and C. Kirkpatrick (2000) "Financial regulation in developing countries." *The Journal of Development Studies*, 37(1), pp. 1–24.

Caballero, J. (2012) Do surges in international capital inflows influence the likelihood of banking crises? Cross-country evidence on bonanzas in capital inflows and bonanza-boom-bust cycles, IDB Working Paper Series IDB-WP-305. Washington DC: Inter-American Development Bank.

Calderón, C. and M. Kubota (2012) Gross inflows gone wild: Gross capital inflows, credit booms and crises, The World Bank Policy Research Working Paper WPS6270, November 2012. Washington DC: The World Bank.

Calvo, G. A., Leiderman, L., and C. M. Reinhart (1994) "The capital inflows problem: Concepts and issues." *Contemporary Economic Policy*, 12(3), pp. 54–66.

Calvo, G. A., Leiderman, L., and C. M. Reinhart (1996) "Inflows of capital to developing countries in the 1990s." *The Journal of Economic Perspectives*, 10(2), pp. 123–139.

Chea, A. C. (2011) "Global private capital flows and development finance in sub-Saharan Africa: Exemplary performers, lessons for others, and strategies for global competitiveness in the twenty-first century." *Journal of Sustainable Development*, 4(5), pp. 18–31.

Choong, C.-K., Lam, S.-Y., and Z. Yusop (2010) "Private capital flows to low-income countries: The role of domestic financial sector." *Journal of Business Economics and Management*, 11(4), pp. 598–612.

Čihák, M. and R. Podpiera (2005) Bank behaviour in developing countries: Evidence from East Africa, IMF Working Paper WP/05/129. Washington DC: International Monetary Fund.

Dabla-Norris, E., Honda, J., Lahreche, A., and G. Verdier (2010) FDI flows to low-income countries: Global drivers and growth implications, IMF Working paper WP/10/132. Washington DC: International Monetary Fund.

Deléchat, C., Kovanen, A., and J. Wakeman-Linn (2008) "Sub-Saharan Africa: Private capital fueling growth." *IMF Survey Magazine*, May 22, pp. 1–5. Washington DC: International Monetary Fund.

Deléchat, C., Ramirez, G., Wagh, S., and J. Wakeman-Linn (2009) Sub-Saharan Africa's integration in the global financial markets, IMF Working Paper WP/09/114. Washington DC: International Monetary Fund.

De Vita, G. and K. S. Kyaw (2009) "Growth effects of FDI and portfolio investment flows to developing countries: a disaggregated analysis by income level." *Applied Economic Letters*, 16(3), pp. 277–283.

Eichengreen, B. and A. K. Rose (2014) Capital controls in the 21st Century. Washington, DC: Brookings Institution.

Esso, L. J. (2010) "Long-run relationship and causality between foreign direct investment and growth: Evidence from ten African countries." *International Journal of Economics and Finance*, 2(2), pp. 168–177.

Furceri, D., Guichard, S. and E. Rusticelli (2011) The effect of episodes of large capital inflows on domestic credit, OECD Economics Department Working Papers No. 864. Paris: Organization for Economic Co-operation and Development.

Gottschalk, R. and C. Azevedo Sodre (2008) The liberalization of capital outflows in CIBS. What opportunities for other developing countries? UNU-WIDER Research Paper No. 2008/68. Helsinki: World Institute for Development Economic Research.

Griffith-Jones, S. and J. Ocampo (2009) The financial crisis and its impact on developing countries, UNDP Working Paper, January 2009. New York: United Nations Development Programme.

Grilli, V. and G. M. Milesi-Ferretti (1995) Economic effects and structural determinants of capital controls, IMF Working Paper WP/95/31. Washington DC: International Monetary Fund.

Gupta, S., Powell, R., and Y. Yang (2006) Macroeconomic challenges of scaling up aid to Africa: A checklist for practitioners. Washington DC: International Monetary Fund. Available at: www.imf.org/external/pubs/ft/afr/aid/2006/eng/aid.pdf.

IMF (2008) Regional economic outlook. Sub-Saharan Africa, April 2008. Washington, DC: International Monetary Fund.

IMF (2009) The implications of the global financial crisis for low-income countries, March 2009. Washington DC: International Monetary Fund.

IMF (2010) Sub-Saharan regional economic outlook. Back to high growth? April 2010. Washington DC: International Monetary Fund.

IMF (2011) Sub-Saharan regional economic outlook. Recovery and new risks, April 2011. Washington DC: International Monetary Fund.

IMF (2012a) Liberalizing capital flows and managing outflows, IMF Staff Paper, 13 March 2012. Washington DC: International Monetary Fund.

IMF (2012b) The liberalization and management of capital flows: An institutional view. Washington DC: International Monetary Fund.

Johnston, B. R. and N. T. Tamirisa (1998) Why do countries use capital controls? IMF Working Paper WP/98/181. Washington DC: International Monetary Fund.

Kaminsky, G., Reinhart, C., and C. Vegh (2004) "When it rains, it pours: Procyclical capital flows and macroeconomic policies." In: *NBER Macroeconomics Annual 2004*, ed. by Mark Gertler and Kenneth Rogoff (Cambridge MA: MIT Press), pp. 11–53.

Kawai, M. and S. Takagi, (2008) A survey of the literature on managing capital inflows, ADB Institute Discussion Paper No. 100. Tokyo: Asian Development Bank Institute. Available at: www.adbi.org/files/dp100.managing.capital.flows.lit.survey.pdf.

Korinek, A. (2011) The new economics of capital controls imposed for prudential reasons, IMF Working Paper WP/11/298. Washington DC: International Monetary Fund.

Laban, R. and F. Larrain (1997) "Can a liberalization of capital outflows increase net capital inflows?" *Journal of International Money and Finance*, 16(3), pp. 415–431.

Lamine, K. M. and D. Yang (2010) "Foreign direct investment effect on economic growth: Evidence from Guinea Republic in West Africa." *International Journal of Financial Research*, 1(1), pp. 49–54.

Lartey, E. K. K. (2008) "Capital inflows, Dutch disease effects and monetary policy in a small open economy." *Review of International Economics*, 16(5), pp. 971–989.

Lindgren, C.-J., Garcia, G., and M. Saal (1996) Bank soundness and macroeconomic policy. Washington DC: International Monetary Fund.

Lopez-Mejia, A. (1999) Large capital flows: A survey of causes, consequences, and policy responses, IMF Working Paper WP/99/17. Washington DC: International Monetary Fund.

Lumbila, K. N. (2005) What makes FDI work? A panel analysis of the growth effect of FDI in Africa, Africa Region Working Paper Series No. 80.

Magud, N. and Reinhart, C. M. (2006) Capital controls: An evaluation, Working Paper 11973. Massachusetts: National Bureau of Economic Research.

Magud, N. E., Reinhart, C. M., and E. R. Vesperoni (2012) Capital inflows, exchange rate flexibility, and credit booms, IMF Working Paper WP/12/41. Washington DC: International Monetary Fund.

Murinde, V. (2009) Capital flows and capital account liberalization in the post-financial crisis era: Challenges, opportunities and policy responses, African Development Bank Working Paper 99, July 2009. Tunisi: African Development Bank.

Ndambendia, H. and M. Njoupouognigni (2010) "Foreign aid, foreign direct investment and economic growth in sub-Saharan Africa: Evidence from pooled mean group estimator (PMG)." *International Journal of Economics and Finance*, 2(3), pp. 39–45.

Obwona, M. B. (2001) "Determinants of FDI and their impact on economic growth in Uganda." *African Development Review*, 13, pp. 46–81.

O'Connell, S., Adam, C., Buffie E., and C. Pattillo (2007) "Managing external volatility: Central bank options in low-income countries." In: *Monetary Policy in Emerging Market and Other Developing Countries*, ed. by Nicoletta Battini (New York: Nova Science Publishers), pp. 1–30.

Ostry, J. D., Ghosh, A. R., Habermeier, K., Chamon, M., Quereshi, M. S., and D. B. S. Reinhardt (2010) Capital inflows: The role of controls, IMF Staff Position Note 10/04. Washington DC: International Monetary Fund.

Ostry, J. D., Ghosh, A. R., Habermeier, K., Laeven, L., Chamon, M., Qureshi, M. S., and A. Kokenyne (2011) Managing capital inflows: What tools to use? IMF Staff Discussion Note SDN/11/06. Washington DC: International Monetary Fund.

Ostry, J. D., Ghosh, A. R., Chamon, M., and M. S. Quereshi (2012) "Tools for managing financial-stability risks from capital inflows." *Journal of International Economics*, 88(2), pp. 407–421.

Reinhart, C. M. and V. R. Reinhart (1999) "On the use of reserve requirements in dealing with capital flow problems." *International Journal of Finance and Economics*, 4(1), pp. 27–54.

Reinhart, C. M. and G. Calvo (1999) The consequences and management of capital inflows: Lessons for sub-Saharan Africa, MPRA Paper No. 7901.

Reinhart, C. M. and V. Reinhart (2008) Capital flow bonanzas: An encompassing view of the past and present, NBER Working Paper 14321, September 2008. Massachusetts: National Bureau of Economic Research.

Reinhart, C. M. and K. S. Rogoff (2008) This time is different: A panoramic view of eight centuries of financial crises, NBER Working Paper 13882, March 2008. Massachusetts: National Bureau of Economic Research.

Rusuhuzwa, T. K. and J. Baricako (2009) The global financial crisis, slowing private capital inflows and economic growth in Rwanda and Burundi. Paper presented at the African Economic Conference 2009 "Fostering Development in an Era of Financial and Economic Crises", 11–13 November 2009, Addis Ababa, Ethiopia. Available at: www.afdb.org/fileadmin/uploads/afdb/Documents/Knowledge/2009%20AEC-%20The%20Global%20Financial%20Crisis%20Slowing%20Private%20Capital%20Inflows%20and%20Economic%20Growth%20in%20Rwanda%20and%20Burundi.pdf.

Seetanah, B. and A. J. Khadaroo (2007) Foreign direct investment and growth: New evidences from sub-Saharan African countries. Available at: www.csae.ox.ac.uk/conferences/2007-EDiA-LaWBiDC/papers/169-Seetanah.pdf.

Shen, C.-H., Lee, C.-C., and C.-C. Lee (2010) "What makes international capital flows promote economic growth? An international cross-country analysis." *Scottish Journal of Political Economy*, 57(5), pp. 515–546.

Slavov, S. (2011) *De jure* versus *de facto* exchange rate regimes in sub-Saharan Africa, IMF Working Paper WP/11/198. Washington DC: International Monetary Fund.

Spiegel, S. (2012) "How to evade capital controls . . . and why they can still be effective." In: *Regulating Global Capital Flows for Long-Run Development*, Pardee Center Task Force Report, March 2012, ed. by K. P. Gallagher, S. Griffith-Jones and J. A. Ocampo (Boston: Boston University Creative Services).

Sukar, A., Ahmed, S., and S. Hassan (2007) "The effects of foreign direct investment on economic growth: The case of Subsaharan Africa." *Southwestern Economic Review*, 34, pp. 61–74.

Tekin, R. B. (2012) "Economic growth, exports and foreign direct investment in least developed countries: A panel Granger causality analysis." *Economic Modelling*, 29, pp. 868–878.

te Velde, D. W., Ackah, C., Ajakaiye, O., Aryeetey, E., Bhattacharya, D., Cali, M., Fakiyesi, T., Fulbert, G. A., Jalilian, H., Jemio, L. C., Keane, J., Kennan, J., Massa, I., McCord, A., Meyn, M., Ndulo, M., Rahman, M., Setiati, I., Soesastro, H., Ssewanyana, S., Vandemoortele, M. and others (2009) The global financial crisis and developing countries: Synthesis of the findings of 10 country case studies, ODI Working Paper 306. London: Overseas Development Institute.

Toulaboe, D., Terry, R., and T. Johansen (2009) "Foreign direct investment and economic growth in developing countries." *Southwestern Economic Review*, 36(1), pp. 155–170.

UNCTAD (2013) Capital account regulations and global economic governance: The need for policy space, Policy Brief No. 28, November.

UNDP (2011) "Private capital flows: Foreign direct investment and portfolio investment." In: *Towards Human Resilience: Sustaining MDG Progress in an Age of Economic Uncertainty*, September 2011. New York: United Nations Development Programme.

Williamson, J. and M. Mahar (1998) A survey of financial liberalization, essays in international finance No. 211. Princeton, NJ: Department of Economics, Princeton University.

4 Assessing capacity constraints for effective financial regulation in Sub-Saharan Africa

Ricardo Gottschalk[1]

Introduction

Financial systems in African low-income countries (LICs) have relatively low levels of integration with the global financial system, when compared with those systems of most other countries around the world. Their less integrated systems have been pointed out as a critical factor to explain why the financial transmission channels were less important than the macro-economic and trade channels in explaining the impacts of the 2007–2008 global financial crisis on the African continent. It also explains why most of their financial systems escaped virtually unscathed from the crisis. However, Africa is not entirely insulated from financial globalisation, nor is it immune from its potentially destabilising effects, or from the challenges it creates for national financial regulatory authorities. In an increasingly financially globalised world, African LICs face at least three inter-connected challenges concerning their financial systems:

1) Whether and how to adopt complex financial standards designed for developed financial systems;
2) How to address the challenges arising from the presence of foreign banks in their jurisdictions;
3) How best to manage risks from a more integrated financial system with the rest of the world, as a result of capital account liberalisation (CAL).

This chapter maps the regulatory challenges and capacity constraints facing African LICs for effective financial regulation and supervision. It does not cover all challenges and constraints facing African LICs; it focuses on those relating to the three inter-connected issues enumerated above. The mapping exercise is based essentially on available material. The broader aim is to help 'bridge on-going discussions on reforming financial regulation at the global level and measures needed to strengthen financial stability and growth in Africa'.[2]

In addressing capacity issues, the chapter asks capacity for what? Nowadays, developing country regulatory and supervisory capacities are being assessed in terms of their ability to implement and use with efficacy standards of international best practice, but, since the global financial crisis, a wave of criticism has emerged towards complex regulatory approaches for financial systems, and the need of simpler rules (see next section). Thus, in a sense, the benchmark for capacity assessment is being set too high and inappropriately. These countries can settle on simpler rules more in line with their specific needs, and it is in this light that capacity in developing countries should be discussed.

This chapter in the second section discusses the implementation, in Africa, of complex international financial standards designed for developed financial systems, focusing on the question: how feasible or desirable is it to implement such standards in African jurisdictions? The third section discusses the regulatory challenges that foreign banks create for African regulators. The fourth section analyses the risks that CAL creates, focusing in particular on currency mismatches, which may constitute an important threat to the stability of African financial systems. The fifth section concludes.

Complex international financial standards designed for developed financial systems: implementation assessment

International financial standards designed by standard setting bodies such as the Basel Committee on Banking Supervision (BCBS) and coordinated by the Financial Stability Board (FSB) are designed having in mind developed and emerging countries.

Since the global financial crisis, the tide of opinion is growing against the financial rules at the national levels that are based on such standards. A main issue is their complexity. Haldane and Madouros (2012), Hoenig (2012) and others have forcefully made the point that complex rules are not only less effective but, in fact, they can even be detrimental. Proposals to revert financial regulation back towards simpler rules[3] have sprung up. Even the BCBS has looked into this issue through the establishment of a Task Force on Complexity and Comparability.[4]

The criticisms revolve around two main issues: the effectiveness of complex rules in helping avoid bank failures and financial crises, and the sheer scale of resources they require, in terms of sophisticated risk assessment models, large databases and number of regulators in each jurisdiction. A McKinsey study on Basel III (the latest Basel Capital Accord, approved after the global crisis) and the European banking system finds that, with the new capital adequacy framework, complexity rises in the areas of design, data quality and reporting, and operations, and that many banks have 'vastly underestimated' the required efforts as well the financial costs for regulatory compliance (Harle et al., 2010). These criticisms and findings are relevant for developed countries and their financial systems, but even more so for developing and especially LICs, which lack financial, technical and human resources to adopt these rules.

However, faced by growing complexities, for instance those embedded in the latest capital accords (i.e. Basel II and III), African LICs appear to feel that adoption of the most complex approaches that the latest accords recommend for capital determination is a way to signal they are adopting standards of international best practice, even if they are not the most appropriate to meet their needs. There is a concern that unless they adopt the most complex approaches, their financial institutions could be penalised, for example in the form of higher international borrowing costs (Beck et al., 2011, Chapter 5). Thus, complexity is a relevant issue for LICs, including – and as discussed further below, especially – when it relates to capital standards. Thus, in the case of the Basel capital rules, a main challenge facing African regulators is their limited technical capacity to validate and monitor the more complex models that banks might choose for adoption; equally important, they lack sufficiently large and reliable databases to run the models. Investment in personnel to enhance their capacity to perform their regulatory/supervisory role adequately creates the risk of having them poached by the banks, since the pool of skilled workers at the country level often is limited.

African countries, facing these constraints, seem to be slowly recognising that their initial expectations about what is feasible or achievable were overly optimistic. Evidence of this is that, following the creation of the Basel II framework in 2004 and their proposed implementation to start in 2006–2007, African countries are slowly tracking back on their initial plans to adopt the most complex approaches, or even to move from Basel I (the initial capital framework adopted in 1988) to Basel II, at least within the time frame that they were initially envisaging to accomplish this change.[5] By comparing consecutive surveys of the Financial Stability Institute (FSI) conducted in 2006, 2008, 2010 and 2012, Table 4.1 shows that, between 2006 and 2008, the percentage of jurisdictions intending to adopt Basel II had increased slightly from 71 to 75 per cent of the total number of respondents, remained constant between 2008 and 2010, but then declined between 2010 and 2012 to 67 per cent (although this last statement is based on a sample size of only 12 countries against 16 and 20 in earlier years).

These results, at first view, are counter-intuitive since expectations are that, with time, countries would be able to understand the new capital rules better, invest in capacity building and gain confidence to adopt them. But what seems to have happened is the opposite. As time went by, countries seem to have realised

Table 4.1 Number of African jurisdictions adopting (or intending to adopt) Basel II

*FSI surveys**	*2006*	*2008*	*2010*	*2012***
No. of survey respondents	17	16	20	12
Respondents intending to adopt Basel II	12	12	15	8
% in total	71	75	75	67

Source: Based on the Financial Stability Institute (FSI) surveys carried out between 2006 and 2012.

Notes:
* The FSI 2012 Survey comprises the following African jurisdictions: Botswana, Democratic Republic of Congo, Egypt, Gambia, Madagascar, Mauritius, Morocco, Mozambique, Namibia, Tanzania, Uganda and West African Economic and Monetary Union (WAEMU). The jurisdictions covered by the 2006–2010 FSI surveys are not disclosed.
** Not perfectly comparable with previous years, since results were quantified by the author based on individual qualitative country information from the FSI Survey, and therefore subject to his own interpretation.

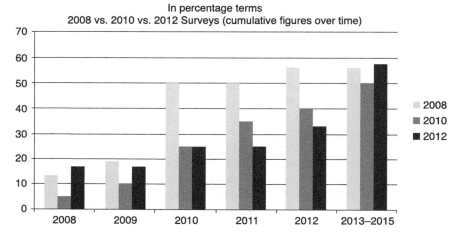

Figure 4.1 African jurisdictions adopting Basel II standardised approach for credit risk, in percentage terms

Source: Based on Financial Stability Institute (FSI) surveys of 2008–2012.

Note: 2008 vs. 2010 vs. 2012 surveys (cumulative figures over time).

that the rules were not appropriate to them, even though, as noted earlier, Basel II does provide for simpler alternatives, and allows for flexibility, in terms of time frame for adoption.

Among countries still intending to adopt Basel II, responses of the 2008, 2010 and 2012 FSI surveys show that those countries opting for the standardised approach for credit risk have gradually slowed down their plans for its adoption over the 2008–2015 time frame (Figure 4.1).

In addition to this slowdown over time, the FSI surveys also show that there has been a gradual withdrawal of countries' intentions to adopt the advanced IRB approach (Figure 4.2), which are those requiring the most sophisticated models to determine risk weights for different categories of assets.

Table 4.2 summarises the number of African jurisdictions adopting the different Basel II credit risk approaches, showing, in 2012, the beginnings of a preference for the standardised approach.

Clearly, the FSI surveys show that there has been some readjustment of expectations and about what is being set as feasible and achievable by African countries.

This chapter explores next what specific capacity constraints African countries face, how common these constraints are across countries, what initiatives have been taken to overcome them and how successful these initiatives have been. This analysis draws mainly on three sources: IMF and World Bank Financial Sector Assessment Programs (FSAPs) and their variants for 19 African countries, undertaken between 2002 and 2011;[6] the 2012 KPMG Africa Banking Survey based on 14 countries;[7] and the World Bank Survey (2012) on "Bank Regulation

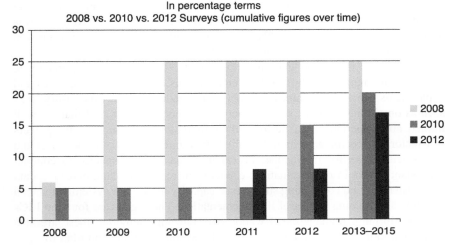

Figure 4.2 African jurisdictions adopting Basel II A-IRB approach for credit risk, in percentage terms

Source: Based on Financial Stability Institute (FSI) surveys of 2008–2012.

Note: 2008 vs. 2010 vs. 2012 surveys (cumulative figures over time).

Table 4.2 Number of African jurisdictions adopting the different Basel II credit risk approaches over 2007–2015

	2007	*2008*	*2009*	*2010*	*2011*	*2012–2015*
Standardised	1	1		1		4
FIRB				1		1
AIRB				1		1

Source: Financial Stability Institute (FSI) Survey 2012.

and Supervision", comprising 31 countries.[8] In looking at capacity issues, the chapter does not pool together the information from the three sources. Instead, it looks at these separately, and therefore takes into account possible biases from each source as well as both similar and contradictory information between them, which can provide important insights about where African countries stand on these issues.

IMF-World Bank FSAPs

Taking together the FSAP reports on the regulatory and supervisory frameworks for the financial sectors of different African jurisdictions, the non-compliance with a number of the 25 Basel Core Principles (BCPs) for banking regulation and supervision can be identified as a common thread. Non-full compliance with the

BCPs might be a reason as to why countries seem to have slowed down on their plans to move from Basel I to Basel II capital frameworks. From a logical viewpoint and given their limited resources, they may have realised that it was important first to achieve full BCPs compliance, and only then make the transition from Basel I to Basel II and III implementation.

Critical capacity-related gaps identified in the various FSAP reports relate first to a low number of staff in the Central Banks and regulatory agencies and departments, which undermines their ability to conduct critical supervisory tasks such as on-site inspections; second, there is a general lack of staff that are well trained and experienced to perform their regulatory and supervisory powers satisfactorily. Specific gaps include skilled and trained accountants, actuaries and others with expertise in finance; IT capacity; analytical capacity to conduct supervisory tasks in risk evaluation; capacity for reviewing data, detecting data inconsistencies and conducting stress tests; capacity to monitor systemic financial stability, and training for Basel II implementation. These gaps are found in LICs such as Burundi, Madagascar, Rwanda and Tanzania, although these are also found in middle-income countries, such as Botswana, Namibia and Mauritius.

Specifically in relation to the Basel capital adequacy framework, critical issues include lack of sufficient supervisory capacity in risk based approach, and to carry out stress testing to assess whether levels of capital requirements are sufficient. A further Basel related issue is lack of large and/or reliable databases, better methods of retrieval, processing and storage of data, and capacity to review and detect data inconsistencies, which are expertise needed in risk assessment. Countries that have foreign banks lack interaction with the home supervisors to identify and assess home country risks and how the home supervisor practises consolidated supervision. The need to interact with home country supervisors partly arises from the fact that, in highly dollarized countries, foreign banks have high levels of concentration of deposits in parent banks, implying portfolio concentration and country risks.

Regional regulatory bodies seem to face similar capacity issues, despite the fact that, in principle, these bodies should be less resource constrained due to a pooling of resources from the member countries. The Central African Banking Commission (COBAC), which is the regulatory body for the Economic and Monetary Community of Central Africa (CEMAC), suffers from acute shortage of staff, which limits considerably its ability to conduct its functions in the countries under its supervision, for example in implementation of new prudential regulation and on-site supervisions.[9] In the Central African Republic, Chad and Gabon, FSAP country reports have highlighted inadequate supervisory capacity by COBAC to carry out both off-site and on-site inspections, in addition to data collection and analysis to support off-site supervision. COBAC is clearly under-resourced, despite the fact that, of the six CEMAC member countries, two are middle-income countries and one is upper-income, according to the World Bank classification.[10] CEMAC's shortage of staff seems to reflect a tension between the resources the regional regulatory body needs to operate with effectiveness and the need to maintain the limited resources available at the country level.

The FSAP report on Senegal, however, indicates that the Central Bank of West African States (BCEAO), which is the regional banking regulator for the West African Economic and Monetary Union (WAEMU), has been historically better equipped and staffed, with a developed supervisory infrastructure in place, to carry out its supervisory duties.[11] The differences between WAEMU and CEMAC seem, in part, to do with the fact that BCEAO is better resourced than COBAC, possibly because of having a clearly established authority as the regional regulator in the region, whereas in the case of COBAC it seems that a significant part of the regulatory role is still in the hands of national authorities, thereby weakening COBAC independence and depriving it of the critical resources it needs to perform its supervisory role adequately. Moreover, BCEAO seems to have benefited significantly from cooperation with France's regulatory authorities. This might be missing in the case of COBAC.

The FSAP reports this chapter draws on cover the 2002–2011 period. On the one hand, this creates the problem that some of the information provided may be outdated. On the other hand, this relatively long time span permits identification of actions that have been undertaken over the period to remedy problems, and of how much has been achieved. In the period covered by the FSAP reports, it is possible to notice that, in a number of countries, significant progress has been made on BCP compliance, and on putting in place much needed regulatory and supervisory infrastructure. However, in areas such as numbers of supervisors and training to enhance staff's technical capacity, progress has been uneven and, on the whole, largely insufficient. Where staff has been adequately trained, a partial staff loss to the private sector has occurred – for example, in Uganda. Of course, the loss of staff to the private sector is not limited to bank supervision; rather, it is a generalised problem affecting other areas of the public sector as well.

What can be said, as a way of preliminary assessment, is that technical capacity gaps exist in different areas, ranging from IT to data reviews and systemic risk evaluation. These gaps are common across countries of different income categories, although more prevalent among LICs and CEMAC member countries. Initiatives have been undertaken to fill these gaps, such as strengthening regulation and supervisory guidelines, expanding staff skills and risk management capacity. However, progress has been partial and uneven, with larger gaps remaining among LICs.

This assessment, based solely on the FSAPs, should be interpreted cautiously. While evidence on shortage of supervisory staff and training are important gaps, the IMF and the World Bank place considerable emphasis on capacity about managing tasks such as using risk assessment models and conducting complex model-based stress tests that may not be the most suitable or pertinent for LICs.

The KPMG Survey

The chapter turns next to the KPMG Africa Banking Survey. The survey covers 14 African countries and is intended to provide basic information on Africa for those considering investing in the continent, particularly in the banking sector. It is structured around a set of questions ranging from a country's regulatory regime to its legal and tax environment, banking environment, skills availability, physical environment and governance and reporting issues.

The analysis that follows groups the countries in the surveys according to their income levels.

Looking at what regulatory approach countries adopt, the picture that emerges is that, first, the institutional approach, in which financial firms are regulated according to their legal status rather than what functions they perform, is dominant among LICs. Diversity is found to a greater extent across low-middle income and upper-middle income countries. In these groupings, the functional, hybrid and twin peaks approaches are commonly adopted, together with the institutional approach. The dominance of the institutional approach among LICs might be associated with their possibly less developed financial systems, in which financial activities are more clearly segmented among financial firms.

Second, all countries are in the process of adopting Basel II, albeit at different speeds, with upper-middle income countries more advanced, having in virtually all cases reached full implementation. Some countries are also working on implementing Basel III, such as Tanzania, Nigeria, South Africa and Zimbabwe.

To some extent, this positive outlook regarding adoption of Basel II diverges from the findings of the FSI Survey of 2012, which overlaps in the countries it covers and which was published at around the same time. According to the FSI Survey, some LICs of Africa – such as Gambia, the Democratic Republic of Congo, Tanzania and Uganda – are still working on the BCP and moving only very slowly towards Basel II implementation.

The divergence between the two surveys may be explained by how responses are provided to different questionnaire formats. At the same time, it may as well be indicating that reporting countries to the KPMG survey attempt to portrait a more positive outlook having in mind potential private investors to their econo-mies. If this is the case, then a further reason for countries opting for standards of best practice is to attract or at least not to discourage FDI. The KPMG Survey shows that in almost all cases, countries' regulation on FDI has very low restrictions or none at all.

Third, in terms of skills availability, taking the country as a whole, the survey shows that the countries harbour highly skilled labour forces, and have training courses available in banking. Thus, skills shortage is not emphasised by the coun-tries, except in a few cases: Zimbabwe highlights limited knowledge available in derivative instruments, Nigeria points to limited depth of skills, and Botswana and Namibia stress critical shortage of professionals. These reported results con-trast strongly with the IMF FSAPs and academic surveys conducted in the past (see Gottschalk and Griffith-Jones, 2010).

Fourth, most countries have stock exchanges where shares and bonds are traded, but only South Africa has active derivatives markets, while Kenya is planning to introduce exchanges of derivatives; the regional stock market of the WAEMU has bonds as the main exchange in the region. Although the survey lacks detail, overall the capital markets are under-developed and therefore opportunities for banks to trade with securities other than government bonds are limited. The main risks the Survey brings to the fore relate to exchange rate risks, due to a combination of dollarization and high level of foreign bank ownership across countries. Other risks are those associated with concentration of assets in a few banks: in Uganda, the top four have 70 per cent of market share; foreign banks in Ghana hold 51 per cent of bank assets; the top four in Nigeria hold 44 per cent of total assets; and a few "old players" in Senegal have 75 per cent of market share.

The World Bank Survey

The chapter next turns to the World Bank Survey on Bank Regulation and Supervision conducted in 2011 with results made available in 2012 – the WB 2012 Survey henceforth.[12] The WB 2012 Survey covers 31 African countries, as mentioned earlier. It is very comprehensive, providing information on a wide range of aspects of banking regulation and supervision. The topics (general and specific) covered by the survey which are relevant to this chapter and which it therefore discusses are: number of supervisors, years of experience, qualifications and hours of training; and number of on-site supervisions by bank, to capture information on availability of resources and therefore complement and/or contrast with FSAP information; plans to adopt Basel II and what approach is being considered for adoption, to complement information from the FSI (which captures changes in intentions over time but is not sufficiently detailed) and KPMG; and asset diversification requirements to capture concentration risks, which links up to macro-prudential regulation discussed below in the context of Basel III.

Table 4.3, which summarises information on resource availability, shows that the number of supervisors among low-income African countries range from

Table 4.3 Resource availability in African countries[1,2]

	Number of bank supervisors	Number of supervisors with more than ten years of experience	Percentage of supervisors with postgraduate degree	Number of on-site supervisors by bank in the last five years
Burundi	26	4	8	2
Ethiopia	27	4	4	3
Gambia	20	5	60	4
Kenya	60	30	80	–
Madagascar	19	12	–	–
Malawi	25	11	50	5
Mozambique	–	–	–	7
Sierra Leone	34	15	70	5
Tanzania	52	19	90	5
Uganda	79	29	38	5
Zimbabwe	45	8	50	2

(Continued)

Table 4.3 (Continued)

	Number of bank supervisors	Number of supervisors with more than ten years of experience	Percentage of supervisors with postgraduate degree	Number of on-site supervisors by bank in the last five years
WAEMU	46	–	80	–
Low-income countries*	26	14	25	4
Low-middle income countries	157(34)	109(23)	32	3
Upper-middle income countries	39	13	32	4

Source: World Bank 2012 Bank Regulation and Supervision Survey database.

Notes:
[1] All individual countries reported in the table are low-income. For the country groupings, the figures are simple averages from the countries covered in the survey and for which information is available.
[2] (–) means no information is available.
* Without WAEMU. ( ) Without Egypt and Nigeria.

19 to 79, with no clear evidence as to what stands behind the differences in numbers across countries, apart from the possible fact that countries with larger numbers have invested more in expanding resources and capacity due to their more diverse and complex supervisory needs. For example, Kenya with 60 and Uganda with 79 supervisors notably are two African countries with financial systems facing higher levels of international integration. Income per capita levels may also explain differences, since the average number of supervisors goes up from low-income to low-middle and to upper-middle income countries. Population size also matters: Egypt and Nigeria, two populous countries, have far higher numbers of supervisors than all the other African countries. No discernible pattern can be found in number of supervisors with more than ten years of experience or the percentage with postgraduate degrees. At one extreme, Ethiopia has very few experienced supervisors – four in total and the percentage with postgraduate degrees is only 4 per cent. At the other extreme, in Tanzania, nearly two-fifths of its supervisors have more than ten years of experience, and the percentage of supervisors with postgraduate degrees is 90 per cent. Number of on-site supervisors per bank in the last five years varies across countries between two and seven, with just a very weak link between these numbers and total number of supervisors per country: when countries of all income categories are pooled together, the correlation index between these two variables is just 0.17.

Resource availability across countries, therefore, seems to vary significantly depending on how it is measured, with no clear correlation patterns across different measures. The explanatory factors probably are varied too, but it is fair to conjecture that countries with more available resources are those with higher absolute and per capita income levels, and those which have prioritised enhancing their regulatory and supervisory capacities.

Table 4.4 Regulatory capital adequacy regime[1]

	Regulatory capital regime (end of 2010)	Timetable for Basel II implementation	Basel II approach for credit risk
Burundi	Basel I	2012	Simplified standardized
Ethiopia	Basel I	–	Simplified standardized
Gambia	Basel I	2014	–
Kenya	Basel I	–	–
Madagascar	Basel I	–	–
Malawi	Basel I	2014	–
Mozambique	Basel I	2014	–
Sierra Leone	Basel I	2014	–
Tanzania	Basel I	–	–
Uganda	Basel I	–	–
Zimbabwe	Basel II for market risk	2012	Standardized
WAEMU	Basel I	2015	–
Low-income countries	One country adopting Basel II		One country adopting standardized
Low-middle income countries	One country adopting Basel II	2012–2015	One country adopting standardized
Upper-middle income countries	50% of countries adopting Basel II	2008–2012	Standardized; one country adopting IRB and A-IRB

Source: World Bank 2012 Bank Regulation and Supervision Survey database.

Note:
[1] All individual countries reported in the table are low-income. For the country groupings, the figures are simple averages from the countries covered in the survey and for which information is available.

Table 4.4, on regulatory capital adequacy regime, shows that most low- and lower-middle income African countries were still adherent to Basel I regulatory capital regime in 2010, with plans to move to Basel II only in 2014–2015, or even after, and indicating their preferences for either the simplified standardised or the standardised approaches. Among upper-middle income African countries, 50 per cent responded to be already under Basel II or planning to have it adopted by the end of 2012, with just one country adopting the IRB and the A-IRB approaches. These survey responses confirm what have been unveiled by the other sources: a slowdown in intentions to move from Basel I to Basel II, and an overwhelming preference for the simpler approaches, especially among the poorer countries.

Challenges in relation to adoption of Basel III

Basel III, announced in October 2010, has brought macro-prudential regulation to the forefront of discussions on regulatory reforms. A major challenge for LICs is how to implement an effective macro-prudential regulation to address the risks arising from the link between financial systems and the macro-economy. The risks they face often are different in nature from those faced by developed countries. Important macro risks developed countries face arise from the use of complex financial instruments and the close inter-connectedness among banks. African LICs face macro risks arising from external shocks that may affect macro-economically important sectors with large banking liabilities. LICs therefore need a macro-prudential framework that is adapted to their specific needs, for example by including in their framework a set of monitoring indicators that are relevant to them (Bagyenda et al., 2011). However, financial regulation experts claim that up to now the emphasis in African LICs has been on micro-prudential regulation and that in most countries a macro-prudential framework is lacking, partly because they lack the resources and have limited technical capacity available to develop such a framework. Thus, according to this assessment, there is a need to build up technical capacity so that regulators are equipped with the tools to detect risks developing from macro-financial links. Moreover, it is also seen as necessary to develop the ability to translate macro-prudential analysis into macro-prudential policy making (Dijkman, 2012).

In view of this assessment, the question is: how fast have they been or how far have they gone in transitioning from micro-prudential towards macro-prudential regulation? At the same time, going back to the debate between complex rules which are hard to adopt versus simpler rules better aligned with needs, the questions might well be re-cast as: how much do they have in place and is what they already have sufficient to meet their needs?

African regulators make the important point that, like Basel I and II, reforms under Basel III maintain a focus on capital adequacy requirements, which may not be as relevant for Africa as it may be for developed countries. A reason is that, in Africa, banking systems already hold capital in excess of the minimum regulatory requirements, so the proposed reforms on raising both relative and absolute capital ratios (the latter through introducing leverage ratios) will have little effect in Africa. In their view, what is necessary in Africa is to address the higher degree of volatility in the value of their banks' assets, by imposing quantitative restrictions on the risk exposures of banks' asset portfolios, an approach which has not been favoured by the Basel Committee in the past many years. Still in their view, what Africa needs is a broad range of restrictions which, according to them, the region has retained despite the change in focus of international regulation from quantitative restrictions to capital adequacy regulation (Bagyenda et al., 2011).

As pointed out above, macro-prudential regulation in Africa should address macro risks arising from external shocks, such as commodity price shocks and natural disasters. Bagyenda et al. (2011) also stress external capital flows and their sudden reversibility as an important source of external shocks. Unlike more traditional commodity price shocks that tend to operate through their impacts on sectors with large bank liabilities, thus implying a credit risk for banks, shocks from capital flows impose risks through the liability side of a bank's balance sheet. This is the case when such flows are sources of non-core funding, with the latter accounting for a significant share of the total liabilities of banks.[13]

Despite their differences, all these sources and types of external shocks share in common the fact that they can cause a large exchange rate adjustment and destabilise the whole financial system. This can happen when currency mismatches are large within banks or within companies to which banks have loaned.

Table 4.5, which summarises guidelines, actions and indicators regarding systemic risks, provides a general idea of the extent to which African countries are, or not, addressing systemic risks, and whether the tools they have in place are the most appropriate to meet their needs, given their specific economic characteristics.

Table 4.5 shows, first, that virtually all African countries do have rules in place to limit banks' ability to lend to a single borrower or to a group of inter-related borrowers. This limitation is a critical macro-prudential rule because banks may be overly exposed to a dominant sector of the economy – say coffee producers in Uganda, which when affected by a shock can cause great distress to the entire banking system and the economy more broadly.[14] Table 4.5 also shows that nearly 50 per cent of African jurisdictions have guidelines to address asset diversification, which is a tool that can be very relevant, especially when specified to encourage asset diversification across different economic sectors facing different risks. Next, the table shows that, in responding to whether countries use tools to capture systemic risk, it can be seen that many countries use a wide range of tools, including bank capital ratios, bank profitability ratios, growth in bank credit, sectoral composition of bank loan portfolios, and foreign exchange position of banks.[15] Specifically in relation to liquidity risks, the WB survey shows (though it is not in Table 4.5) that African countries also have regulation in place on liquidity requirements.

The other indicators in Table 4.5 have more to do with tools and regulations that Basel III has highlighted as important to address systemic risk, such as stress tests, tools to restrict large or inter-connected institutions and counter-cyclical regulation to influence cycles of credit flows. African countries seem to have stress tests, but in most cases these are used at the bank level rather than at a system-wide level. Few countries have tools to restrict large or inter-connected institutions and only a few countries have counter-cyclical tools in place to address risks associated with credit booms. Other constraints that financial sector regulation experts have stressed as critical for Africa include data availability needed for measurement (Dijkman, 2012).

In the 2000s, a number of African countries witnessed a very rapid increase in credit as a proportion of GDP – in Benin and Swaziland, it almost doubled; in Malawi, Mali, Tanzania and Sierra Leone, it increased by threefold or more (see Chapter 1 in this book). These developments, of course, should be closely monitored by the banks' supervisory authorities, and, if Basel III is correct, counter-cyclical tools, such as capital buffers (i.e. higher capital ratios on the upside of the credit cycle), should be adopted to moderate credit growth when the economy is booming, and encourage it when the economy is in a downturn. However, Nigam (2013) questions the possible efficacy of counter-cyclical buffers for Africa. First, because, according to the author's own data analysis for

Table 4.5 Addressing systemic risks[1]

	Banks limited in their lending to a single (or group of inter-related) borrowers	Guidelines on asset diversification	Indicators/tools used to capture systemic risk[2]	Stress test for assessing systemic stability[3]	Tools to restrict large or inter-connected institutions	Counter-cyclical regulation for credit flows
Burundi	Yes	No	Wide range	–	No	No
Ethiopia	Yes	Yes	Wide range	Yes (B/S)	Yes	No
Gambia	Yes	Yes	Bank liquidity ratio	Yes (S)	No	Yes
Kenya	Yes	Yes	Sectoral composition of bank loan portfolios	Yes (B)	No	No
Madagascar	Yes	No	Bank capital ratio	No	No	No
Malawi	Yes	Yes	Wide range	Yes	No	No
Mozambique	Yes	No	Sectoral composition of bank loan portfolios	No	No	Yes
Sierra Leone	Yes	No	Bank liquidity ratio	Yes (B)	No	No
Tanzania	Yes	Yes	Wide range	Yes (B)	No	No
Uganda	Yes	No	Sectoral composition of bank loan portfolios	Yes (B)	Yes	Yes
Zimbabwe	Yes	Yes	Wide range	Yes	No	No
WAEMU	Yes	Yes		Yes (B)	Yes	No
Low-income countries	Yes			Yes		
Low-middle income countries	Yes	3 of 7 Yes	Wide range except Swaziland	Yes	2 of 7 Yes	1 of 7 Yes
Upper-middle income countries	Yes	2 of 7 Yes	Wide range except Angola	Yes, except Botswana and Namibia	3 of 7 Yes	4 of 7 Yes

Source: World Bank 2012 Bank Regulation and Supervision Survey database.

Notes:
[1] All individual countries reported in the table are low-income. For the country groupings, the figures are simple averages from the countries covered in the Survey and for which information is available.
[2] The tools considered are: bank capital ratios; bank leverage ratios; bank profitability ratios; bank liquidity ratios; growth in bank credit; sectoral composition of bank loan portfolios; FX position of banks; bank non-performing loan ratios; bank provisioning ratios; stock market prices; housing prices.
[3] B stands for stress test at the bank level, and S at system-wide level.

Kenya, Tanzania and Uganda, it is hard to find a strong, positive correlation between credit patterns and real GDP growth in these countries. Lack of synchronisation between these two variables would imply that a capital increase triggered by, say, a gap between credit to GDP ratio and its long-term trend crossing a pre-determined threshold, may not necessarily happen when the economy is booming. Second, the role of a credit boom in overheating an economy in Africa tends to be rather small, given their low credit-to-GDP ratio relative to developed economies; third, increases in the minimum regulatory capital in Africa probably will not be binding, given Africa's capital levels already well beyond regulatory minimum.

Thus, the picture that emerges on macro-prudential regulation to address systemic risks is that Africa may not yet be up to scratch, if assessment is undertaken using Basel metrics, such as stress tests. Nevertheless, the region seems to be doing rather well – though further assessment is warranted – if one takes into account the sort of rules and tools that African countries have in place to address their specific needs.

Presence of foreign banks

African countries are known for having banking systems with high levels of concentration, in terms of asset holdings, liabilities or market shares (Beck et al., 2011; Table 4.7). In addition, many African LICs have foreign banks in their jurisdictions. This often means that the banking system in Africa is not only concentrated, but in many cases, foreign banks dominate the system. According to Table 4.6, over 50 per cent (and in a few cases, over 70 per cent) of total bank assets are held by foreign-owned banks. In principle, national regulators have the power to impose their choice of regulatory regimes on banks operating within their jurisdictions. In countries where technical capacity is limited or the financial system is still under-developed, regulators may have as their preferred choice simple regulatory rules, deemed as sufficient to address the country needs. However, foreign banks may challenge these rules, opting instead for more complex regulatory approaches. In light of this, national regulators have to invest in building technical capacity to validate and monitor the use of the models foreign banks wish to adopt. In case national regulators do recommend the adoption of a simpler regulatory approach, their challenge is to have it accepted by the foreign banks. As Y. V. Reddy, ex-Governor of the Reserve Bank of India (RBI), puts it 'international banks enjoy significant influence over the political economy in several countries'. Although his assertion relates to international banks operating mainly in developed country markets, it applies well to African countries, where these banks probably are 'too powerful to regulate' (Reddy, 2012).

The emphasis on macro-prudential regulation since the global crisis has brought to the spotlight the need for greater cooperation between host and home regulators in Africa. Cooperation would permit host regulators to follow and be updated on how supervision of subsidiaries is done by home supervisors, and to

Table 4.6 Banking concentration and presence of foreign banks[1]

	Of commercial banks, % of total assets held by five largest banks (2010)	% of banking system's assets in hands of foreign-controlled banks (own 50% or more of equity) (2010)
Burundi	87	16
Ethiopia	84	0
Gambia	72	80
Kenya	50	37
Madagascar	82	100
Malawi	83	29
Mozambique	92	92
Sierra Leone	74	62
Tanzania	64	49
Uganda	61	75
Zimbabwe	54	46
WAEMU	21	73
Low-income countries	55	60
Low-middle income countries	53	62
Upper-middle income countries	87	67

Source: World Bank 2012 Bank Regulation and Supervision Survey database.

Note:
[1] All individual countries reported in the table are low-income. For the country groupings, the figures are simple averages from the countries covered in the survey and for which information is available.

have access to data. However, IMF FSAPs indicate that cooperation is limited, possibly with the exception of the WAEMU BACEAO regulator, which has historically maintained close links with French regulators. This lack of cooperation is problematic. It leaves host regulators powerless and creates serious systemic risks to the host country, since host regulators do not know whether banks' headquarters are sufficiently solid or even what their policy is in case their subsidiaries come to face acute funding needs; and there is no guarantee that home supervisors pay attention to or are aware of the situation of their banks in specific locations around the world.

The lack of cooperation, therefore, also is a missed opportunity for capacity building. Supervisory colleges, which have been created in Africa for those countries with cross-border banking, have become important, and to an important extent African regulators are happy with how these colleges operate and the benefits they bring, in terms of exchange of information between their peers and in terms of technical advice they receive from developed country mentors that participate in their meetings. But African regulators also note that, while exchange of information is taking place regionally, there is still a great lack of cooperation with home supervisors from developed countries (see Gottschalk, 2015 and also Chapter 10 in this book).

Risks associated with capital account liberalisation

Increased capital account liberalisation may result in inflows of foreign bank lending and portfolio capital, which in turn have the potential to create serious currency mismatches in banks' balance sheets. Moreover, foreign banks may magnify the risks, given the ease with which they can tap into foreign sources of funding for their lending and other activities in the host country. It is thus necessary that countries have in place a supervisory framework for monitoring adequately the size of these mismatches and how they evolve over time. These mismatches imply serious exchange rate risks, which materialise very quickly and strongly when a country faces a sudden and sharp exchange rate adjustment as a result of external shocks. Supervisors have to look at mismatches within banks and within firms to which banks lend, and have real time based surveillance and be alert to sudden changes to minimise risks. A further issue is that capital account liberalisation may lead to adoption of new financial instruments and higher levels of inter-connectedness within national financial systems as well as internationally. These developments can be quick, requiring the ability to understand and detect the new risks that arise, and the resources to monitor them closely. However, although important, close monitoring is not sufficient; it is important to have rules that prevent mismatches going out of control, and restrictions on financial innovation.[16]

African countries are aware of these risks, and some have home-grown measures to address some of them, which can be applied by other countries, too. For example, in 2005, the Central Bank of Mozambique adopted the so-called Aviso No 5, according to which banks lending in dollars to non-exporting firms have to make provisioning corresponding to 50 per cent of the total loan value.[17]

As for stronger restrictions to reduce exchange rate risks, African countries such as Ethiopia, Cameroon and Tanzania, have fairly restricted capital accounts of their balance of payments, although for debt inflows liberalisation may rather be the case. Restrictions on the capital account probably are a most effective way to prevent currency mismatches in the domestic economy, although the downside is lack of access to external funding by banks.

Restrictions on external capital do not, however, entirely eliminate the risk of currency mismatches in Africa. A main reason is that many African economies are dollarized, due to aid flows. So, even countries that have fairly closed capital accounts for external private capital still can have large currency mismatches in their banking systems and in the economy at large and therefore face significant exchange rate risks. The motivation for Mozambique's Act No 5 was not that the economy was attracting large volumes of external private capital, but that its banks had large foreign currency denominated liabilities, in the form of dollar bank deposits, associated with foreign aid.

Table 4.7 shows that, in Mozambique in 2010, 29 per cent of the total liabilities of commercial banks were denominated in foreign currency. Gambia, Sierra Leone, Tanzania and Uganda had even higher percentages in that year. While these percentages are high, it is important to see to what extent the liabilities

Table 4.7 Foreign assets and liabilities in the banking sector[1]

	% of assets of commercial banks denominated in foreign currency (2010)	% of liabilities of commercial banks denominated in foreign currency (2010)	Regulators' monitoring of forex position of banks to assess systemic risk
Burundi	20	18	
Ethiopia	–	–	Yes
Gambia	34	34	
Kenya	–	–	
Madagascar	21	19	
Malawi	10	12	Yes
Mozambique	17	29	
Sierra Leone	22	31	
Tanzania	31	33	Yes
Uganda	25	30	
Zimbabwe	100	100	Yes
WAEMU	7	6	
Low-income countries	21	23	
Low-middle income countries	8	7	4 of 7 Yes
Upper-middle income countries	27	29	5 of 7 Yes

Source: World Bank 2012 Bank Regulation and Supervision Survey database.

Note:
[1] All individual countries reported in the table are low-income. For the country groupings, the figures are simple averages from the countries covered in the survey and for which information is available.

denominated in foreign currency match with banks' assets in foreign currencies. Still according to Table 4.7, the percentages of assets and liabilities in foreign currency roughly match in a number of countries, such as Burundi, Gambia and Tanzania. However, in a few countries, such as Mozambique and Sierra Leone, the gap is over 10 percentage points, implying important risks, especially because the higher percentage is on the liability rather than assets' side, making sudden and sharp currency devaluations particularly dangerous. Despite these mismatches, only a few countries in their responses to the WB 2012 Survey indicate that they monitor the foreign exchange position of banks as part of their assessment of systemic risk (see final column of Table 4.7). This seems to be a clear supervisory gap in the region.

Of course, elimination of mismatches in the banking sector alone does not totally eliminate risks. If banks offer loans denominated in foreign currency to companies whose markets are domestic and therefore do not generate revenues in foreign currency, still banks will be bound to face a credit risk, which may materialise in the event of a sudden and large exchange rate devaluation, because it would affect companies' ability to honour their commitments in foreign currency. In this respect, Mozambique's Act No 5 mentioned earlier is particularly well designed, since it precisely targets banks' loans to companies whose earnings are not in foreign, but in domestic currency.

The problem with these measures is that, given banks' liabilities in dollars, the latter still need to find ways to have assets in the same currency to avoid currency mismatches. Given this basic problem, risks are not eliminated, but just transferred to other agents or transfigured into another type of risk. Having liabilities in dollars, but facing restrictions to lend in the same currency, banks are left with the alternative of having assets denominated in foreign currency, for example in the form of bank deposits in their parent banks abroad. In this case, risks probably are smaller, but they still exist, to the extent that this alternative creates asset portfolio concentration risks. This is a further reason as to why cooperation between home and host regulators is so important.

The above discussion shows that there is not an easy, short-term solution to risks associated with currency mismatch. The issue requires a medium- to long-term strategy, for instance in the form of attempts to steer the financial sector development towards de-dollarization. It would be a wise way forward that can increase monetary policy effectiveness and contribute to the development of more robust financial systems in Africa.

Conclusion

This chapter raises the general point that regulatory challenges and capacity limitations facing Africa should be examined and judged with caution. This is partly because the African region includes countries of different levels of development, with challenges and needs in the area of banking regulation and supervision varying considerably across countries. And partly because, recently, international standards designed by committees and forums dominated by developed and emerging economies have been challenged both from within (i.e. regulators from developed countries) and outside (i.e. regulators from African LICs). These challenges raise questions about standards of international best practice, and therefore making it more difficult to make judgements about what African countries already have in place for effective banking regulation and supervision, and what is still missing.

A further issue, particular to this chapter, is that much of the assessment it conducts draws on surveys that are based on multiple choice questions or that require binary answers, therefore lacking depth.

Having these caveats in mind, the mapping exercise in this chapter shows that African countries, and African LICs in particular, face significant regulatory challenges, for example regarding what capital adequacy framework to adopt and how to regulate foreign banks, which in a number of cases have a dominant presence. They also face important regulatory and supervisory gaps – examples that came up in the chapter include a lack of counter-cyclical tools to address systemic risks (though the usefulness of this tool in the African context has been questioned by African regulators); insufficient assessment of foreign exchange position of banks, needed to guard against risks associated with currency mismatches; and limited available capacity, for example in terms of number of experienced supervisors for effective regulation and supervision of their banking systems.

In addition to this general, initial assessment, the chapter makes evident that, most of all, further investigation is needed to understand what the key issues and challenges are in the opinion of African regulators, and what, in their views, are the necessary actions to improve banking regulation and supervision in their own countries to ensure that their banks are robust and ready to fulfil their primary role, which is supporting inclusive and sustainable growth.

Notes

1   This chapter is a shorter version of a paper prepared under the ESRC-DFID project "Financial regulation in low-income countries: Balancing inclusive growth with financial stability", and presented at the workshop project in Accra on 10–11 September 2013. Comments from Charles Harvey and Accra workshop participants, and research assistance of Piotr Winter are greatly appreciated. The usual caveats apply.

2   This quote is extracted from the ESRC-DFID project proposal.

3   See, for example, Haldane and Madouros (2012).

4   Cornford (2012) provides an excellent summary of these recent trends.

5   When initially published in 2004, Basel II introduced a menu of different approaches for capital determination: i) the standardised approach, which involves changing risk weights based on assessments made periodically by rating agencies; ii) the simplified standardised approach, quite similar to Basel I, to which fixed weights are assigned as well iii) the internal-ratings-based approach (IRB), which is based on banks' own risk assessment models for capital determination, and which uses the probability of default (PD) variable as input to run the model, and whose weights are non-fixed; and iv) the advanced IRB approach (A-IRB), which is also based on banks' own risk assessment models for capital determination, but differing from the IRB approach in that it uses the loss given default as the input variable instead. Approaches iii) and iv) are understood as the more complex ones, since they require sophisticated internal risk models for capital determination, and which are data intensive.

6   In addition to the FSAP reports, information has been drawn from the FSAs (Financial Sector Assessments) and the FSSA (Financial System Stability Assessment), all available on the IMF and World Bank websites. Reports from the following jurisdictions were consulted: Botswana, Burundi, Cameroon, Central African Republic, CEMAC, Chad, Gabon, Madagascar, Malawi, Mauritius, Mozambique, Namibia, Niger, Rwanda, Senegal, South Africa, Tanzania and Uganda.

7   The KPMG survey covers the following countries: Botswana, Ghana, Kenya, Mauritania, Mauritius, Morocco, Namibia, Nigeria, Senegal, South Africa, Tanzania, Uganda, Zambia and Zimbabwe.

8   The World Bank Survey covers the following African countries: Angola, Benin, Botswana, Burkina Faso, Burundi, Egypt, Ethiopia, Gambia, Ghana, Guinea-Bissau, Kenya, Lesotho, Madagascar, Malawi, Mali, Mauritius, Morocco, Mozambique, Namibia, Niger, Nigeria, Senegal, Seychelles, Sierra Leone, South Africa, Swaziland, Tanzania, Togo, Tunisia, Uganda and Zimbabwe.

9   CEMAC member countries are: Cameroon, Central African Republic, Chad, Equatorial Guinea, Gabon and Republic of Congo.

10   Based on the World Bank classification of July 2012, which was the latest available on-line at the time of writing this paper.

11   The WAEMU member countries are: Benin, Burkina Faso, Cote d'Ivoire, Guinea Bissau, Mali, Niger, Senegal and Togo.

12 Previous World Bank surveys on Bank Regulation and Supervision were made available in 2001, 2003 and 2007.
13 To address this less stable source of funding and therefore reduce liquidity risks facing banks, Basel III proposes the introduction of a liquidity coverage ratio (LCR), which means a minimum level of highly liquid assets that banks should hold to be able to meet their financial obligations.
14 Whether developed countries also have such restrictions or not, the point is that, for them, this is not so relevant, since the risk of portfolio loan concentration is much smaller, given that their loan opportunities often are far greater.
15 Table 4.7 shows, nevertheless, that the foreign exchange position of banks is an indicator used only by some countries.
16 Concerns with currency mismatches in the economy more broadly rather than just within the banking sector gained prominence already with the East Asian crisis in the late 1990s. Following the crisis, the emphasis by the then Financial Stability Forum (FSF) was on monitoring, control and reporting systems. That is, banks were advised to monitor carefully the foreign currency exposures of their borrowers, the extent to which they have access to foreign exchange to service their debts and whether they have hedged against foreign exchange risks (FSF, 2000, p. 29).
17 See Aviso No 5, Banco de Mocambique website.

References

Bagyenda, J., Brownbridge, M. and Kasekende, L. (2011) "Basel III and the Global Reform of Financial Regulation: How Should Africa Respond? A Bank Regulator's Perspective". Paper prepared for AERC input to Connect-USA project on global financial reform, February, Bank of Uganda.

Beck, T., Maimbo, S., Faye, I. and Triki, T. (2011) "Financing Africa: Through the Crisis and Beyond". The World Bank, Washington DC.

Cornford, A. (2012) "Of Dogs, Frisbees and the Complexity of Capital Requirements". SUNS-South-North Development Monitor, 19 November. Also at: www.mapping finance.org/article/89/Of-Dogs-Frisbees-and-the-Complexity-of-Capital-Requirements. html#.VlXcA7_7Prc.

Dijkman, M. (2012) "Making Macro-Prudential Supervision Work for Africa". Africa Finance Forum, 4 June. Also at: http://aff.mfw4a.org/africa-finance-forum-blog/author/miquel-dijkman.html.

Financial Stability Institute (Various Years) "Implementation of the New Capital Adequacy Framework in Non-Basel Committee Member Countries: Summary of Responses to Basel II Implementation Survey". Bank for International Settlements, Basel.

FSF (2000) "Report of the Working Group on Capital Flows". Financial Stability Forum. 25–26 March.

Gottschalk, R. (2015) "What Financial Regulation for Stability and Financial Inclusion in Africa? The Views of Regulators of Ethiopia, Kenya and Lesotho". ODI Working Paper 414. March.

Gottschalk, R. and Griffith-Jones, S. (2010) "Basel II Implementation in Low-Income Countries: Challenges and Effects on SME Development". In: Gottschalk, R. (ed.) *The Basel Capital Accords in Developing Countries: Challenges for Development Finance.* Palgrave Macmillan, UK, pp. 75–96.

Haldane, A. and Madouros, V. (2012) "The Dog and the Frisbee". Speech at the Federal Reserve Bank of Kansas City's 366th economic policy symposium, "The Changing Policy Landscape", Jackson Hole, Wyoming, 31 August.

Harle, P., Luders, E., Peparides, T., Pfetsch, S., Pappensieker, T. and Stegemann, V. (2010) "Basel III and European Banking: Its Impact, How Banks Might Respond, and the Challenges of Implementation". McKinsey Working Papers on Risk, No 26. McKinsey & Company, November.

Hoenig, T. (2012) "Back to Basics: A Better Alternative to Basel Capital Rules". Address to the American Banker Regulatory Symposium, Washington DC, 14 September.

IMF-World Bank FSAPs, various reports.

KPMG (2012) "African Banking Survey", KPMG, May, South Africa.

Nigam, P. K. (2013) "Procyclicality of Credit and the Counter-Cyclical Capital Buffer: A Critical Analysis for East Africa". Working Paper Draft, Bank of Uganda, Kampala, Uganda.

Reddy, Y. V. (2012) "Society, Economic Policies, and the Financial Sector". The Per Jacobsson Foundation Lecture 2012, Basel, Switzerland, 24 June.

World Bank (2012) "Bank Regulation and Supervision Survey". The World Bank, Washington DC.

5 Financial regulation in Kenya

Balancing inclusive growth with financial stability

Francis M. Mwega[1]

Introduction

Since the global financial crisis, many countries have prioritized stability by strengthening financial regulation. Given that the primary purpose of finance is to facilitate productive economic activities, regulation should aim at maintaining financial stability and promoting economic growth. This is a delicate balancing act, as too great a focus on stability could stifle growth, while a dash for growth is likely to sow the seeds of future crises.

This chapter analyses the potential tradeoffs between regulation, stability and growth in Kenya, a small open economy which is highly vulnerable to domestic and external shocks, but with a lightly regulated financial system and a fairly open capital account. To make the analysis manageable, it focuses mainly on the banking sector, although capital markets, pension funds and other financial institutions may facilitate more long-term finance if banks do not provide them sufficiently. The chapter is organized around six main issues. The second section analyzes the size and growth of the financial sector and its linkages to economic performance; the third section investigates the role of foreign banks, state-owned banks and development finance institutions (DFIs); the fourth section examines the evolution of financial inclusion in the country; the fifth section discusses access and cost of credit; the sixth section explains prudential regulations; while the seventh section analyzes the management of capital flows in the country. The eighth section concludes.

Size and growth of the financial sector

The financial sector in the context of Kenya's Vision 2030

The starting point of the chapter is an analysis of the role of the financial sector in Kenya's Vision 2030, the country's development blueprint which was launched in 2008 (Kenya, 2007). The Vision identifies financial services as one of seven sectors that are the key drivers of the economy, and aims to create "a vibrant and globally competitive financial sector that will create jobs and also promote high levels of savings to finance Kenya's overall investment needs". It envisages a dynamic financial sector comprised of banks, the capital market, insurance, pensions, development finance and financial co-operatives (SACCOs). The Vision therefore aims to revamp Kenya's already fairly diversified financial sector.

The Kenya Vision 2030 was to be flexibly implemented in successive five-year Medium-Term Plans (MTPs), with the first MTP covering the period 2008–2012 (already completed), and the current second MTP covering the period 2013–2017 (Kenya, 2013). The flagship projects and policies that were to be implemented during the First MTP (2008–2012) included: i) transformation of the banking sector to bring in fewer stronger, larger scale banks; ii) development and execution of a comprehensive model for pension reform; iii) pursuance of a comprehensive remittances strategy; iv) formulation of a policy for the issuing of benchmark sovereign bonds; and v) implementation of legal and institutional reforms required for a regional financial centre.

According to the Second MTP (2013–2017), some of these projects and policies have not been implemented at all or have been implemented only partially. The MTP attributes this to a number of factors, including: i) the post-election violence of 2007–2008; ii) adverse weather impacting the agricultural sector and the economy; and iii) the global financial crisis and the subsequent worldwide economic slowdown. Nevertheless, the Second MTP identifies some of the following key process achievements under the First MTP:

- Increased efficiency of financial services that directly supports improved credit access by reducing transaction costs such as interventions in the payments system, capital markets infrastructure and credit referencing, although the MTP does not indicate how these efficiency gains were measured.
- Introduction of credit reference bureaus first rolled out in July 2010. By December 2013, the two licensed credit referenced bureaus (Credit Reference Bureau Africa Limited and Metropol Credit Reference Bureau Limited) had received a total of 3.5 million credit requests from banks and more than 53,000 requests from individual customers. Revised regulations allowing for sharing of positive and negative credit information by banks and deposit-taking microfinance institutions were gazetted in January 2014.
- Implementation of policies to enhance the stability of the financial system, focused on the deposit-taking institutions, which account for the largest proportion of the assets in the system. Oversight of insurance, pension and other investment funds had also been strengthened with all the regulators adopting the Basel risk-based approach to the supervision of institutions or entities under their regulation.[2]

Financial sector and economic performance

A lot of work has been done on the relationship between the size of the financial sector and economic performance (for a review, see Chapter 3 in this book). Many studies find a close linkage between financial deepening, productivity and economic growth. For example, it is estimated that policies that would raise the M2/GDP ratio by 10 per cent would increase the long-term per capita growth rate by 0.2–0.4 per cent points (Easterly and Levine, 1997;

Ndulu and O'Connell, 2008). In the simple AK model, the financial sector promotes the growth of the economy by raising the saving rate; the marginal productivity of capital, and the proportion of savings that is channelled to investment.[3] However, while low-income countries (LICs) need to increase the size of their financial sectors, there are limits to this. Beyond a certain level, financial sector development becomes negative for economic growth, both through heightened financial instability and the misallocation of financial resources. The same applies to a too rapid growth of private sector credit which might lead to output volatility and adverse growth effects (see Chapter 1 in this book).

Kenya has a well developed financial system for a country of its income level (Beck and Fuchs, 2004). The country's level of financial development is not too far off from the predicted level in a global cross-country model (Allen et al., 2012). Christensen (2010) classifies Kenya as a frontier market economy whose financial market is advanced, but not to the same extent as those of emerging markets, e.g. S. Africa, given that its M3/GDP ratio was about 34 per cent compared with an average of 63 per cent for emerging market economies. It is therefore unlikely that the size of Kenya's financial sector is beyond the threshold to negatively impact on economic growth. Chapter 1 in this book also shows that credit expansion in Kenya has been relatively modest in their study period (at 19.5 per cent over 2000–2010) compared with other selected sub-Saharan African (SSA) countries, perhaps because of the relatively dominant influence of the IMF and the World Bank programs in policy-making in the country with their bias towards tight monetary policies.

Two measures of the depth and coverage of financial systems is the M2/GDP and private credit/GDP ratios. As seen in Figure 5.1, while the M2/GDP ratio in Kenya closely tracks that of LICs, it is far below that of middle-income countries

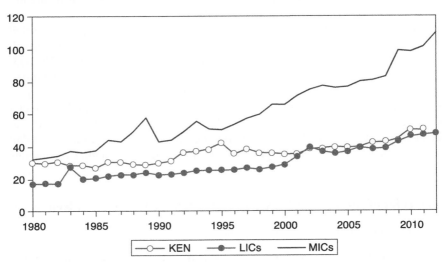

Figure 5.1 M2 as percentage of GDP in Kenya versus LICs and MICs

Source: World Bank, World Development Indicators.

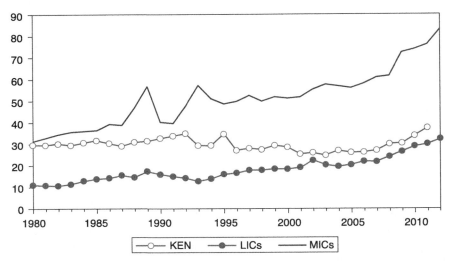

Figure 5.2 Domestic credit to the private sector as percentage of GDP in Kenya versus LICs and MICs

Source: World Bank, World Development Indicators.

(MICs), with a clear divergence over time. Figure 5.2 also shows a similar pattern with respect to credit to the private sector to GDP ratio, with the Kenya ratio tending to decline from the early 1990s. Between 1980–2011, Kenya's ratio increased from 29.5 per cent to 37.4 per cent, while for MICs it went from 31 per cent to 76 per cent. With the country aspiring to MIC status by 2030, it apparently has a long way to go in building its financial sector.

The Kenya National Bureau of Statistics (KNBS) provides quarterly GDP growth data since 2000. Figure 5.3 shows four-period moving average growth rates in financial intermediation and overall GDP in Kenya over 2001Q1–2013Q3. Granger causality tests show significant causality from financial intermediation to growth at three and four lags at the 5 per cent level, with the other lags non-significant (Table 5.1), supporting Kenya Vision 2030 designation of the financial sector as one of the drivers of growth in Kenya, at least in the short-run.[4] On an annual basis, the financial sector growth has consistently outpaced the real GDP growth since 2009; hence the potential need for macro-prudential regulations should this trend continue or accelerate.

The roles of foreign banks, state-owned banks and DFIs in Kenya

Foreign and state-owned commercial banks

Opinion on the merits of foreign banks and state-owned banks has shifted considerably since the global crisis. While foreign banks can bring valuable skills, technology and capital, they can also bring risks. Evidence from the recent global

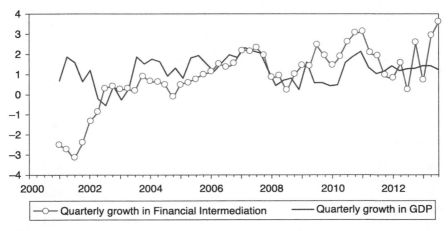

Figure 5.3 Quarterly growth in financial intermediation and GDP in Kenya, 2001Q1–2013Q3

Source: Kenya National Bureau of Statistics (www.knbs.go.ke).

financial crisis shows that countries where foreign banks dominate the market could suffer negative lending shocks, as turmoil in the home markets cause parent banks to withdraw capital from the developing countries where they operate. Critics of foreign bank participation therefore argue that foreign banks may have an overall negative effect on financial deepening and inclusion. The existing empirical literature has, however, not provided unambiguous findings on the repercussions of foreign banks for financial development and inclusion and neither has the African experience (Beck, 2013).

Similarly, there has been a change in the negative perception of state-owned commercial banks, with some studies finding that these banks performed a valuable counter-cyclical role in some countries; while others find them to be associated with higher rates of economic growth (see Chapter 2 in this book). The challenge, therefore, is to design and regulate them so that they can successfully fulfil their development mandate, while avoiding the well-documented failures of the past.

Kenya currently (in September 2014) has 43 banks, accounting for about two-thirds of the financial system's assets. In terms of shareholding, the Central Bank identifies 14 banks with foreign ownership, accounting for 32.2 per cent of net assets in 2012. The Central Bank also identifies six banks with state ownership accounting for 24.8 per cent of net assets in the same year, with the government having majority ownership in three of these, which account for 4.2 per cent of net total assets (Consolidated Bank; Development Bank of Kenya; and the National Bank of Kenya).[5] The remaining 23 are local private banks, accounting for 43.0 per cent of the banking sector's net assets. Hence Kenya's banking system is dominated by local private banks and foreign banks.[6]

We next examine the relative performance of the 14 foreign banks and the six banks with state ownership *versus* the local private banks in the country.

Table 5.1 The performance of commercial banks in Kenya by ownership

	Foreign banks	Banks with state ownership	Banks with majority state ownership	Local private banks	All banks
Return on assets, %					
2009	3.6	2.8	3.7	3.8	3.6
2010	4.7	3.7	4.2	4.8	4.6
2011	4.7	4.1	3.1	4.8	4.7
2012	5.2	4.1	1.4	4.8	4.9
Return on capital, %					
2009	36.7	30.0	27.2	30.3	32.3
2010	46.1	23.4	30.8	46.6	40.7
2011	50.6	44.9	27.6	50.4	49.1
2012	51.9	38.0	12.7	50.9	48.0
Average cost of funds, %					
2009	3.0	2.7	3.5	4.0	3.4
2010	2.2	2.1	2.9	3.4	2.7
2011	2.5	2.3	3.8	3.8	3.0
2012	4.9	5.3	7.6	7.0	6.0
Efficiency ratio, %					
2009	53.1	66.4	64.4	58.8	60.0
2010	47.1	61.4	58.0	51.6	53.6
2011	45.8	56.8	63.1	51.6	52.0
2012	50.7	57.0	74.8	52.0	53.9
Non-performing loans to advances ratio, %					
2009	4.5	9.7	10.1	6.4	6.7
2010	3.6	6.4	6.6	5.1	5.0
2011	2.7	4.4	6.5	3.7	3.6
2012	2.4	5.2	8.8	3.6	3.7

Note: Return on assets (ROA) is the ratio of profits before tax to average total assets (at beginning and end of the year); while return on capital (ROC) is measured as the return to the average core capital. The cost of funds ratio is a measure of how cheaply or expensively a bank gets resources from its two sources of funds: a) deposits from customers; and b) borrowing. The efficiency ratio is measured by taking the total operating expenses, which include the bank's overheads, and weighting them against the total operating income.

Oloo (2013) proposes a number of indicators to identify the different strengths and weaknesses of Kenyan banks and provides data on individual banks, which we aggregate into the various ownership components, weighted by the value of assets in 2012. These include the rates of return on assets and capital; cost of funds; efficiency ratio; and the ratio of non-performing loans (see Table 5.1).

The foreign banks have done as well as local private banks with both having an average rate of return on assets of 4.6 per cent over 2009–2012, ahead of banks with state ownership (3.7 per cent) and state-owned banks (3.1 per cent), perhaps because the latter two perform some social functions, for example having more rural branches. Hence, lower returns (and higher non-performing loans (NPLs) of state-owned banks) may reflect higher-risk lending. The poorer performance could also be attributed to the legacy in the past of poor governance and massive interference by the state in their management.

The same pattern is repeated in the other indicators. Foreign banks have on average done slightly better on the rate of return on core capital (46.3 per cent) over 2009–2012 when compared with local private banks (44.6 per cent), ahead of banks with state ownership (34.1 per cent and 24.6 per cent, respectively). One should also note the massive increase in return to capital for foreign and local private banks, reflecting the overall good performance of the banking sector in recent years. They also have the lowest cost of funds (index of 3.2 per cent) together with banks with state ownership (index of 3.1 per cent and 4.5 per cent, respectively) and local private banks (index 4.6 per cent). The doubling of funding costs for all banks in 2012 reflects a tightening of monetary policy in 2011 to deal with a high rate of inflation and depreciation of the exchange rate. Foreign banks are also the most efficient (with an average score of 49.1 per cent) slightly ahead of local private banks (score of 53.5 per cent), with banks with state ownership the least efficient (scores of 60.4 per cent and 65.1 per cent, respectively). Banks with majority state ownership seem to have become less efficient. Finally, foreign banks have the lowest non-performing loans ratio (average 3.3 per cent over 2009–2012), followed by local private banks (4.7 per cent) and banks with state ownership (6.4 per cent).

It is therefore apparent that foreign banks largely behave like local private banks, except that they have cheaper sources of finance due to their reputation capital. With similar profit levels, this implies that local private banks compensate by charging higher lending rates. In 2013, their average retail lending rates were 10.7 per cent compared to 9.5 per cent of foreign banks. Foreign banks are also very diverse so that it is difficult to generalize their behaviour. They include, for example, i) the traditional multinational banks from Europe and the USA (Barclays, Citibank, Habib A.Z. Zurich and Standard); ii) banks from Asia and the Middle East (Bank of Baroda, Bank of India, Gulf African Bank, Habib Bank and Diamond Trust Bank); iii) pan-African banks (Bank of Africa, United Bank of Africa and Ecobank); and iv) Islamic banks (First Community Bank and Gulf African Bank).

Challenges of regulating Kenyan banks in other countries

In Kenya, some banks have expanded their branch networks in the region. By December 2012, 11 Kenyan banks had established 282 branches in neighbouring countries (Uganda 125, Tanzania 70, Rwanda 51, Burundi 5 and South Sudan 31). Such banks pose an increasing challenge for regulators across Africa (Beck, 2013). Financial integration implies that the negative externality costs of bank failure go beyond national borders that are not taken into account by national regulators and supervisors. Close cooperation can help internalize these cross-border externalities.

Central banks in Eastern African countries have, for example, signed a Memorandum of Understanding (MOU) to facilitate information sharing and supervisory cooperation for regional banking groups. The East African Central Banks are also currently working to harmonize their banking sector supervisory rules and practices as a prerequisite for the envisaged East African Monetary Union (EAMU). The recently established Committee of African Bank Supervisors as part of the African Association of Central Banks can give this cooperation further impetus, by enabling informal exchange of information and experiences and networking possibilities. However, based on the experience of European countries, there should be a focus on proper preparation for resolution, as non-binding MOUs and Colleges of Supervisors whose activities involve mainly information exchange are of limited use in times of bank failure (Beck, 2013).

Development finance institutions[7]

It has long been known that commercial banks will under-supply long-term finance, and under-serve key sectors, such as agriculture or small and medium-sized enterprises (SMEs), and that these 'market failures' are more acute in LICs. Although DFIs are an obvious solution, they were widely seen as inefficient and ineffective, generally and in Africa. This perception has shifted significantly since the recent global financial crisis, where some countries with significant DFIs saw them fill the gap left by the commercial banks. The success of DFIs in countries as diverse as Brazil, South Africa and Germany has shown that it is possible to get positive impact and avoid many pitfalls (Griffith-Jones and Cozzi, Forthcoming).

There is no doubt that DFIs in Kenya could play a significant role in the financial sector by providing long-term finance (CBK, 2013). This is recognized under Vision 2030, where DFIs are expected to contribute towards enhanced financial access and investment goals. But the sector remains small. The six existing DFIs account for less than 1 per cent of the assets of the banking sector and had lent only Ksh.6.8 billion (approximately $80.73 million) as of June 2012, a small value when compared with Ksh 1,224.11 billion (approximately $14.53 billion) of credit to the private sector from the county's banking sector (CBK, 2013). Hence, these DFIs supplied only about 0.6 per cent of the banking sector credit to the private sector.

According to a Presidential Task Force on Parastatals Reform (2013), the role of DFIs has atrophied since the mid-1980s which the Task Force attributes to the DFIs' inability to respond successfully to the change to a liberal policy regime in the 1980s and 1990s; narrow credit focus and limited sources of financing from donors and government; as well as poor governance, coupled with ineffective management and low staff morale. The Task Force therefore advocates consolidating DFIs under a Kenya Development Bank (KDB) with sufficient scale, scope and resources to play a catalytic role in Kenya's economic development by providing long-term finance and advisory services. There may be a case for the government or donors to increase capital of such a bank, combined with an effort at good governance and regulation, so that a larger KDB has a more positive impact on Kenyan development, SMEs and possibly infrastructure or other key sectors.

The CBK (2013) calls for the introduction of prudential regulation and supervision consistent with a DFI mandate – for example the standards of the Association of African DFIs (AADFI) – as done in several countries including Tanzania, Nigeria, China, Swaziland and Korea, which already regulate and supervise DFIs. An effective regulatory and supervisory framework should adequately address the potential risks faced by DFIs by tailoring them to suit their unique features.

Financial inclusion in Kenya

Trends and patterns of financial inclusion

Financial inclusion in Kenya has been monitored through financial access surveys of which three so far have been conducted: in 2006, 2009 and 2013. These surveys reveal that Kenya's financial inclusion landscape has undergone considerable change. The proportion of the adult population using different forms of formal financial services has increased from 27 per cent in 2006, to 41 per cent in 2009 and stood at 67 per cent in 2013, the highest in Africa (Table 5.2). Overall, the proportion of the adult population totally excluded from financial services has declined from 39.3 per cent in 2006 to 31.4 per cent in 2009 and to 25.4 per cent in 2013. With a decline of 35 per cent between 2006 and 2013, this has substantially exceeded Vision 2030's expectations.

Formal financial institutions are defined broadly to include commercial banks, deposit-taking microfinance institutions (DTMs), foreign exchange bureau, capital markets, insurance providers, deposit-taking SACCOs (DTSs), mobile phone financial service providers (MFSP), Postbank, NSSF, NHIF, credit-only MFIs, credit-only SACCOS, hire purchase companies and the government. The informal financial sector includes informal groups, shopkeepers and merchants, employers, and money lenders who are all unregulated under structured law provisions.

The last decade has therefore seen a massive increase in access to financial services in the country. Deposit accounts have, for example, increased from about 2 million to 18 million while loan accounts have increased from 1 to 3 million since 2007.[8] This is reflected in Table 5.3 which shows a substantial increase in the use of bank services, from 13.5 per cent in 2006, to 17.1 per cent in 2009 and to 29.2 per cent in 2013. However, the most dramatic increase is usage of mobile

Table 5.2 Financial inclusion and exclusion in Kenya, per cent

	2006	*2009*	*2013*
Formal	27.4	41.3	66.7
Informal	33.3	27.2	7.8
Excluded	39.3	31.4	25.4

Source: Financial Sector Deepening Kenya (2013).

Table 5.3 Overall use of financial services, per cent

Usage of:	2006	2009	2013
Banks	13.5	17.1	29.2
SACCOs	13.5	9.3	9.1
Microfinance institutions	1.8	3.5	3.5
Informal groups	39.1	29.5	27.7
Mobile money financial services	0.0	28.4	61.6

Source: Financial Sector Deepening Kenya (2013).

money services from virtually 0 per cent in 2006 to 28.4 per cent in 2009 to 61.6 per cent in 2013, at the expense of SACCOs and other informal groups. Mobile banking has introduced alternative channels for financial service provision to conventional banking and has provided clear, quick and convenient platforms to conduct a range of financial transactions.

Is regulation of M-PESA and other mobile money platforms adequate?

The success of M-PESA in Kenya is often used to argue for a light-touch regulatory approach, under which mobile banking was allowed to flourish. Possible systemic and individual users' risks seem to require careful evaluation, however. It is clearly important to enable, rather than stifle, innovation but it is also clear that regulation should be comprehensive in the longer term.

In responding to this tradeoff, the CBK admits that the technology used to deliver the mobile money services carries inherent threats, the main ones being operational risk, financial fraud and money laundering.[9] However, prior to the launch of mobile banking services by the various companies, the CBK requires them to provide a detailed risk assessment, outlining all potential risks and satisfactory mitigating measures they have put in place. Following the enactment of the National Payments System Act in 2011, all payment service providers offering money transfer services fall under the CBK's regulatory framework. There is supervision as well as regulation to make sure there are no micro problems, with mobile money companies in conjunction with banks providing saving and credit facilities such as M-Shwari. This of course may offend the Know Your Customer (KYC) doctrine in banking, with implications for financial stability and consumer protection, as well as fair competition with banks.

The Kenya Bankers Association (KBA) has, for example, complained that the Mobile Network Operators (MNOs) offer services similar to those offered by banks, yet they are not subject to similar regulations.[10] The KBA argues that there is a blurred line between what constitutes taking deposits from customers as done by MNOs and taking deposits for savings as done by banks. The e-float, for example, which is kept in special accounts in banks by MNOs, is not subject to deposit insurance, undermining the security of such deposits in case of a bank failure or financial crisis. The response by MNOs is that the possibility of such risks making a huge impact on clients is very rare as the e-float is relatively small, and it is distributed across several banks.

Financial inclusion (innovations) and macroeconomic stability in Kenya

The Central Bank of Kenya (CBK)'s monetary policy has two pillars. The first is a monetary programme that assigns a prominent role to monetary aggregates, as reflected by the announcement of targets for the growth of the M3 and its components and which assumes a stable income velocity and money multiplier. The second pillar is the Central Bank Rate (CBR), introduced in July 2006, in accordance with Section 36(4) of the CBK Act, to signal the stance of the monetary policy.

The increased financial inclusion through financial innovations does not seem to have compromised the conduct of monetary policy and therefore financial stability. First, the stock of e-money is backed 100 per cent by accounts held at commercial banks. The mobile money e-float is also a small proportion of the other monetary aggregates in terms of size for it to matter much for monetary policy. Weil et al. (2011) estimate the outstanding stock of M-PESA e-float at 1.6 per cent of M0 and 0.4 per cent of M1.

Second, while there has been increased instability in monetary relationships post-2007, reflected in a decline in the income velocity of circulation and an increase in the money multiplier undermining the conduct of monetary policy, stability seems to have been re-established since 2010. Velocity which is the ratio of nominal GDP to money supply (M3X) declined significantly from a monthly average of 2.50 in 2006 to 2.1 in 2010 and stabilized at that level thereafter. Similarly, the money multiplier increased from a monthly average of 5.5 in 2006 to 6.0 in 2010 and stabilized at that level (Figure 5.4). The demand for money also shows stability post-2010 (Weil et al., 2011), to suggest that the mobile money market is stabilizing after a period of fast growth.

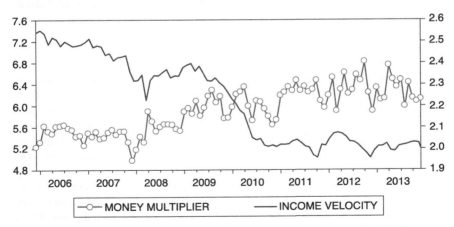

Figure 5.4 The money multiplier and income velocity in Kenya, December 2005 to December 2013

Source: Central Bank of Kenya.

Access and cost of credit in Kenya

Banks lending to SMEs in Kenya

The World Bank (2013) finds that access to credit for SMEs in Kenya is still limited, where the SMEs account for about 90 per cent of all enterprises in the country, according to the Kenya Private Sector Development Strategy 2006–2010. Only 67 per cent of the firms that made it to the 2013 Top 100 Mid-Sized Companies' survey turned to lenders for credit lines and overdrafts, although the study does not say whether they actually got the credit. Most of the surveyed entrepreneurs cited the high cost of credit as the reason for cash flow challenges they face, leaving them with no recourse but to dig deeper into their personal savings or turn to family friends to raise funds for day to day operations.

The study notes, however, that there is some evidence that Kenyan banks are actually ahead of their counterparts in Nigeria and South Africa in lending to the SMEs. From field surveys, about 17.4 per cent of total bank lending goes to SMEs in Kenya, compared to only 5 per cent in Nigeria, and 8 per cent in South Africa. These numbers are supported by the innovations in the banking sector that suggest a strong appetite for SME lending. These innovations started through microfinance-rooted institutions scaling up to becoming commercial banks and now include innovations with lending models and technology in the retail banking segment by other institutions, most notably Equity Bank.

On policy, the study recommends that tapping the full growth and job-creating potential of the SME sector will entail a move towards providing growth capital and not just working capital, for example, by tapping private equity providers in the region. Improving the listability of SMEs as well could increase their access to equity finance. In fact, about 28 per cent of firms surveyed in the Top 100 Mid-Sized Companies said they were considering listing on the Nairobi exchange, which now has a special segment, the Growth Enterprise Market Segment (GEMS) for SMEs.[11]

Cost of credit and interest rate spreads in Kenya

One of the key criticisms of the Kenyan banking sector is that the cost of credit and the interest rate spread remains high, at an average of 10.02 per cent over 2005–2013 (Figure 5.5). According to the critics of commercial banks, there have been many developments that have taken place in the country that should have significantly reduced the spread (Oloo, 2013). These include: i) improvements in technology (ATMs, mobile phones, etc.) that have reduced the cost of doing business, and the need for human resource requirements; ii) agency banking, with 26,000 agents (in May 2014) available to banks at nominal cost; iii) introduction of a credit reference bureau to reduce information asymmetries and risk; and iv) the opening of Currency Centres across the country, which has reduced costs associated with transporting cash for the banks.

Table 5.4 compares interest rate spreads in Kenya versus a few selected comparator countries over 2000–2012. The spreads are on average relatively

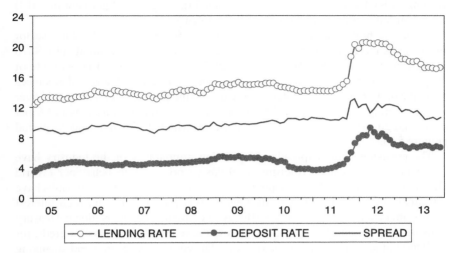

Figure 5.5 The interest rates spread in Kenya (*ex post* lending minus deposit rate)
Source: Central Bank of Kenya.

higher in Kenya than in Malaysia, Botswana, South Africa, Nigeria and Tanzania, with only Uganda having a higher spread. The spreads in Kenya decreased until 2005, but then were either stable or increased. The high spread in Kenya may reflect the comparably higher lending by Kenyan banks to SMEs that are perceived to have a higher risk premium. Within the country, commercial banks

Table 5.4 Comparative analysis of commercial banks' *ex post* spreads in Kenya and selected countries, per cent

Year	Malaysia	Botswana	South Africa	Nigeria	Kenya	Tanzania	Uganda
2000	4.31	6.06	5.30	9.58	14.24	14.19	13.08
2001	3.75	5.66	4.40	8.18	13.03	15.25	14.19
2002	3.32	5.75	4.98	8.10	12.97	13.11	13.53
2003	3.23	6.45	5.20	6.50	12.44	11.47	9.09
2004	3.05	5.90	4.74	5.48	10.10	9.94	12.86
2005	2.95	6.48	4.58	7.42	7.80	10.52	10.85
2006	3.34	7.59	4.03	7.16	8.50	8.93	9.61
2007	3.24	7.60	4.01	6.65	8.18	7.39	9.84
2008	2.95	7.87	3.51	3.51	8.71	6.73	9.78
2009	3.00	6.29	3.17	5.07	8.84	7.06	11.20
2010	2.50	5.86	3.37	11.06	9.81	7.98	12.49
2011	2.00	5.85	3.33	10.32	9.42	8.18	8.81
2012	1.81	7.39	3.31	8.39	8.15	5.95	10.08
Average	3.04	6.52	4.15	7.49	10.17	9.75	11.19

Source: World Bank, World Development Indicators.

lending to SMEs have a higher *ex post* spread (average of 12 per cent in 2013) than their lending in general (average 9.5 per cent).[12]

Alongside high lending interest rates and wide spreads, the banking sector profits have increased over time. Profits before tax increased from about US$70 million in 2002 to US$1,256 million in 2012, an average annual growth rate of 39 per cent. The major sources of income were interest on loans and advances (average of 49.6 per cent of total income during the period) which increased over time reflecting an increase in the spread; and fees and commissions (14.6 per cent), and government securities (19.8 per cent) which declined during the period (Figure 5.6).

The persistently high spreads and growing profitability of the industry have left it open to repeated criticisms of collusive price-setting behaviour (World Bank, 2013; Oloo, 2013). In the popular press and elsewhere, Kenyan banks have repeatedly been portrayed as using their market power to extract high interest rates from businesses, especially SMEs. As a consequence, the National Treasury constituted a committee in 2013 to address the relatively high cost of credit for both individuals and business enterprises.[13] The committee recommended, among other actions, that all banks use a transparent pricing framework known as the Kenya Banks' Reference Rate (KBRR), comprised of an average of the CBR and the 91-days Treasury Bill Rate. The commercial banks would then price their flexible rate loans at KBRR+k, where k is a premium to be loaded to the reference rate depending on the banks cost of doing business, the borrowers credit profile and the loan product type. The KBRR was launched in July 2014 at an initial rate of 9.1 per cent to be effective for six months. Commercial banks were given one year to migrate all loans to the new framework and inform borrowers. In addition, the committee recommended the promotion of full disclosure of bank charges to facilitate informed decision making, entailing the introduction of the Annual Percentage Rate (APR) by the Kenya Bankers Association. Other recommendations were: i) fast tracking the modernization of the lands and company registries to facilitate quicker collateral process; ii) fast tracking regulations for sharing of banking infrastructure, and so on.

There have been several studies of interest rate spreads in Kenya (Abdul et al., 2013; Were and Wambua, 2013; World Bank, 2013). According to this literature, there are four determinants of the spreads: a) macroeconomic factors; b) the state of financial sector development; c) industry-specific factors; and d) bank-specific factors.

a) Macroeconomic environment. The size of the spread will depend on the macroeconomic environment and the country's monetary policy stance. There is, for example, a high correlation between the spread and the CBR in Kenya. The CBK, for example, raised the benchmark interest rate by nearly 300 per cent (from 6.3 per cent to 18 per cent) in less than three months in late-2011. As a result, banks raised their lending and deposit rates. After August 2012, when the central bank started to lower the policy rate as inflation moderated, bank lending rates were not as responsive, with the asymmetric behaviour perhaps reflecting inadequate competition. Although banks did eventually lower their lending rates, the interest rate spread remained high.

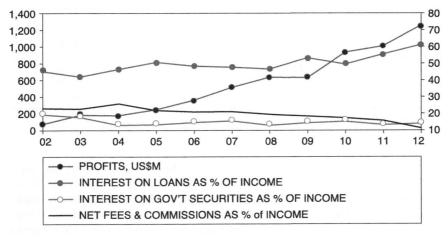

Figure 5.6 The performance of the banking sector, 2002–2012

Source: Central Bank of Kenya.

b) Financial sector development. Cross-country studies show that large interest spreads are associated with low levels of financial sector development. In general, spreads in the East Asia and Pacific region are lower than in SSA. And within SSA, the most advanced market (South Africa) exhibits small spread. The spreads in LICs averaged 11.4 per cent compared to 7.4 per cent in MICs over 1990–2012 (Figure 5.7). Figure 5.7, however, shows that spreads have not come down much since 1990 either in LICs or MICs so that, in fact, they are higher, though lower than in mid-1990s.

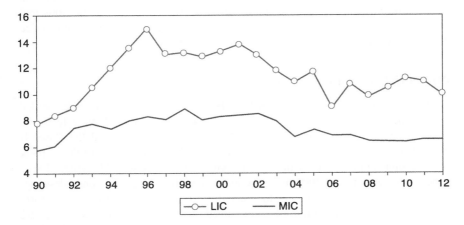

Figure 5.7 Spreads in LICs and MICs

Source: World Bank, World Development Indicator. Missing LIC spreads were extrapolated.

Table 5.5 Ex post spread decomposition in Kenya, per cent

	2009	2010	2011	2012
Profit	41.6	47.6	51.4	47.9
Bad loans provisions	7.9	8.6	3.6	4.3
Overhead costs	44.6	38.1	38.7	40.2
Reserves	5.9	5.7	6.3	7.7
Total	100	100	100	100

Source: World Bank (2013).

   c) Industry-specific factors: overhead costs. Kenya banks justify the high spreads as due to the difficult business environment they operate in (Oloo, 2013). The main argument is that dispute resolutions take too long and are costly, while national infrastructure services (e.g. electricity) are expensive and unreliable. They also cite the high cost of attracting, training and maintaining human resources. Salaries and other forms of labour compensation make up a large part of their overhead, as the scarcity of skilled financial sector workers leads to high turnover and compensation packages geared to retain scarce skills (World Bank, 2013). Most banks estimate that salaries make up 50 per cent of their overhead cost despite the fact that Kenya has a fairly well-developed pool of banking skills. There is additionally a problem in Kenya, as well as world-wide, that bankers' salaries tend to be extremely high, compared to other sectors, as supported by recent research that shows that there is a high premium attached to the remuneration in the financial sector. Nevertheless, the largest portion of spreads is explained by profits in recent times (Table 5.5).

   d) Bank-specific factors: lending risk premium. The difference between market lending rates and short-term T-bill rates can be interpreted as the risk premium, and reflect the market's perception of risk. Over and above the actual risk perception, where information gaps on credit history or market conditions and other deficiencies in the financial infrastructure persist, banks are likely to price these deficiencies through a higher risk premium (World Bank, 2013).

Prudential regulations in Kenya

In 1988, the Basel Committee issued the Basel I Accord which assesses banks' capital adequacy requirements in the context of the credit risk they face and advocates risk-based supervision. In 2004, the Committee issued the Basel II Accord which set rigorous risk management requirements to ensure that a bank holds capital appropriate to the risk to which it is exposed. The Accord was to be implemented from 2007 by G10 countries, with more time given to developing countries, as they were yet to meet the prerequisites for the new accord. In December 2010, the Committee announced proposals dubbed Basel III. These latter proposals include the strengthening of capital adequacy and liquidity requirements as well as counter-cyclical macro-prudential measures.

Table 5.6 Selected prudential and financial stability indicators for the banking sector,
2011–2013

	Dec-11	*Dec-12*	*Dec-13*	*Statutory requirement*
Core capital to total risk Weighted assets ratio	18.0%	18.9%	19.5%	8.0%
Total capital to total risk Weighted assets ratio	21.0%	21.9%	23.2%	12.0%
Core capital/deposits	15.6%	16.3%	17.3%	8.0%
Liquidity ratio	37.0%	41.9%	38.6%	20.0%
Gross non-performing loans to gross loans ratio	4.4%	4.5%	5.0%	N/A
Return on Assets (ROA)	3.4%	3.8%	3.6%	N/A
Return on Equity (ROE)	30.3%	34.2%	28.9%	N/A

Source: Central Bank of Kenya.

The CBK continues to regulate banks mainly based on Basel I but was in the process of formulating a policy position on Basel II implementation (KPMG, 2012). New guidelines that came into force in January 2013 contain some features of Basel II and Basel III on capital adequacy requirements, including a 2.5 per cent capital buffer to be implemented by December 2014 (Oloo, 2013). Overall, Kenya has endeavoured to implement the Basel Accords for ensuring financial stability of the country's financial sector. The prudential and financial stability indicators seem to show that the financial sector is sound (Table 5.6). All the banks have in the recent past met the four minimum capital requirements with large margins.[14] In addition, the NPL/Assets ratio has decreased from a high of 22.6 per cent in 2001 to a low of 4.3 per cent in 2007, and as of December 2013 averaged 5 per cent, an indication that the banking systems asset quality has generally improved over time. As well, the Return on Assets (ROA) and Return on Equity (ROE) have generally shown an upward trend since 2002. Although these data show a very strong banking system, there may be some risks such as currency mismatches that are not fully addressed, undermining the strength of the banking system.

The CBK has focused mainly on micro-prudential regulation which relates to factors that affect the stability of individual banks and less so on macro-prudential regulation which relates to factors which affect the stability of the financial system as a whole. In the latter case, changes in the business cycles may influence the performance of banks; hence the Basel III proposal for counter-cyclical capital buffers to provide the way forward for future macro-prudential regulation, which should take into account the growth of credit and leverage as well as the mismatch in the maturity of assets and liabilities. Murinde (2012) argues that review of macro-prudential regulations should encompass the broader aspects of financial services regulation, such as depositor protection or deposit insurance and the safety of the payments system which have received some attention from the CBK.

The regulatory toolkit in Kenya has also relied substantially on quantitative measures such as the structure of banking assets and liabilities such as restrictions on banks' large loan concentrations and foreign exchange exposure limits (Kasekende et al., 2011). As well, according to KPMG (2012), capacity for implementing different regulations and supervision, such as lack of information and insufficient staff, do not seem to be a major constraint. In a group of 11 SSA countries, Kenya is found to have the second largest number of supervisors (60), the largest number of supervisors with more than ten years of experience (30) and the largest percentage of supervisors with a postgraduate degree (80) (see Chapter 4 in this book).

The management of capital flows in Kenya

Kenya has in the last decade experienced a large increase in the current account deficit (Figure 5.8). The current account recorded an average deficit of 1.8 per cent of GDP in 2006, generally widening over in the subsequent years. By 2012, the deficit had risen to an average of 10.6 per cent of GDP and by July 2014 to 10.8 per cent of GDP, mainly due to increased imports in the context of a stagnant export sector.[15] Imports of machinery and other equipment have, for example, continued to account for a higher proportion (about one-quarter) of the import bill. These are essential for enhancing future productive capacity of the economy.[16]

The high overall current account deficit is mainly financed by short-term net capital inflows, except in a few episodes when net long-term official flows dominate. Short-term capital flows have typically accounted for more than 50 per cent of total financial flows. This is a major source of potential vulnerability for the economy and for financial stability. The easy reversibility of these inflows

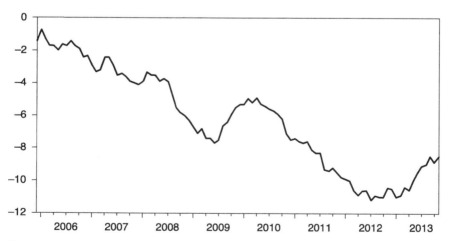

Figure 5.8 Twelve-months cumulative current account deficit as percentage of GDP, December 2005–November 2013

Source: Central Bank of Kenya.

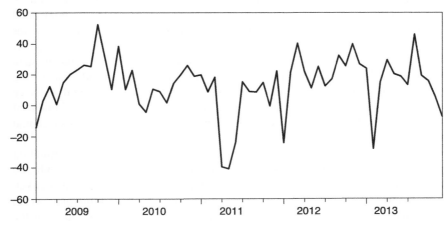

Figure 5.9 Net foreign purchases as percentage share of equity turnover in Kenya, January 2009–December 2013

Source: Central Bank of Kenya.

increases the risk of a 'sudden stop' or a reversal as a shift in market sentiments creates a flight away from domestic assets (O'Connell et al., 2010). This could lead to depletion of reserves, sharp currency depreciation and a decline in stock prices, as happened during the 2007–2008 global crisis (Mwega, 2010). Conditions have, however, stabilized since then. Despite the large current account deficit, Mwega (2013) shows that the real exchange rate was only slightly misaligned in 2012, with an overvaluation of about 4.3 per cent. With the elasticity of real exchange rate (RER) with respect to nominal exchange rate (NER) of about 0.76, it would require a depreciation of only about 5.5 per cent to close this gap so that the exchange rate pressure was minimal. The CBK also performs stress tests, for example, of the impact of the shilling depreciation on foreign exchange exposure ratio. In one typical result (January 2014), none of the banks would breach the foreign exchange exposure limit of 10 per cent if the shilling value declined by 20 per cent.

The CBK has not in the past collected information on foreign participation in the government securities market until recently. Between December 2013 and July 2014, foreign participation in government securities averaged only 6.6 per cent, 40.2 per cent in Treasury bills and 59.8 per cent in Treasury bonds. Longer maturities provide protection against rapid withdrawals that can put pressure on the balance of payments. Figure 5.9, on the other hand, shows the net foreign purchases in Kenya's Nairobi Stock Exchange (NSE) as percentage of equity turnover over January 2009–December 2013. Net purchases averaged 14.7 per cent of equity turnover and were negative in only a few months: January 2009 (–13 per cent), May 2010 (–3 per cent), April–June 2011 (–23 per cent to –40 per cent), December 2011 (–23 per cent), February 2013 (–27 per cent) and December 2013 (–6 per cent).

Management of the short-term capital flows in Kenya could be enhanced by building reserves (for example to the six-months cover initially recommended by the East African Community) to guard against reversals. Some countries have implemented more radical policies such as unremunerated reserve requirements that reduce attractiveness for short-term lenders, as well as asking such flows to be in the country for a certain minimum period, in addition to the pursuit of a competitive and stable real exchange rate, which may both enhance competitiveness for exports and thus growth, as well as defend financial stability, by reducing current account deficits, and making reversals of capital flows less likely.

Besides monetary policy actions to neutralize the effects of the net capital on domestic liquidity, the CBK relies mainly on foreign exchange reserves to enhance the country's capacity to absorb shocks that impact the foreign exchange market. The statutory requirement is that the CBK endeavour to maintain foreign reserves equivalent to four months' import cover. The CBK does not participate in the foreign exchange market to defend a particular value of the Kenya shilling but may intervene to stabilize excess volatility in the exchange market.

There are no explicit measures to regulate currency mismatches in lending to banks and companies, except indirectly through foreign currency exposure limits. As seen in Figure 5.10, while foreign currency advances and deposits have increased over time, their ratio has been fairly stable over 2007–2013. While this is welcome, there may be mismatches at the individual bank or company level, which can be problematic. There are no counter-cyclical capital account management measures on inflows of short-term capital to the country, which could be desirable, especially once the current account deficit is reduced.

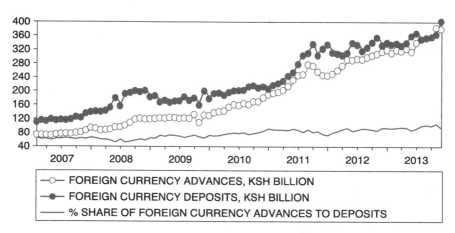

Figure 5.10 Foreign currency advances and deposits in Kenya, January 2007–December 2013

Source: Central Bank of Kenya.

Conclusions

This chapter has examined the relationship between the financial sector, stability and growth in Kenya, looking at structural and regulatory issues. On the size and growth of the financial sector, Kenya's M2/GDP and private credit/GDP ratios closely track those of LICs, but they are far below those of MICs, with a clear divergence over time. With the country aspiring to MIC status by 2030, it therefore has a long way to go in building a strong financial sector to support growth and development.

In terms of specialized institutions, DFIs in Kenya play a small role in the economy. The six existing DFIs account for less than 1 per cent of the assets of the banking sector and supplied only about 0.56 per cent of the banking sector credit to the private sector. In the area of financial inclusion, Kenya is faring better. The proportion of the adult population totally excluded from financial services has declined significantly from 39.3 per cent in 2006 to 25.4 per cent in 2013. The massive increase in access to financial services in the country since 2006 is mainly due to enhanced usage of mobile money services from virtually 0 per cent in 2006 to 61.6 per cent in 2013, making Kenya a global leader in the use of mobile phone platforms.

Notwithstanding, Kenya still has a way to go in terms of financial inclusion, even though its banks are ahead of their counterparts in Nigeria and South Africa in lending to SMEs.

A key issue facing the Kenyan banking sector is that the cost of credit and the interest rate spread remains high (at an average of 10.02 per cent over 2005–2013). The persistently high spreads and growing profitability of the industry have left it open to repeated criticisms of collusive price-setting behaviour, particularly for large banks.

The CBK continues to regulate banks based mainly on Basel I. New guidelines that came into force in January 2013 contain, however, some features of Basel II and Basel III on capital adequacy requirements. The regulatory toolkit in Kenya has also relied substantially on other variables such as restrictions on banks' large loan concentrations and foreign exchange exposure limits.

Finally, Kenya has in the last decade experienced a large increase in the current account deficit and been financed by short-term net capital inflows. The easy reversibility of these inflows increases the risk of a 'sudden stop' or reversal as a shift in market sentiments creates a flight away from domestic assets, leading to depletion of reserves and sharp currency depreciations.

Management of the short-term capital flows in Kenya could be enhanced by building reserves to guard against reversals. Some countries have implemented capital account management, for example, by asking such flows to be in the country for a certain minimum period. Kenyan policy makers may consider such policy actions to reduce the country's vulnerability to external shocks.

104 Francis M. Mwega

Notes

1 Paper Prepared for the ESRC-DFID Project on Financial Regulation in Low-Income Countries: Balancing Inclusive Growth with Financial Stability. I am grateful to Stephany Griffith-Jones, Stephen Spratt and Ricardo Gottschalk for their comments on an earlier draft of the paper.
2 Other achievements were: i) progress towards the formation of the Nairobi International Financial Centre; and ii) the enactment of the Anti-Money Laundering and Combating Financing of Terrorism Act in 2009.
3 Mwega and Ndung'u (2008) explain Kenya's growth performance from the 1960s to the early 2000s. They first identified economic growth episodes, based on cross-country neoclassical and endogenous growth models. They find that economic growth roughly tracked growth in physical capital, a conclusion that is supported by a number of other studies that conclude that private investment has been the strongest and the most significant contributor to the country's economic growth, and which requires long-term finance and low cost of credit. There is, however, some evidence that the efficiency of capital use worsened over time (reflected in an increased incremental capital output ratio or reduced total factor productivity growth) especially in the public sector activities, reducing the growth effects of investment.
4 In contrast, the KNBS reports growth data on a quarter-on-quarter basis to remove the seasonal effects. By ignoring the intermediate values, none of the Granger causality tests are significant.
5 The other three banks are CFC Stanbic, Housing Finance and Kenya Commercial Bank.
6 The assets shares a decade earlier in 2002 were foreign banks 49.5 per cent, public banks 25.5 per cent and local private banks 25 per cent. There has therefore been a substantial change in the composition of banks' assets in favour of local private banks and, to a lesser extent, public banks at the expense of foreign banks, reflecting the entry of large local banks such as Equity Bank (2004) and Family Bank (2007), which converted from building societies. Mwega (2011) provides a detailed account of the historical evolution of Kenya's banking sector.
7 DFIs are state-owned institutions created to provide medium- and long-term finance to various sectors in the economy. They are therefore owned and mainly financed by the Treasury and are governed by their own Acts of Parliament. The six existing DFIs in Kenya service commerce and industry (Industrial and Commercial Development Corporation, IDB Capital and Kenya Industrial Estates); agriculture (Agricultural Finance Corporation); tourism (Kenya Tourist Development Corporation) and building and construction (National Housing Corporation).
8 Interview with the Governor, Central Bank of Kenya. *EastAfrican*, August 24–30, 2013.
9 Interview with the CBK Governor in Oloo (2013). This section draws on this interview.
10 See the *Daily Nation*, 26 January 2014, 'Banks revive battle with money service providers'.
11 Only one firm (Home Afrika) has so far listed in this segment.
12 Comparable data for 2014 are 11 per cent and 8.6 per cent respectively so that the spreads declined in 2014.
13 As well, the Competition Commission has launched its own investigation into the price-setting behaviour of commercial banks which is ongoing in 2014.
14 The high liquidity ratio, for example, reflects the fact that about 50 per cent of the value of liquid assets comprise of investments in government bonds which are difficult to liquidate without banks incurring capital losses.
15 However, there have been concerns about the quality of the balance of payments data and the size of the current account deficit. Among these concerns are: i) the services

account is highly aggregated, affecting the quality of data; ii) data is available only for remittances channeled through the formal channels and iii) there is a large uncaptured component in cross border trade.

16 According to a CBK estimate, excluding heavy machinery and industrial equipment would reduce the current account deficit to a sustainable 4.2 per cent of GDP in the year to July 2014.

References

Abdul, Farida; Sheila M'Mbijjewe; Isaya Maana and Joseph Wambua (2013) *An Empirical Analysis of the Determinants of Interest Rate Spreads In Kenya.* Paper Presented at a Central Bank of Kenya Retreat, Naivasha, June 2013.

Allen, Franklin; Elena Carletti; Robert Cull; Jun Qian; Lemma Senbet and Patricio Valenzuela (2012) *Resolving the African Financial Development Gap: Cross-Country Comparisons and a Within-Country Study of Kenya.* National Bureau of Economic Research (NBER) Working Paper 18013.

Beck, T. (2013) *Cross-Border Banking and Financial Deepening: The African Experience.* Paper presented at an AERC Workshop, December 2013.

Beck T. and M. Fuchs (2004) *Structural Issues in the Kenyan Financial System.* World Bank Policy Research Working Paper 3363, July.

CBK (2013) *The Role of Development Financial Institutions in Kenya.* Paper presented at the 2013 Annual Association of African Development Finance Institutions Forum. Serena Beach Hotel, Mombasa, Kenya, 14 November 2013.

Christensen, Benedicte Vibe (2010) "Have Monetary Transmission Mechanism in Africa Changed? In Bank of International Settlements", *Central Banking in Africa: Prospects in a Changing World Roundtable.*

Easterly, William and Ross Levine (1997) "Africa's Growth Tragedy: Policies and Ethnic Divisions." *Quarterly Journal of Economics*, Vol. 112, No. 4.

Financial Sector Deepening Kenya (FSDK) (2013) *FinAccess National Survey 2013.*

Griffith-Jones, Stephany and Giovanni Cozzi (Forthcoming), *Investment Growth: A Solution to the European Crisis.* Forthcoming Chapter in a Book by Mazzucato and Jacobs.

Kasekende L.A.; J. Bagyenda M. and Brownbridge (2011) *Basel III and the Global Reform of Financial Regulation: How Should Africa Respond? A Bank Regulator's Perspective.* (Available online under: www.new-rules.org/storage/documents/g20-fsb-imf/kasakende.docx.)

Kenya (2007) *Kenya Vision 2030: The Popular Version*, Nairobi. www.vision2030.go.ke.

Kenya (2013) *Kenya Vision 2030: Second Medium Term Plan 2013–2017*, Nairobi. www.vision 2030.go.ke.

KPMG (2012) *Africa Banking Survey.* www.kpmg.com.

Murinde, V. (2012) "Bank Regulation in Africa: From Basel I to Basel II, and Now at Crossroads." In: Victor Murinde (Ed.), *Bank Regulatory Reforms in Africa.* London: Palgrave Macmillan.

Mwega F. M. (2010) *The Effects of the Global Financial Crisis: A Case Study of Kenya Phase II.* Paper prepared for the Overseas Development Institute (ODI), London, January 2010. Available on the Internet.

Mwega, F. M. (2011) "The Competitiveness of the Financial Services in Africa: A Case Study of Kenya." *African Development Review*, Vol. 23, No. 1, pp. 44–59.

Mwega F. M. (2013) *Real Exchange Rate Misalignment and Implications for the Nominal Exchange Rate Level in Kenya*. Paper presented at a Central Bank of Kenya Retreat, Naivasha, June 2013, now available on the CBK website.

Mwega, Francis and Njuguna Ndung'u (2008) "Explaining African Economic Growth Performance." In: B. J. Benno, S. A. O'Connell, J.-P. Azam, R. H. Bates, A. Fosu, J. W. Gunning and D. Njinkeu (Eds), *The Political Economy of Economic Growth in Africa, 1960–2000: Volume 2: Country Case Studies*. Cambridge: Cambridge University Press, pp. 325–368.

Ndulu, B. J. and S. A. O'Connell (2008) "Policy Plus: African Growth." In: B. J. Ndulu, S. A. O'Connell, R. H. Bates, P. Collier and C. S. Soludo (Eds), *The Political Economy of Economic Growth in Africa, 1960–2000*. Cambridge: Cambridge University Press.

O'Connell, Stephen; Benjamin O. Maturu; Francis M. Mwega; Njuguna S. Ndung'u and Rose W. Ngugi (2010) "Capital Mobility, Monetary Policy, and Exchange Rate Management in Kenya" In: Christopher S. Adam, Paul Collier and Njuguna S. Ndung'u (Eds), *Kenya: Policies for Prosperity*. New York: Oxford University Press, pp. 172–210.

Oloo, Ochieng (2013) *Banking Survey 2013*. Nairobi: Think Business Ltd.

Weil, David; Issac Mbiti and Francis Mwega (2011) *The Implications of Innovations in the Financial Sector on the Conduct of Monetary Policy in East Africa*. (Available online under: www.theigc.org/sites/default/files/weil_mbiti_and_mwenga_0.pdf.)

Were, Maureen and Joseph Wambua (2013) *Assessing the Determinants of Interest Rate Spread of Commercial Banks in Kenya: An Empirical Investigation*. KBA Working Paper WPS 04 12/2.

World Bank (2013) *Kenya Economic Update: Reinvigorating Growth with a Dynamic Banking Sector*. Kenya: The World Bank.

6 Financial regulation in Ghana

Balancing inclusive growth with financial stability

Charles Ackah and Johnson P. Asiamah

Introduction

There is an extensive literature on the link between financial development and economic growth (see for example Bencivenga and Smith, 1991; Pagano, 1993; King and Levine, 1993; Levine, 1997). Well-functioning financial systems serve a vital purpose by offering savings, payment, credit, and risk management services to individuals and firms. Financial inclusion is important for development and poverty reduction. It is defined by the IMF *Global Financial Development Report 2014* as the proportion of individuals and firms that use financial services. There is a large literature on the linkages between access to finance and economic development (see Levine, 1997). Several models elucidate how financial exclusion and, especially, lack of access to finance can lead to persistent income inequality or poverty traps, as well as lower growth (Aghion and Bolton 1997; Banerjee and Newman 1993; Galor and Zeira 1993).

Following the global financial crisis, many countries are beginning to prioritize financial stability through regulation, and seeking to balance such policy priorities with the promotion of inclusive growth, especially in poor countries. In many cases, reforms have been put in place aimed at building stronger supervisory and regulatory frameworks whilst financial sector policy in general is focused on pursuing growth and development, as well as creating inclusive growth to support social stability and equity.

This chapter is a case study of Ghana, a small open economy that has sustained decades of first- and second-generation reforms since the early 1980s. It identifies and analyzes the key obstacles or gaps in the financial sector for funding inclusive growth. The chapter also discusses why financial stability matters in an increasingly globalized world and the challenges in securing and safeguarding financial stability while pursuing financial inclusion. The second section analyzes the structure and role of the financial sector in the Ghanaian economy; the third section examines issues in financial inclusion in the country; the fourth section discusses access and cost of credit; the fifth section discusses the issues relating to capital flows and financial stability; the sixth section discusses prudential regulations; while the seventh section provides a summary of the issues and conclusions.

Structure and role of the financial sector in the Ghanaian economy

The financial sector in Ghana's economic development strategy[1]

The medium-term national development policy framework – *Ghana Shared Growth and Development Agenda 2010–2013* – is the over-arching policy framework that provides the broad policy parameters for economic growth and development in Ghana.[2] The policy thrust of Ghana's second medium-term Private Sector Development Strategy (PSDS II) is about developing a thriving private sector that creates jobs and enhances livelihoods for all. The development of a well-functioning financial system to serve the vital purpose by offering savings, payment, credit, and risk management services to individuals and firms is a key policy objective in the development agendas of the State.

Both policy documents have underscored the crucial role of finance for furthering growth, innovation, and prosperity in Ghana. Government's financial sector strategies for economic development and poverty reduction revolve around two policy prongs. They are: 1) financial sector policies for long-term shared economic growth; and 2) enhanced access (inclusiveness) in the Ghanaian financial sector (MOFEP, 2012).

The Government of Ghana recognizes that shared economic growth is the surest way to sustained reduction in poverty in the country and that in order to attain shared economic growth there is the need to ensure the availability of medium- to long-term financing, deepen the resource mobilization of the banking system, ensure that banks want to and can safely lend these resources, and enable productive formal sector firms to find the mix of equity and debt finance they need to grow, as well as tools for risk management (MOFEP, 2012).

The second policy prong is concerned with improving the access of low-income households and microenterprises to financial services. Thus, Ghana's economic development framework identifies that the most pressing needs in Ghana's financial sector are to:

- increase the availability of credit;
- lower the cost of credit to productive enterprises; and
- extend the reach of basic savings, payments, credit, and insurance services for low-income people, the smallholder farmers, and microenterprise.

The financial sector in Ghana: structure, conduct, and performance

Financial sectors in Africa are expected to support growth by mobilizing sufficient savings, intermediating savings at low cost and long maturity to investors and consumers, and helping companies and individuals manage risks. In Ghana, the efficiency and effectiveness with which the financial sector has played these roles has been limited but is improving. Effective banking systems expand financing opportunities for both large and microenterprises, while also supporting financial sector development.

Structural reforms in the financial sector

The Ghanaian financial sector is largely dominated by banks.[3] The banking industry is fairly saturated, comprising 27 commercial banks (up from 16 in the year
2000), 137 rural and community banks, and 58 non-banking financial institutions
including finance houses, savings and loans, leasing and mortgage firms.

Ghana's financial system has gone through a process of liberalization, restructuring, and transformation over the last two decades. The transformation started
as part of the Financial Sector Adjustment Programs (FINSAP I and II), which
was implemented from the late 1980s through the mid-1990s. Prior to the banking
sector reforms in the 1990s, the banking sector in Ghana was dominated by state-
owned banks with official allocation and pricing of credit and as a consequence,
the banking system was uncompetitive and the intermediation process was
inefficient. The banking sector was characterized by limited innovation and suitable governance structures. In many cases, credit decisions lacked commercial
considerations, resulting in several bank failures. The financial reforms involved
the privatization of the state-owned banks, licensing of new banks including
foreign ones, the restructuring of the financially distressed banks, the improve-
ment of the regulatory and supervisory framework, and the promotion of non-
bank financial institutions (MOFEP, 2012). Since the reforms, the financial
sector has seen rapid development in terms of growth in number and variety of
financial institutions and services. As a result, today Ghana has a more dynamic
and diversified financial system.

Financial sector development issues

The developments in Ghana's financial sector can be gleaned from the level of
financial intermediation and financial deepening. As can be seen from Figures 6.1

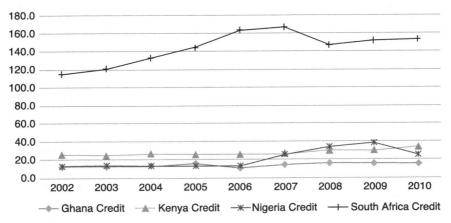

Figure 6.1 Trends in domestic credit to private sector, in percentage of GDP

Source: African Development Indicators, 2013.

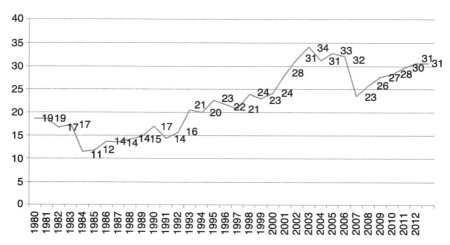

Figure 6.2 Money supply, M2 percentage of GDP

Source: World Bank, World Development Indicators.

and 6.2, credit provided to the private sector as a proportion of GDP has significantly increased over time, but it is still low when compared with other comparator countries. At the same time, the rapid expansion of banking activities has resulted in more than 100 per cent growth in the banking sector's assets over the past two decades. The broad money (M2/GDP) ratio has also shown significant increase over time and reached 32 per cent in 2012 compared to 15 per cent in 1992. One common characteristic of the banking system in Africa is that a large number of banks invest in government securities, primarily treasury bills. This is symptomatic of a highly dysfunctional banking intermediation and it is responsible for the low level of private credit provision that we observe in many African countries (Allen, Otchere and Senbet, 2011).

Ghana's banking sector in 2013 suggests that the banking industry remained strong in terms of financial soundness indicators such as asset growth, solvency, liquidity, and profitability. The Capital Adequacy Ratio (CAR) for the industry as in July 2014 was about 16 per cent, beyond the prudential limit of 10 per cent (Table 6.1). Asset penetration, measured as the ratio of total assets to GDP,

Table 6.1 Capital adequacy ratio-industry, per cent

Item	Jul.-07	Jul.-08	Jul.-09	Jul.-10	Jul.-11	Jul.-12	Jul.-13	Jul.-14
RWA/total assets (RHS)	66.1	77.3	78.3	68.5	65.3	74.4	67.4	70.5
CAR	14.5	14.4	14.7	19.3	17.0	15.5	18.6	16.2
TIER 1 CAR	13.3	13.0	13.0	18.5	15.4	13.6	16.8	14.6

Source: Bank of Ghana.

Table 6.2 Profitability indicators, per cent

Item	Jul.-07	Jul.-08	Jul.-09	Jul.-10	Jul.-11	Jul.-12	Jul.-13	Jul.-14
Gross yield	15.1	15.9	20.0	21.3	9.6	8.7	10.4	12.7
Int. payable	7.3	6.9	11.0	10.7	3.7	2.8	3.9	4.1
Asset utilisation	14.5	16.1	20.1	19.5	9.0	8.9	10.1	10.5
Interest margin to total assets	7.0	7.1	7.7	9.3	4.2	4.2	5.2	5.3
Interest margin to gross income	48.3	44.2	38.4	47.7	46.9	46.9	51.3	50.2
Profitability ratio	15.7	14.5	13.8	12.6	14.8	22.0	22.5	23.7
Return on assets (%) before tax	3.7	3.2	3.3	3.2	3.5	4.6	5.5	6.3
Return on equity (%) after tax	24.4	23.0	23.7	19.3	18.1	26.7	27.7	31.4

Source: Bank of Ghana.

was 40.5 per cent indicating continued deepening of the financial sector in the economy. In contrast to low investment yields of 2 per cent in global financial markets, banks in Ghana on average had Return on Equity (ROE) of over 20 per cent and Return on Assets (ROAs) of over 5 per cent (Table 6.2). This is apparently consistent with the high interest spreads in the industry in Ghana.

Ghana's impressive record on financial sector development may entail new risks in an environment of high credit growth. The Central Bank has noted that non-performing loans (NPLs) have increased since 2007, after recording a consistent year-on-year decline from 22.7 per cent in 2002 to as low as 6.4 per cent in 2007 (Table 6.3). There is a relatively high ratio of NPLs in Ghana compared to peer countries. The ratio for the industry in Ghana was 12.8 per cent in 2013. The Central Bank is reportedly taking steps to encourage banks to write-off long outstanding "loss" accounts with 100 per cent provisioning, that otherwise tend to overstate the true NPL ratios. For example, when the loss category was accounted for, the NPL ratio as at June 2013 declined to 4.7 per cent, which

Table 6.3 Bank non-performing loans to total gross loans, per cent

Year	Ghana	Kenya	Nigeria	South Africa
2002	22.7	18.1	21.4	2.8
2003	18.3	34.9	20.5	2.4
2004	16.3	29.3	21.6	1.8
2005	13.0	25.6	18.1	1.5
2006	7.9	N/A	9.3	1.1
2007	6.4	10.6	9.5	1.4
2008	7.7	9.0	7.2	3.9
2009	16.2	7.9	36.1	5.9
2010	17.6	6.3	20.1	5.8

Source: World Bank, 2013 and MOFEP, 2012.

compares favourably with NPL ratios in other peer countries such as South Africa. The Central Bank is therefore focusing on applying provisioning rules on overdraft facilities as well as tackling issues related to the build-up of unclaimed deposit balances or dormant accounts.

The role of domestic and foreign banks

The banking system in Ghana consists of the Central Bank and deposit taking institutions. The Central Bank is technically independent of government control, but in practice it works closely with the Ministry of Finance and helps formulate and implement macroeconomic policies of the government. The deposit taking institutions are made up of local banks and branches or subsidiaries of foreign banks. Foreign banks have played an important role in banking development in Ghana; their share in total banking assets has increased significantly.

Indeed, the foreign dominance in the Ghanaian banking sector is high, with 15 of the 27 commercial banks in the sector having foreign majority equity. Six of the 15 foreign banks are African banks, accounting for about one-third of total banking assets in Ghana. The recent expansion of pan-African banks in West Africa is contributing to stronger competition and financial deepening. But it has also increased risks. Financial distress in one country can spill over more easily to other countries when markets are integrated; and more complex financial linkages and exposures across markets can strain the monitoring ability of supervisory agencies. In this context, effective supervision becomes both more important and more difficult.

There are ongoing efforts at promoting financial integration in West Africa, which include strengthening of financial sector regulation and supervision. There is, however, the need to further strengthen effective mechanisms for crossborder cooperation in particular, information sharing, and crisis management. One major lesson that the global financial crisis has provided is the importance of regional cooperation, regional policy dialogue, and harmonization of financial sector supervision.

In Ghana, sustained financial sector restructuring and transformation has succeeded in creating one of the most vibrant financial services centres in the sub region.

Looking back, the entry of foreign banks and investors into the financial services industry has increased competition in the banking industry as well as the introduction of strong business practices, technology, products, and risk management systems, and has given impetus to dynamic efficiency in the industry. Traditional domestic private banks have also held their own, and grown particularly fast, as they accounted for 22 per cent of assets as at the end of 2012 compared with only 12 per cent in 2005.

The Bank of Ghana has currently embarked on an upgrading of financial sector legislation and supervisory practices to deal with the growing complexities of an evolving financial landscape with increased foreign participation and a growing role of microfinance institutions. The resolve is to continue to pursue financial sector development, focusing on enhancing depth, access, efficiency, and stability.

In sum, while the opening up of the banking industry to national, pan-regional, and foreign banks could be a key contributor to the development of the country, efforts must be intensified to create the appropriate regional regulatory framework to encourage more financial integration while stemming the inherent risks. This calls for the coordination of financial regulation, through information sharing about systemically important institutions, applying common rules across jurisdictions, and creating a common level field. There should also be common enforcement through shared cross-border regulatory and supervisory agencies.

Issues in financial inclusion

There is a growing recognition of the importance of financial inclusion for economic and social development. Considerable evidence abound that indicate that the poor benefit enormously from access to finance and to basic financial services such as payments, savings, and insurance services. However, while financial inclusion has important benefits, boosting financial inclusion is not trivial. If care is not taken, efforts to promote financial inclusion can lead to defaults and other negative effects. The global financial crisis, precipitated by the subprime mortgage crisis in the United States in the 2000s, indicates that things can get out of hand, especially if credit starts growing rapidly.

According to the Alliance of Financial Inclusion (AFI), financial inclusion refers to all initiatives that make formal financial services available, accessible, and affordable to all segments of the population. Particular attention should be directed to the segment of population that have been historically excluded from the formal financial sector due to their peculiar characteristics, regarding their income level and volatility, gender, location, type of activity, and level of financial literacy. In general, the concept of financial inclusion goes beyond improved access to credit to include improved access to savings and risk mitigation products, a well-functioning financial infrastructure that allows individuals and companies to engage more actively in the economy, while protecting consumers' rights.

The AFI suggests a three-dimensional framework for accessing finance inclusively, which borders on access, usage, and quality of financial services available to users. It is in these areas that the work done under the FinScope Ghana 2010 survey comes in handy. The survey aimed at establishing credible benchmarks and indicators of access, provide insights into regulatory and market obstacles to growth and innovation, and highlight opportunities for policy reform and innovation in product development and delivery.

According to the survey, access to financial services in Ghana is higher in urban than in rural areas since urban areas are generally equipped with infrastructure that support services including financial services. Besides, the level of literacy beyond secondary education is quite appreciable, constituting more than half of the population with less than 25 percent with no formal education at all. Prominent among the factors cited for influencing how people interact with financial services are: access to amenities, infrastructure, and wealth profiles. People whose livelihoods are constrained by access to basic amenities rarely prioritize usage of financial services, since their primary focus is on survival issues. The survey revealed that a significant proportion of Ghanaians aged 15 years or more do not have access to basic amenities. The divergence in terms of the lack of access to social amenities is more pronounced in the rural areas. It also came out that only 12 per cent of Ghanaian adults earn most of their income in the form of wages and salaries. The formal financial institutions tend to target these groups due to the regularity and less volatile nature of their sources of income. The bulk of adults from both the rural and urban sectors earn their income on an irregular and inconsistent basis. In the rural area, most incomes are generated through farming and from own businesses, whereas in urban areas self-employment and remittance from a household member are important sources of income.

In terms of usage of financial services, the survey revealed that about 44 per cent of Ghanaian adults do not use any form of financial product or mechanism (be it formal or informal) to manage their financial lives. Some 40 per cent use formal financial services and about 29.4 per cent use informal financial services. The proportion of the population that makes use of informal products and services demonstrates the significance of the informal sector in Ghana. Within the formal sector, the banks play a more dominant role than the non-bank formal financial institutions. Some 34 per cent of Ghanaian adults have a bank account, and about 20 per cent use products from non-bank financial institutions. Notwithstanding, about 73.1 per cent of Ghanaian adults claim that none of the income they receive passes through a bank account. The proportion of adults who received all their income as cash was 60.6 per cent in urban areas and 82.0 per cent in rural areas. In fact most Ghanaians, both in the rural and urban areas, prefer to receive their income in cash. The FinScope survey 2010 findings illustrate the interwoven nature of the link between people's livelihoods and the extent to which they engage with the financial system.

Cost of and access to credit

High interest rate spreads and low credit availability to the private sector have been persistent problems in Ghanaian banking in spite of recent financial sector reforms. Ghanaian businesses have complained incessantly over the past few years about how high interest rates are squeezing the life out of the enterprises. The financial reform process in Ghana resulted in changes in the structure of the banking sector to a market-based regime. In spite of the positive results of these reforms, the interest rate spread remains excessively and persistently high. As a consequence, credit availability to the private sector remains limited.

Figure 6.3 reviews the trends in interest rate spreads for Ghana and three comparator African nations – Nigeria, South Africa, and Kenya. The data indicates that in all the years under review, Ghana's interest rate spread far exceeded that of the three African countries; South Africa reported the lowest spread. Indeed, it is

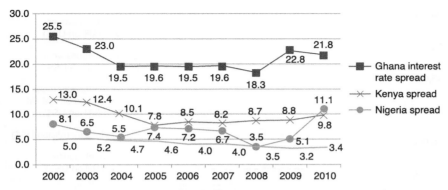

Figure 6.3 Trends in interest rate spread, per cent

Source: African Development Indicators, 2013.

reported that Ghana has the highest lending rates in Africa and one of the highest in the world. In spite of growth in the number of banks in the industry, banks continue to charge high interest rates far above the policy rate. Also, the spread between the lending and deposit rates continues to be overly high. Competition in the banking sector appears to be weak. Ghanaian banks incur high overhead costs and their pre-tax returns on assets and equity are among the highest in sub-Saharan Africa due to their wide interest margins. A competitive market is designed to be more efficient; firms are required to operate at the minimum cost of production, which will then lead to a manageable interest rate spread. However, this has not been the case with Ghana's banking sector over the past two decades.

Issues in capital flows and financial stability

The increased access to external financing led to substantial capital flows to Ghana in recent years. This has been handy given Ghana's persistent current account deficits of its balance of payments over the years – see Table 6.4.

Table 6.4 Current account balance

Year	Current account balance (BoP, Million US$)	Current account balance (% of GDP)
2005	−1,104.6	−10.3
2006	−1,056.1	−5.2
2007	−2,378.8	−9.6
2008	−3,327.4	−11.7
2009	−1,897.2	−7.3
2010	−2,747.3	−8.5
2011	−3,503.9	−8.9
2012	−4,777.5	−11.4

Source: World Bank.

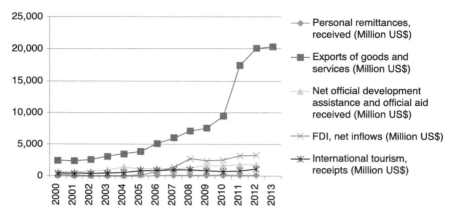

Figure 6.4 Sources of capital flows to Ghana, in million US$

Source: World Bank, World Development Indicator.

Foreign aid constitutes an important source of development finance in Ghana. As with many other aid recipient countries, Ghana receives aid in the form of budgetary and project support. In Ghana, both the level and proportion of aid (% of Gross National Income (GNI)) have increased from the levels observed in the early 1990s. Net Official Development Assistance (ODA) increased from under US$300 million in 1990 to peak at about US$928 million in 2004. It decreased over the 2005–06 period (when Ghana was undergoing the HIPC initiative) but has since increased, and reached about $820 million in 2009 (Figure 6.4). The Aid to GNI ratio has followed a similar trend although it is less pronounced. It increased from about 4.6 per cent in 1990 to a peak of about 10.7 per cent in 2004 but fell to about 5.4 per cent in 2009. The ratio has fallen consistently since 2009 to 4.9 per cent in 2012.

Capital flows in the form of foreign direct investment (FDI) and portfolio investment have also gained some prominence over the years. Indeed, total private capital flows, consisting of FDI and other private capital, has increased since 2000. FDI, in particular, has become an important component of total private capital flows, particularly since 2006 (see Figure 6.5). FDI to Ghana is dominated by the resource-seeking type and so the increases observed from about 2006 would have been accounted for largely by the mining sector.

Financial development requires an enabling environment. The probability that a country will suffer a banking crisis depends on global contagion and domestic factors (Forbes and Warnock, 2012 and IMF, 2013). The global financial crisis and the subsequent U.S. Federal Reserve's "tapering announcement" in May 2013, which contributed to capital outflows from some sub-Saharan African frontier markets and exchange rate depreciations, are clear testaments of how imbalances and instability in the international economy create instability in financial markets and real sectors of developing countries, with adverse growth

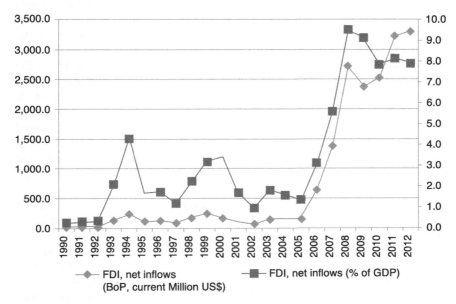

Figure 6.5 Contribution of FDI to Ghana's GDP
Source: Word Development Indicators and Bank of Ghana.

impacts. It is, therefore, of utmost importance to keep a watchful eye on risks or threats to macroeconomic and financial stability in order to avoid a real crisis.

Generally, the year 2013 saw a pickup in threats to Ghana's financial system and to the economy more broadly stemming from both external and domestic sources. The Ghanaian economy has faced significant macroeconomic challenges due, in part, to high and extraordinary fiscal and current account deficits during 2012–2013. These weak fundamentals reflected growing and unsustainable levels of government spending in the run up to the general elections of 2012. Fiscal expansion was partly financed by foreign borrowing, thereby increasing Ghana's vulnerability to sudden capital flow reversals. In 2013, high deficits in both the fiscal and current accounts were registered in the context of low levels of foreign reserves, with the current account deficit alone reaching 13.2 per cent of GDP. Private capital flows (including FDI) fell as a percentage of GDP from 7.4 per cent in 2012 to 6.6 per cent in 2013. Net international reserves fell from $3.2 billion in December 2012 to $2.1 billion by the end of 2013 and $1.7 billion by January 2014 covering only less than one month of imports of goods and services. In 2014, government debt rose past 60 per cent of GDP, raising concerns about fiscal sustainability and the risk of debt distress.

Threats to stability from external sources related mainly to increased global financial market volatility on the back of the US Fed's perceived indication to end its accommodative monetary policy by tapering bond purchases. Exchange rates adjusted sharply towards the end of 2013 as the rate of depreciation recorded 14.7 per cent for the year 2013. In early 2014, there was additional pressure on the exchange rate following the announcement of new reform measures in the foreign exchange markets. Hence, the Ghana Cedi depreciated by more than 17.6 per cent during the first quarter of 2014 compared to 1.1 per cent during the corresponding period in 2013. The other main threats to the outlook included a fragile global economic recovery and a further deceleration of growth in major emerging markets, which could weaken exports through lower commodity prices or reduce inflows of aid and FDI with dire consequences for planned and ongoing resource development projects in Ghana. Continued lower global commodity prices will also weaken current account balances and put pressure on the domestic currency with its attendant destabilizing consequences for financial stability.

The growing economic imbalances and the less favourable external environment resulted in heightened financial fragility and uncertain expectations, which led to rapid outflow of capital and increased the probability of a severe crisis.

In early February 2014, the Central Bank announced a number of foreign exchange restrictions to counter sharp depreciation of the domestic currency and thus restore stability in the foreign exchange markets. Commercial banks and other financial houses were banned from issuing cheques and cheque books on foreign exchange accounts and foreign currency accounts. No bank should grant a foreign currency-denominated loan or foreign currency-linked facility to a customer who was not a foreign exchange earner. The Central Bank also prohibited offshore foreign deals by resident and non-resident companies, including exporters in the country.

The Ghanaian Cedi continued to fall after the Central Bank had introduced the exchange rate restrictions – between January and September 2014, the Cedi had fallen by about 40 per cent against the US dollar, but then the currency stabilized after the infusion of $2.7 billion into the economy as a result of a US$1 billion Eurobond floatation and $1.7 billion cocoa syndicated loan facility.

Measures to protect the financial system in particular were mainly macro-prudential and included reduction in the Net Open Positions (NOPs) of banks, and a requirement for banks to keep statutory reserves in Cedis. Further measures to consolidate financial stability included adoption of risk-based supervision and regulatory participation in regional financial stability bodies aimed at sharing experiences with a view to reducing cross-border contagion.

Issues in prudential regulation

Bank failures create serious negative externalities that ultimately lead to a loss of confidence in the financial system. This creates the need for the supervision and regulation of individual banks.

The Bank of Ghana is directly in charge of regulating and monitoring the banking sector. The Bank of Ghana serves as a lender of last resort to all banks irrespective of ownership. Thankfully, Ghana does not yet have to worry too much about systemically important, too big to fail banks and financial institutions. Nevertheless, the Central Bank is quite active in building up supervisory capabilities of early identification and addressing any incipient systemic risks. Routine stress test exercises are mandatory for banks to identify vulnerabilities.

The regulatory and legal regime in Ghana has evolved over the years to meet the changing structure of the Ghanaian banking industry as well as the risk levels associated with the pace of expansion. These prudential regulations relating to banking and non-banking financial business aim at achieving a sound and efficient banking system in the interest of depositors and other customers of these institutions and the economy as a whole.

In recent times, the Bank of Ghana has reviewed upwards the minimum capital required for commercial banks to operate in the country to 120 million Cedis from the 60 million Cedis it set previously. The bank has also reviewed upwards new capital requirements for other financial institutions. Savings and loans companies will now be required to have 15 million Cedis as their new minimum capital from the 7 million Cedis required earlier. The rural and community banks are now required to have a minimum capital of 300,000 Cedis up from 150,000 Cedis previously.

These prudential and legal regulatory reforms over the years, coupled with upgrading the skills and competences of the supervisory staff, have ensured that the Ghanaian banking system continues to be sound, well-liquid, and adequately capitalized. Ghana has already adopted risk-based Basel II capital adequacy regime and preparatory work for adoption of the revised Basel III version, and its liquidity coverage standards are in progress.

Summary and conclusion

In Ghana, sustained financial sector restructuring and transformation has succeeded in creating one of the most vibrant financial services centres in West Africa. The liberalization of the sector led to an influx of foreign banks and investors, mostly leading brands from Nigeria, South Africa, and beyond. Certainly, these investments were apparently driven by good economic policies and profit opportunities as well as prudential banking supervision, rather than market size.

Ghana has therefore seen a significant increase in the number of banks, including pan-African groups, with a rapidly expanding deposit base. As a dynamic economy with regional importance and large infrastructural needs, Ghana can greatly benefit from, and contribute to, regional financial integration.

Looking back, the entry of foreign banks and investors into the financial services industry in Ghana has increased competition in the banking industry as well as the introduction of strong business practices, technology, products, and risk management systems, and has given impetus to dynamic efficiency in the industry.

Moreover, a number of other challenges remain, including access to credit by the private sector and the high cost of credit, which tends to militate against small-scale businesses. While the authorities have continued to work on these challenges, current macroeconomic challenges continue to hamper efforts to lower the cost of credit and to expand access to credit for most small-scale businesses.

Ghanaian banks are notoriously the most profitable in the sub region. This suggests there is a role for government, in the form of regulatory (and even more forceful) intervention to promote competition and prevent abuse of market power. There may be a good case for considering the introduction of competition (antitrust) and consumer protection laws to protect consumer welfare. Whereas banks often attribute the high lending interest rates to rigidities in their funding costs, particularly related to banks' term deposit liabilities, there are also instances where particular subsidized funds that are to be administered by these banks for the benefit of small and medium-scale enterprises are also priced as regular loans. This effectively frustrates government efforts to enhance access to finance for the benefit of the vulnerable and the excluded, who have no options other than to go to money lenders who also quote extremely high rates.

On prudential regulation, the Central Bank has been proactive in reforming the banking system, and has reviewed upwards again the minimum capital required for commercial banks to operate in the country. The Central Bank has also set itself to enhance the institutional infrastructure for prudential regulation, such as the establishment of a Deposit Insurance scheme and also an orderly framework for dealing with problem banks in the future, among others. These prudential and legal regulatory reforms over the years coupled with upgrading the skills and competences of the supervisory staff have ensured that the Ghanaian banking system continues to be sound, well-liquid, and adequately capitalized. This notwithstanding, there remain significant counterparty risks as well as cross-border risks resulting from increasing integration of the financial markets in the sub region as a result of the expansion of regional banks.

Finally, on the management of capital flows, Ghana continues to attract significant amounts of flows including ODA, FDI, and portfolio flows among others. While such openness could have clear benefits in helping to fill the resource gap, there are potential risks particularly from sudden stops and capital flow reversals that one must be mindful about. The phenomenon of increasing financial integration in the sub region and the high interest shown in investing in Ghana's banking sector could raise cross-border risks that could crystallize in the absence of effective regulation. It is, however, positive to note that the Central Bank is engaging with other supervisory authorities in regional countries for information sharing and collaboration to stem such potential risks.

Notes

1   This section draws on the Financial Sector Strategic Plan II (FINSSP II) (MOFEP, 2012).
2   The GSGDA was to be implemented within a four-year term covering the period 2010–2013 (recently completed). A new policy framework was then drafted to cover the period 2014–2017.
3   The insurance market is relatively well developed, with more than 30 companies competing on the market, with a high level of foreign participation. Capital markets have also been developing at a rapid pace.

References

Aghion, P. and P. Bolton (1997) "A theory of trickle-down growth and development", *Review of Economic Studies*, 64(2): 151–72.

Allen, Franklin, Isaac Otchere, and Lemma W. Senbet (2011) "African financial systems: A review", *Review of Development Finance*, 1: 79–113.

Banerjee, A. and A. Newman (1993) "Occupational choice and the process of development", *Journal of Political Economy*, 101: 274–98.

Bencivenga, V. and B. Smith (1991) "Financial intermediation and endogenous growth", *Review of Economic Studies*, 58(2): 195–209.

Forbes, Kristin J. and Francis E. Warnock (2012) "Capital flow waves: Surges, stops, flight, and retrenchment", *Journal of International Economics*, 88(2) (November): 235–51.

Galor, O. and J. Zeira (1993) "Income distribution and macroeconomics", *Review of Economic Studies*, 60: 35–52.

IMF (International Monetary Fund) (2013) *Global Financial Stability Report*, October 2013: 93–125.

King, R. and R. Levine (1993) "Finance, entrepreneurship and growth: Theory and evidence", *Journal of Monetary Economics*, 32(3): 513–42.

Levine, R. (1997) "Financial development and economic growth: Views and agenda", *Journal of Economic Literature*, 25: 688–726 (June).

MOFEP (2012) *Financial Sector Strategic Plan II*. Ministry of Finance and Economic Planning. Republic of Ghana, April. 119 pages.

Pagano, M. (1993) "Financial markets and growth: An overview", *European Economic Review*, 37(2–3): 613–22.

7 Financial regulation in low-income countries

Balancing inclusive growth with financial stability – the Nigerian case[1]

Olu Ajakaiye and Sheriffdeen Tella

Introduction

The global financial crisis caught many countries unprepared and thus had devastating effects on many individual country's economic and particularly financial systems and the world at large. It sent both policy makers and academics involved in financial matters to the drawing board with the intention to bring about short, medium and long term stability into the banking system and prevent future catastrophe. For the Central Bank of Nigeria (CBN), it was time to undertake immediate review of its consolidation reform programmes, more so when the global crisis had started causing financial instability and attendant effects on the Nigerian economy.

The Nigerian banking system has witnessed substantial policy and regulatory developments in the last five decades, having seven distinct phases of banking reforms.[2] At the time of the recent global financial crisis, the banking sector was in its sixth phase, started in 2004. This phase was regarded as the *era of bank consolidation*, designed to ensure a diversified, strong and reliable banking sector, to ensure the safety of depositors' money, play an active developmental role in the Nigerian Economy and become competent and competitive players both in the African and global financial systems; it was also aimed at encouraging the emergence of regional and specialised banks (CBN, 2004).

This chapter, like the others in this book, investigates the effects of the existing regulations on the structure of the financial system and specifically the banking sector in Nigeria. The second section describes the structure and role of Nigeria's financial sector; the third section discusses recent initiatives to address issues in financial inclusion; the fourth section analyzes capital flows and financial stability; and the fifth section concludes.

Structure, size and role of the Nigerian financial sector

The structure of the Nigerian financial system has not witnessed dramatic changes in the last two decades or more despite policy changes. The structure can be divided broadly into banking and non-banking financial sectors. The banking sector has commercial banks, merchant banks, development or specialised banks, community/microfinance banks and their regulatory authorities (e.g. Central Bank of Nigeria and Nigerian Deposit Insurance Corporation) while the non-bank financial institutions (NBFIs) comprise insurance companies, pension funds and the stock exchange, regulated by the Security and Exchange Commission (SEC), the National Insurance Commission (NAICOM) and National Pension Commission (PENCOM).

The physical and operational structure of the banking sector had witnessed structural expansion and contraction in tandem with changing reforms. The reforms, involving regulation, deregulation and re-regulation, were basically carried out to ensure stability, instill confidence in the banking system and improve efficiency. The financial reforms of 2004 were undertaken against the background of:

i) The existence of 89 deposit money banks with weak capital base. The total capitalisation of the banking system in 2004 was equivalent to the capital of the fourth largest bank in South Africa.

ii) The aggregate banking credit to the domestic economy was far below 20 per cent of the GDP. Thus, the contribution of the banking sector to the growth in the real economy was quite low.

iii) The sector was oligopolistic in nature with high wealth concentration within the ten largest banks. Within themselves, they accounted for over 50 per cent of the industry's total assets/liabilities.

iv) The ratio of banks to population was very low and the payment system encouraged cash-based transactions.

v) There was high cost of operation arising from infrastructural deficits, particularly with respect to inadequate energy power.

vi) Over-dependence on public sector deposits and concentration of activities in foreign exchange trading.

vii) High incidence of non-performing loans. The level of saving in the economy was low while the demand for credit continued to grow. The mismatch resulted in large spread between saving and lending rates. The high lending rates eventually resulted in high incidence of non-performing loans.

viii) The sector was also characterised by poor corporate governance with banks engaging in shady contracts and dealings to meet profitability requirements of the shareholders.

ix) More than one-third of the banks were within marginal and unsound state.

(Soludo, 2004)

Thus, the financial sector invariably led to financial instability and systemic crisis that made banks in need of frequent bailout assistance. Such a financial environment required that the regulatory authorities strengthened the regulatory framework and supervisory capacity through a deep reform agenda introduced in 2004.

The vision of the reform agenda was to:

i) establish a banking system that could rapidly drive Nigeria's economic growth and development;

ii) integrate the Nigerian banking system into the global financial system;

iii) target at least one Nigerian bank in the top 100 banks in the world within the next ten years;
iv) in the long term, make Nigeria Africa's financial hub; and
v) create a new Central Bank of Nigeria (CBN) for the 21st century that is best managed and most effective.

The Central Bank therefore, among other policy initiatives,

i) increased minimum capital requirement from N2 billion ($12 million) to N25 billion ($148.8 million) within a period of 18 months;
ii) introduced a phased withdrawal of public sector funds from banks;
iii) promoted mergers and acquisition among banks;
iv) adopted a risk-focused and rule-based regulatory framework;
v) adopted zero tolerance for late reporting and information rendition; and
vi) introduced greater transparency and accountability in operations.

(Soludo, 2004)

The outcome of the reforms can be gleaned from Table 7.1. Over 85 commercial and merchant banks merged into just 24 mega banks with capital base of minimum of N25 billion. At the end of the consolidation exercise, the number of foreign banks was reduced to four from 11 while the number of indigenous banks was reduced to 21 from 77.

Major implications of the downsizing in the number of banks have been that there were no medium sized banks to service small and medium scale enterprises' needs for funds, which are smaller than what the mega banks that emerged were ready to offer; no government-owned commercial bank was left; the ratio of foreign banks to local banks, which was one to seven reduced to one to six; and the universal banking structure, which was introduced in 2002, became a reality as the distinction between commercial and merchant banks disappeared as a result of the reform.

At the same time, the Nigerian banks became major players in the international financial markets with two banks successfully raising funds from the Eurobond market; moreover, banks such as United Bank for Africa, Zenith Bank, Guarantee Trust Bank and Access Bank moved offshore to open branches in African countries like Ghana, Kenya and Uganda.

Table 7.1 Distribution of number of banks by type of owners, 2000–2010

Status	2000	2001	2002	2003	2004	2005	2006	2007	2008	2009	2010
Privately	76	77	78	77	77	77	21	20	20	20	20
Government	1	1	1	1	1	1	0	0	0	0	0
Foreign	10	11	11	11	11	11	4	4	4	4	4
Total	89	89	90	89	89	89	25	24	24	24	24

Source: Data for 2000 to 2006 was sourced from Abel Ezeoha (2007) while the data for the 2007 to 2010 was sourced from the Analysts Data Services and Resources Limited.

The funding void created by the merger and acquisition of hitherto medium scale banks was expected to be filled by microfinance banks (MFBs). Also, the gap in long term funding required for development was expected to be filled by the new structure of the banks – universal banking. However, it soon became clear that the MFB could not play the expected role; and the newly capitalised banks were more active in the short end of the financial markets, thereby behaving more like commercial rather than universal banks. Commercial banks by nature of their philosophy, which is liquidity and profitability, cannot be expected to lend on a long term basis. This situation, coupled with other recurring problems in the management of the financial sector, led to policy reversal, particularly after the global financial crisis.

Another chapter of the recent banking sector reform began in 2009 with the change in leadership of the CBN and the immediate decision to rescue some banks that were already in distress in order to prevent a crisis of confidence in the system. This led to the suspension of operations of three banks (Bank PHB, Spring Bank and Equatorial Trust Bank) which were nationalised by the CBN due to insolvency, with the injection of N200 billion into them. The Asset Management Company (AMCON), which was a creation of the post-consolidation reforms of 2009, purchased what was referred to as 'toxic' assets of the banks in distress.

At the end of 2010, the structure of the financial institutions shows that:

i) commercial banks or deposit money banks (DMBs – as they are now called) which were 89 before the 2004 bank consolidation, were 24 by 2007 but reduced to 20 in 2011 due to merger/acquisition of four banks that were earlier nationalised by the CBN;

ii) there were five Development Finance Institutions (DFIs), namely: Bank of Industry (BOI), Federal Mortgage Bank of Nigeria (FMBN), Nigeria Export-Import Bank (NEXIM), the Bank of Agriculture (BOA) and the Urban Development Bank of Nigeria (UDBN);

iii) there were five discount houses and 108 finance companies;

iv) the number of MFBs was 866;

v) 101 primary mortgage institutions existed;

vi) Bureaux-de-change (BDC) were 1,959 but in 2011 the number increased by 92 due to new ones that were granted approval during the year to bring the total number of BDC to 2,051;

vii) 690 security brokerage firms were functional;

viii) the number of insurance companies were 73; and

ix) there were five Pension funds custodians and 13 Pension fund administrators.

In addition, Nigeria has one of the most active stock exchanges in Africa, the Nigerian Stock Exchange, plus an emerging commodity stock exchange. The regulatory bodies are:

• National Insurance Commission (NAICOM);
• National Pension Commission (PENCOM);

- Nigerian Deposit Insurance Corporation (NDIC);
- Securities and Exchange Commission (SEC); and
- CBN.

How this new financial structure has had an impact on the growth and development of the real sector of the Nigerian economy and encouraged financial stability are examined next.

The Nigerian banking sector and economic performance

Since the publication of the seminal works of McKinnon (1973) and Shaw (1973) on the importance of the financial sector in promotion of economic growth, the results of studies relating to the role of financial deepening on economic growth remain inconclusive.[3] The importance of the banking sector in particular is emphasised in the literature (King and Levine, 1993). The argument is that a bank-based financial system provides information regarding investment opportunities and direct resources to productive sectors or areas, thus facilitating economic growth (Beck et al., 2011).

Since the 2004 reforms, the Nigerian financial system remains one of the fastest growing and changing financial sectors in Africa in terms of structure, competitiveness and outreach. In this context and as already alluded to, foreign banks are not only part of the domestic banking institutions but Nigerian banks have opened branches in many African countries and outside the continent. This has some implications for stability of the financial sector and the economy (IMF, 2009).

Charles Soludo, Governor of the CBN between 2004 and early 2008, identified some issues he termed 'unfinished businesses' towards the end of his mandate. Among these unfinished businesses were:

i) the need to manage macro vulnerability and volatility arising from integration of the Nigerian economy to the international financial markets and in particular shocks arising from the flow of hot money or portfolio investment; foreign capital flows (FDI and portfolio), which were $433 million in 2003, grew to $9.6 billion in 2007;

ii) the inability to achieve revamping of the payment system with respect to improving Real Time Gross System (RTGS) and overall National Clearing System (NACS) including boosting of electronic banking;

iii) the inability to achieve desired financial deepening, which was just 31 per cent as at the end of 2007;

iv) problems of supervision of international subsidiaries of Nigerian banks and implementation of Basel II provisions;

v) mainstreaming MFBs to achieve the desirable goal of credit delivery to small and medium scale enterprises as well as deepening the capital market; and

vi) the inability to make Nigeria an international financial centre.

At the time that Sanusi Lamido Sanusi assumed office as the Governor of the Central Bank in 2009, he noted that the Nigerian banking system had witnessed dramatic growth post-consolidation, but affirmed that 'neither the industry nor the regulators were sufficiently prepared to sustain and monitor the sector's explosive growth' (Sanusi, 2010). Thus, at that time, the banking sector was again in the mood for distress. Sanusi identified and discussed eight main factors that made it possible for the global financial crisis to turn the Nigerian financial system into a fragile entity. The factors were:

i) macroeconomic instability caused by large and sudden capital inflow;
ii) major failure in corporate governance at banks;
iii) lack of investor and consumer sophistication;
iv) inadequate disclosure and transparency about the financial position of banks;
v) critical gaps in regulatory framework and regulations;
vi) uneven supervision and enforcement;
vii) unstructured governance and management process at the CBN/weaknesses within the CBN; and
viii) weaknesses in the business environment.

(Sanusi, 2010)

In order to correct such a precarious situation, Sanusi proposed a blueprint built around four pillars for reforming the financial system in the next decade. These are:

i) enhancing the quality of banks;
ii) establishing financial stability;
iii) enabling healthy financial sector evolution; and
iv) ensuring the financial sector contributes to the real economy.

It is clear from these pillars that the external focus that had prevailed in CBN policy was then halted. There was also immediate reversal of universal banking and introduction of national and regional banks to diminish the status of mega banking. What is the status of the financial sector today, as a result of these latest changes? Let us consider some statistics.

Table 7.2 shows the ratio of private sector credit to GDP and the ratio of broad money (M2) to GDP. Both ratios represent the level of depth of the Nigerian financial market. The credit to the private sector steadily rose to peak at 36.7 per cent in 2009 from 12.5 per cent in 2004 but a sharp inflexion took place in the trend in 2009 with a steady decline to 19 per cent in 2010 and 16.9 per cent in 2011, before a marginal increase in 2012. The same pattern is noticed in the M2/GDP ratio.

The growth rate of credit to the private sector thus fluctuated widely over the period 2004–2012. For most of the period when consolidation reforms started in 2005 and up to 2008, there was a steady increase in credit to the private sector but the trend changed from 2009 when government borrowing suddenly increased and this resulted in crowding-out the private sector. The massive

Table 7.2 Selected financial indicators of Nigerian banks, 2004–2013

	2004	2005	2006	2007	2008	2009	2010	2011	2012	2013
Credit to private/ GDP %	12.5	12.6	12.3	17.8	28.5	36.7	18.7	16.9	20.6	19.7
M2/GDP %	18.7	18.1	20.5	24.8	33.0	38.0	20.4	19.2	19.5	18.9

Source: CBN Annual Report and Statement of Accounts, 2008 and 2013.

borrowing by the government coincided with the time the government revenue fell due to the global crisis (which affected oil prices) as it was trying to bail out distressed sectors of the economy such as the textile industry, the airlines and recapitalising development banks in the expectation the latter could be able to help revamp the economy.

Another way to look at it is that, between 2006 and 2009, credit to the private sector rose sharply from 12 per cent to 36 per cent of GDP. In real terms (2002 prices), the domestic borrowing by the private sector grew almost fivefold between 2003 and 2009 (see Figure 7.1 and also Chapter 1 in this book).

Figure 7.2 presents savings interest rates, prime lending rates and interest rates spread. The interest rates spread can be used to measure the level of efficiency in the financial market and as such, its high values indicated gross inefficiency of the financial system.[4] The patterns of the interest rates on saving and the inflationary rates, in turn, show that the real interest rates on saving have been negative, which is a disincentive to saving while the positive real interest on loans discourages borrowers and increases their costs excessively.

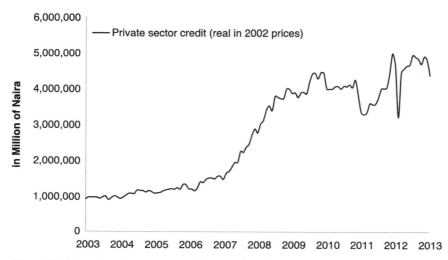

Figure 7.1 Nigerian private sector credit extension, 2003–2013
Source: CBN, 2013.

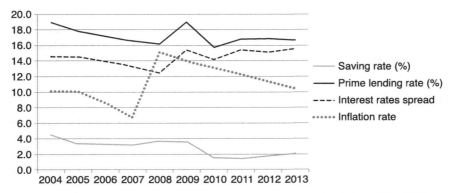

Figure 7.2 Relationships among price variables, interest rates and inflation, 2004–2013

Table 7.3 shows that the increase in the credit to the private sector until 2009 was mainly short term and it can be inferred that, coming at the time of massive capitalisation and consolidation, the banks were in the business to possibly make short term profits rather than investments in real sector to expand production capacity.

As discussed in Chapter 1, fast credit growth can exacerbate vulnerabilities and enhance the risk of financial crises. This became a reality in the case of Nigeria in 2009, when distress in the banking sector was exposed and operation of four banks had to be suspended to prevent systemic failure of the banking system. Non-performing loans as percentage of gross loans rose sharply from 9.5 per cent in 2007 to almost 30 per cent in 2009. In total, nine financial institutions came close to collapse and had to be rescued at the cost of $4 billion. The cost of cleaning up the balance sheets and recapitalising the banks was estimated at about 2.4 trillion Naira, equivalent to almost 8 per cent of GDP (IMF, 2011).

The Nigerian financial crisis shows that there is no reason for complacency about the need for rigorous financial regulation in African economies, especially in the face of rapid credit expansion in many sub-Saharan African (SSA) markets.

Table 7.3 Maturity of DMBs credits/sectorial shares, 2007–2011

Indicator	2007	2008	2009	2010	2011
Short-term (%)	75.8	75.4	70.3	65.3	60.0
Medium-term (1–3 years) %	13.5	14.5	14.3	14.6	15.2
Long-term (3 years above) %	10.7	10.1	15.3	20.1	24.8
Credit to:					
Priority sector (%)	25.9	26.2	25.2	30.4	36.1
Less preferred sector (%)	41.2	42.0	46.9	47.8	45.8
Unclassified (%)	32.9	31.8	27.9	21.8	18.1

Source: CBN Annual Report and Statement of Accounts, 2011.

As importantly, financial stability remains a recurring issue in Nigeria, probably not because of the lack of regulations to check the unwholesome activities that lead to financial instability but the inconsistent and unsustainable manner of enforcing the regulations. This is part of what Ojo (2010) called the maladapted financial system.

Issues in financial inclusion

In a recent study conducted by Ajakaiye et al. (2015), it is stated that inclusive growth is required to address widespread poverty in Nigeria. However, poverty alleviation will not be achieved with the current pattern of credit provision, which is geared towards the short end of the financial market and the non-preferred sectors of the economy.

The issue of financial inclusion has been in the front burner of the activities of the CBN for a long time, but this has not been successful. In the 1970s, the CBN introduced rural banking with the hope of integrating the rural dwellers into the formal banking system, but the project failed largely because the banks complained that the costs of running the rural branches were high and they were unprofitable. In the 1990s, the CBN introduced the People's Bank and the community banks. The former was aimed at addressing the funding needs of informal sector technical/artisan associations organised into co-operative groups. It was a government-funded bank and it eventually collapsed due to lack of transparency and accountability. Many of the community banks, in turn, which were community based, also collapsed and the surviving ones were transformed into MFBs. In addition, the government encouraged the banks to contribute 2 per cent of their profits to the Small and Medium Enterprises Investment Scheme (SMEIS). The impact was imperceptible and, hence, the scheme was discontinued.

So, the CBN, in its attempt to address the need to directly promote financial inclusion and inclusive growth, had to step up its developmental functions. The realisation of the inability of the banking system to promote inclusive growth over the years can be gleaned from a CBN Report (2010:122):

> The real sector plays strategic roles in an economy ... The sector has, however, grossly underperformed as a result of various constraints. The major constraints were poor access to credit, the high cost of credit, inade-quate power supply and other infrastructural challenges. The constraint of credit has been further exacerbated by the impact of the global financial crisis on the economy, as the pool of loanable funds shrank significantly. Against this background, the CBN and the federal government initiated measures to boost credit to the real sector.

The following represent the initiatives which were introduced in 2009 and 2010 by the five specialised or development banks in partnership with commercial banks and the CBN:

i) *N200 billion Commercial Agricultural Credit Scheme (CACS)*: In order to promote commercial agriculture in Nigeria, the Central Bank, in collaboration with the Ministry of Agriculture and Rural Development, established the CACS in 2009. The Federal Government issued a bond worth N200 billion ($1.25 billion) for funding the scheme. By June 2013, N199.37 billion had been disbursed to 273 projects under this scheme and N8.72 billion was repaid by banks for 16 projects financed earlier.

ii) *N200 billion Small and Medium Scale Enterprises Guarantee Scheme (SMECGS)*: The SMECGS was established in 2010 with the main objectives of fast-tracking the development of the small and medium scale enterprises and the manufacturing sector of the Nigerian economy; set the pace for the industrialisation of the economy; and increase access to credit by promoters of the small and medium scale enterprises and manufacturers. The *modus operandi* of the scheme is to guarantee 80 per cent of loans extended by participating banks to the recipients and thus cover risks that have prevented the banks to give credits to the real sector. A total of 52 projects worth N2.2 billion were guaranteed between the inception in 2010 and mid-year 2013.

iii) *N200 billion SME Restructuring/Refinancing Fund*: To improve the financial positions of the DMBs and thereby enhance access of manufacturers to credits, the CBN established the SME Restructuring/Refinancing Fund. The fund serves to re-structure banks' existing loan portfolios to the SMEs and manufacturing sectors. The sources of funding for the project came from N500 billion ($3.13 billion) debenture stock issued by the Bank of Industry (BOI). As at end-December, 2010, the CBN had released N199.67 billion ($1.25 billion) to the BOI, which had disbursed N197.59 billion to participating banks for restructuring/refinancing loans to 539 eligible projects.

iv) *N300 billion Power and Aviation Intervention Fund*: This Fund was established to refinance existing loans and leases and provide working capital for the power and aviation sector. It is to stimulate credit to the domestic power and troubled airline industries. As at mid-June 2013, 41 projects worth N221 billion have been funded.

v) *The Nigerian Incentive-based Risk Sharing System for Agricultural Lending (NIRSAL)* was initiated by the CBN but in collaboration with various stakeholders to solve value-chain lending problems in the agricultural sector. It is a demand-driven credit facility. Banks are free to choose which part of the value chain to support. Many international agencies embraced the programme over time. For example, by June 2013, the German International Cooperation (GIZ) had given grants worth N176 million for four crop projects viz tomato, rice, cocoa and cotton production, and NIRSAL signed a Memorandum of Understanding (MoU) with the United States Agency for International Development (USAID) and the Federal Ministry of Agriculture and Rural Development for technical partnership with a $100 million fund.

On the issue of financial literacy, the CBN claimed that it has been able to sustain its efforts at achieving the broad objective of raising financial inclusion to 80 per cent by 2020. The activities undertaken included the developments of the Financial Literacy Framework to enable people to acquire basic skills on finance-related issues and sensitisation of students in five universities (Gombe State University, Lead City University (Ibadan), University of Nigeria (Nsukka), University of Maiduguri and Adekunle Ajasin University). Financial literacy is very important for financial inclusion in Nigeria given the low level of trust in the banking system and the low literacy rate among the populace.

As part of promoting financial inclusion, the CBN continues to promote e-banking, involving the use of Automated Teller Machine (ATM), Point of Sale machine (POS) as well as internet banking. These are becoming increasingly popular, even in the rural areas. These and other initiatives are relatively nascent such that an assessment of their impact on inclusive growth may be too early. Nevertheless, recent pronouncements by the Government and the new CBN Governor indicate that such initiatives are likely to be sustained and, indeed, stepped up allaying the fears of possible policy reversals on account of changes in leadership of key institutions like the CBN.

Issues in capital flow and financial stability

The IMF, in its Global Financial Stability Report (IMF, 2012) noted the importance of the link between the structure of the financial sector and growth and affirms that preliminary results of the relationship indicate that cross border connections through foreign banks could be beneficial in normal times but a source of instability during crisis. Tella (2009) found that the global financial crisis had transmission effects on the Nigerian capital market; that is, huge capital inflows through the capital market took place, made possible by Capital Account Liberalisation (CAL). The capital inflow into the Nigerian stock market before the global crisis and its subsequent withdrawal at the onset of the crisis created instability in such a market (Figure 7.3) and by extension in the banking sector.

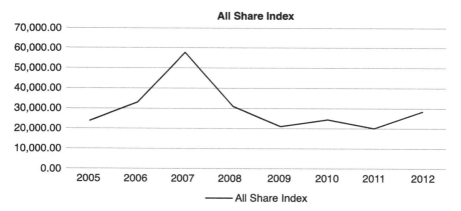

Figure 7.3 Trend in All Share Index of the Nigerian stock exchange

Table 7.4 Five-year average FDI flows to Nigeria, 1995–2011

Periods	FDI inflow (N'M)	FDI outflow (N'M)	FDI net-flow (N'M)	% change in net-flows	FDI as % of GDP
2000–2004	12,794.94	3,215.82	9,579.12	42.31	0.133
2005–2009	531,384.38	78,158.86	453,225.52	4,631.39	2.356
2010–2011	1,126,050	131,025	995,025	119.54	3.077

Source: Authors' computations with data sourced from the Central Bank of Nigeria Statistical Bulletin (various issues).

In truth, the capital account had been liberalised back in 1986, even though there were some times of restrictions. But the CBN's policy of internationalisation of the financial system under the 2004 Consolidation reforms further deepened financial liberalisation and propelled the openness of the economy, thus allowing for the easy inflow and outflow of capital. With respect to FDI, Table 7.4 shows average foreign direct investment flows to Nigeria between 2000 and 2011. The period 2005 to 2009 witnessed huge inflow (and outflow) of capital. The period can be linked with the consolidation reform era, as well as the global financial crisis. We can infer that the consolidation reforms package encouraged capital inflows while the financial crisis encouraged capital outflow.

Table 7.5 presents the international financial investment positions of the country. It can be seen from the table that a large proportion of investment was 'hot money', i.e. portfolio investment which is considered more dangerous for financial stability since it can be withdrawn at short notice. Such withdrawal happened in 2008 causing a significant fall in the Stock Exchange All Share Index. Portfolio investments imply that the transmission mechanism of external funding into the economy was through the banking sector, as the first intermediary of the security markets. The rapid growth in capital flows from the mid-2000s was largely portfolio investments and when the global crisis occurred, it was the source of financial crisis of the Nigerian economy as there was a reversal of funds from the system at the height of the crisis in 2008.

In sum, macroeconomic instability caused by large and sudden capital inflow and then outflows was a major factor of what went wrong with the Nigerian

Table 7.5 International investment positions of Nigeria, 2005–2011

Investment	2005	2006	2007	2008	2009	2010
Total foreign assets	41,417.85	60,475.21	77,498.53	88,463.64	83,928.45	83,668.5
Portfolio investment	2,823.17 (6.82%)	4,349.21 (7.19%)	6,208.32 (8.01%)	10,967.09 (12.4%)	11,797.86 (14.06%)	12,739.73 (15.23%)
Direct investment	302.00 (0.73%)	624.48 (1.03%)	1,506.42 (1.94%)	2,564.69 (2.90%)	4,118.29 (4.91%)	5,041.17 (6.03%)

Source: CBN, 2012.

Note: Figures in parentheses are percentages of total foreign assets.

banking sector in 2009. Since banks were the first recipients of capital inflow and Nigerian banks have often been accused of trading mainly in the foreign exchange market, this was a major channel through which the global financial crisis directly affected the money and capital markets, and hence, the economy in 2008–2009. Other important, albeit indirect, channels include a temporary fall in oil prices which adversely affected the government fiscal position resulting in deficit financing, rising interest rates and crowding out the private sector.

Summary and conclusion

This chapter has set out to identify national risks to financial stability in Nigeria and obstacles or gaps in policy measures that support financial stability towards achieving inclusive growth; and identified issues relating to management of capital accounts, in recent times to support financial stability.

The study focused on the banking sector given the fact that the sector dominates the financial system in terms of number and types of institutions, the volume of funds it controls and volume of transactions among the citizens and business enterprises. The chapter notes the existence of foreign banks but also the insignificant share of their funds in total assets and liabilities of banks. By the same token, Nigerian banks are now engaged in offshore banking.

The chapter argues that the 2004 banking consolidation reform and the 2009 post-consolidation reforms were motivated to address, among other factors, critical gaps in regulatory framework and regulations, inadequate supervision and enforcement of regulations, and, instability caused by capital flows.

The chapter then suggests that the following has become obvious with respect to the Nigerian financial industry:

i) It is very susceptible to instability because of the nature of uses of funds on a short term basis as well as the continuous flow of short term external funds through the banks in the form of portfolio investment or 'hot money'. These factors constitute a risk to financial stability.

ii) Another risk is the continuous policy reversal and inability to see a reform through. This is partly because of rapid change in leadership of the CBN by the government and with each leader introducing new reforms. For example, within the last ten years, the Central Bank has had three governors with different ways of addressing financial instability, inefficiency in the financial system and poor corporate governance in the banking sector.

iii) A third risk is that the government has undue influence on the activities in the financial system as it finances its budget deficits from the banking system resulting in fiscal dominance, rising interest rates and crowding out the private sector.

iv) There is considerable disregard for regulation such that the banks often prefer to be punished for disobeying laws particularly with respect to lending to the preferred sectors of the economy.

v) The liberalisation of the capital account since 1987 and the CBN policy of internationalisation of the banking activities under the 2004 consolidation reforms have created an environment in the foreign exchange market, leading to an increasing movement of short term funds that have destabilising effects.

vi) The CBN and the financial sector generally need additional high quality manpower to supervise and operate the financial system efficiently, as there is the need for constant training for those on the ground.

These concluding remarks lead to the following recommendations on the kind of banking sector environment and activities required to promote financial stability and inclusive growth in Nigeria:

i) Policy consistency and sustainability is imperative. In order to insulate the system from the consequences of changes in leadership, policies and programmes should be institutionalised and depersonalised quickly and effectively.

ii) There should be effective enforcement of regulation by the regulatory authorities in the financial sector to ensure sound and dynamic financial systems and good corporate governance. This calls for strengthening the cooperation and coordination among the regulators in view of the intensifying links among the various components of the Nigerian financial market and between it and the global financial markets.

iii) Manpower development should be accorded priority in the industry in order to meet the emerging challenges posed by the dynamics of domestic and global financial systems, which require proactive and pre-emptive rather than reactive policy initiatives.

Notes

1 This chapter is the Nigerian Case study under the Multi-Country ESRC-DFID-ODU Project on Financial Regulation in Low Income Countries: Balancing Inclusive Growth with Financial Stability led by Stephany Griffith-Jones. We thank all members of the study team for their comments and suggestions on earlier versions of the chapter. The views expressed in the chapter are entirely ours.

2 Details of the phases can be gleaned from Nwankwo, 1980; Soyibo and Adekanye, 1992 and Ajakaiye, 2013.

3 See Easterly and Levine, 1997; Levine, 1997; Ndulu and O'Connell, 2008.

4 This spread figure is significantly higher than the data from the World Bank and the African Development Indicators – see the other chapters in this book.

References

Ajakaiye, Olu (2013) 'Structure and Dynamics of the Nigerian Banking Sub-Sector: Translating Banking Growth to Real Sector Growth in Nigeria', African Centre for Shared Development Capacity Building, Ibadan, Nigeria.

Ajakaiye, Olu, Afeikhena T. Jerome, O. Olaniyan, Kristi Mahrt and O.A. Alaba (2015) 'Spatial and Multidimensional Poverty in Nigeria', WIDER Working Paper no. 2015/135.

Beck, T., A. Domirguc-Kunt and D. Singer (2011) 'Is Small Beautiful? Financial Structure, Size and Access to Finance', World Bank Policy Research Paper, 5806.

CBN (Central Bank of Nigeria) (2004) *Economic Report*. Abuja, Nigeria.

CBN (Central Bank of Nigeria) (2008, 2010, 2011, 2013) *Annual Report and Statement of Accounts*. Abuja, Nigeria.

CBN (Central Bank of Nigeria) (2012) *Annual Statistical Bulletin*. Abuja, Nigeria.

CBN (Central Bank of Nigeria) (2013) *Half Year Report*. Abuja, Nigeria.

Easterly, W. and R. Levine (1997) 'Africa's Growth Tragedy: Policies and Ethnic Divisions', *Quarterly Journal of Economics*, 11(1), 1203–50.

Ezeoha, A. (2007) 'Industrial Development Banking in Nigeria: A Forty Year Failed Experiment', *Journal of Economic Policy Report*, 10(3), 193–203.

IMF (International Monetary Fund) (2009) 'Impact of the Global Financial Crisis on Sub-Saharan Africa', African Department, Washington, DC.

IMF (International Monetary Fund) (2011) 'Nigeria: Staff Report for the 2010 Article IV Consultation,' IMF Country Report. Washington DC.

IMF (International Monetary Fund) (2012) 'Global Financial Stability Report: Restoring Confidence and Progressing on Reforms', Washington DC.

King, R.G. and R. Levine (1993) 'Finance and Growth: Schumpeter Might be Right', *Quarterly Journal of Economics*, 108(3), 717–38.

Levine, Ross (1997) 'Financial Development and Economic Growth: Views and Agenda', *Journal of Economic Literature*, 25, 688–726.

McKinnon, R.I. (1973) *Money and Capital in Economic Development*. Washington DC: Brookings Institution.

Ndulu, B.J. and S.A. O'Connell (2008) 'Policy Plus: African Growth.' In: B.J. Ndulu, S.A. O'Connell, R.H. Bates, P. Collier and C.S. Soludo (eds), *The Political Economy of Economic Growth in Africa, 1960–2000*. New York: Cambridge University Press.

Nwankwo, G.O. (1980) *The Nigerian Financial System*. London: Macmilliam Publishers.

Ojo, J.A.T. (2010) *The Nigerian Maladapted Financial System: Reforming Tasks and Development Dilemma*. Lagos: The CIBN Press Limited.

Sanusi, Lamido (2010) 'The Nigerian Banking Industry: What Went Wrong and the Way Forward', Convocation Lecture presented at the Bayero University, Kano, Nigeria, 26 February.

Shaw, Edward (1973) *Financial Deepening in Economic Development*. New York: Oxford University Press.

Soludo, Chukwuma C. (2004) 'Consolidating the Nigerian Banking Industry to Meet the Development Challenges of the 21st Century', address delivered to the special meeting of the Bankers' Committee, CBN Headquarter, Abuja, 6 July.

Soyibo, A. and F. Adekanye (1992) 'The Nigerian Banking System in the Context of Policies of Financial Regulation and Deregulation', AERC Research Paper 17, December.

Tella, Sheriffdeen A. (2009) 'The Global Economic Crisis and Nigerian Stock Market: Issues on Contagion', *Nigerian Journal of Securities and Finance*, 14(1), March, 101–16.

8 Financial inclusion, regulation and inclusive growth in Ethiopia

Getnet Alemu[1]

Introduction

Ethiopia is a small open and rapidly growing economy with a shallow financial sector and low coverage of financial services. In addition, there is a lack of more sophisticated financing mechanisms such as leasing, and equity funds. The financial sector is highly regulated and closed from foreign competition. However, financial soundness indicators reveal that it is profitable and stable.

The main objectives of this chapter are to identify and analyse:

i) the structure and performance of the financial sector;
ii) regulatory measures used to support financial stability and promote inclusive growth;
iii) the management of the capital account to support financial stability;
iv) advantages and problems of the different mechanisms for such regulation, given country characteristics; and
v) the key national risks to financial stability.

In order to explore these issues, the chapter draws on an extensive literature survey and review of grey material (policy documents, directives, regulations). It also uses extensive secondary data to understand the trends in financial inclusion and to assess the performance and stability of the financial sector. Data was also generated with the help of Key Informant Interviews (KIIs) with senior officials of the financial sector (public and private) and with other major stakeholders.

The Ethiopian economy and the financial sector

The Ethiopian economy has registered remarkable growth in the last decade. Between 2003/04 and 2012/13, average annual real GDP growth rate was 11 per cent. The largest contribution to this double-digit growth came from agriculture (42 per cent) followed by distribution and services (34 per cent) and industry (24 per cent; see Table 8.1).

The development effort can be observed from the high investment rates and imports. The capacity of domestic savings in financing the development effort

Table 8.1 Sectoral contributions to GDP growth rates and GDP growth rates, per cent

Industry	03/04	04/05	05/06	06/07	07/08	08/09	09/10	10/11	11/12	12/13
Agriculture	8.40	7.04	5.71	4.91	3.82	3.13	3.62	4.14	2.23	3.10
Industry	14.34	0.83	0.75	0.96	1.11	1.25	1.50	2.07	1.82	2.11
Distribution & services	−10.97	4.81	5.30	5.94	6.44	5.69	5.41	5.07	4.66	4.45
GDP	11.78	12.67	11.76	11.81	11.37	10.07	10.53	11.28	8.71	9.66

Source: MoFED.

Note:

1 The contribution of each sector to the overall growth of the economy depends on their share from GDP and also on their variability. By differentiating GDP with respect to each sector we can incorporate these two elements.

GDP is given by: $GDP_t = Agr_t + Ind_t + DS_t$

where Agr, Ind and DS stand for agriculture, industry and distribution and services value added and the subscript t stands for time, respectively.

$$\frac{GDP_t - GDP_{t-1}}{GDP_{t-1}} = \left(\frac{Agr_t - Agr_{t-1}}{Agr_{t-1}} \right) \left(\frac{Agr_{t-1}}{GDP_{t-1}} \right) + \left(\frac{Ind_t - Ind_{t-1}}{Ind_{t-1}} \right) \left(\frac{Ind_{t-1}}{GDP_{t-1}} \right) + \left(\frac{DS_t - DS_{t-1}}{DS_{t-1}} \right) \left(\frac{DS_{t-1}}{GDP_{t-1}} \right)$$

of the country is weak, albeit growing. This has contributed to a considerable current account deficit. The per capita income has increased nearly four times (see Table 8.2).

Structure of the financial sector

The Ethiopian financial sector/policies have evolved through three stylized stages: first, financial repression and fostering of state-led industrial and agricultural development through preferential credit (in the socialist regime); second, market-led development through partial liberalization and deregulation (post-1991); and third, financial inclusion mainly through adding private banks and microfinance institutions (MFIs) (since the second half of the 1990s). Proclamation No. 84/1994 that allows the Ethiopian private sector to engage in the banking and insurance businesses and proclamation no. 40/1996 in 1996 that allows the establishment of MFIs mark the beginning of the third stage in Ethiopia's financial sector and opened the opportunity for a broad based financial sector in Ethiopia.

Currently, the Ethiopian financial sector consists of three public banks including the Development Bank of Ethiopia (DBE), 16 private banks, 14 private insurance companies, one public insurance company, 31 microfinance institutions and over 8,200 Saving and Credit Cooperatives (SACCOs) in both rural and urban areas. The ownership structure of the microfinance institutions is mixed, with the big microfinance institutions partially owned by regional states, NGOs and private owners. The government-owned Commercial Bank of Ethiopia (CBE) is the dominant commercial bank and accounts for 70 per cent of total assets of banks as of May 2013 (see IMF, 2013:20). The balance, 30 per cent, is accounted for by the other 15 banks. The CBE is relatively well run and profitable.

Despite those encouraging changes in its structure, the financial sector in Ethiopia still is highly regulated and completely closed to foreign companies. It has no stock market, and the financial market comprising the interbank money and foreign exchange markets as well as the bond and treasury bonds (TBs) market is at an infant stage accommodating limited amounts of transactions (Table 8.3). As a result, the financial sector is dominated by a cash based system.

Size and coverage of financial services

The total capital of the banking sector excluding the central bank reached $1.03 billion at the end of June 2012 which was higher by sixfold compared to 2003/04. Of the total capital, about $0.522 billion (50.7 per cent) was held by the three public owned banks. The total capital of the private banks stood at $0.507 billion (49.3 per cent). Since 2006/07 the private bank's share in the total capital has been increasing (Figure 8.1).

Due to the observed branch expansion especially in recent years, the total deposit (saving/demand/time) mobilization of the banking sector increased significantly from $4.5 billion by the end of June 2005 to $10.7 billion by the end

Table 8.2 Selected macroeconomic indicators

Macroeconomic indicators	03/04	04/05	05/06	06/07	07/08	08/09	09/10	10/11	11/12	12/13
GNS (% of GDP)	25.7	24.1	22.2	27.5	23.2	23.0	24.8	27.2	26.5	28.5
GDI (% of GDP)	29.0	26.0	27.6	24.2	24.5	24.9	27.0	27.9	33.1	33.0
Import (% of GDP)	31.9	35.8	36.9	32.4	31.1	29.0	33.3	32.1	32.0	28.0
Export (% of GDP)	15.1	15.3	14.0	12.8	11.5	10.6	13.8	17.0	13.9	12.7
Per capita GDP (USD)	142	170	205	262	355	414	373	389	510	550

Source: MoFED.

Table 8.3 Structure of the Ethiopian financial sector

Indicators	1998/99	2012/13Q1
Number and composition		
• Commercial banks	8	16
• Development banks	1	1
• Investment banks	0	0
• Insurance companies	9	14
• Mutual fund companies	0	0
• Credit union	N.A	N.A
• Microfinance institutions (MFIs)	11	31
Financial markets		
• Money market	Non-existent	Exist but shallow
• Foreign exchange market	Non-existent	Exist and relatively active
• Securities market		
o TBs market	Non-existent	Exist but shallow
o Bond market	Non-existent	Exist but shallow
o Capital market (stock market)	Non-existent	Non-existent
Number of branches		
• Banks (including DBE)	278	1,376
• Insurance	79	252
• MFIs	N.A	1,385

Source: National Bank of Ethiopia (NBE).

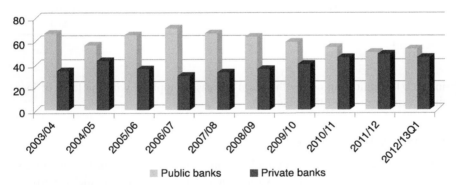

Figure 8.1 Percentage share of total capital of banks

Source: National Bank of Ethiopia (NBE).

of June 2012 (Table 8.4). The three public banks mobilized about 75 per cent of total deposits by the end of June 2005. This share has shown only a modest decline during the following eight years and accounted for 68 per cent in 2012. The CBE alone covered 66 per cent of the total deposits of the banking sector in 2012.

In terms of loan provisions, the banking sector is one of the major sources of financing to the economy by providing loans to individuals, firms and the Government. Total new loans disbursed by the banking sector reached $3.2 billion

Table 8.4 Deposit mobilizations by commercial banks, in million USD

Year	Private	Public	Total	Average exchange rate (USD/Birr)
2004/05	1,128	3,323	4,452	8.6518
2005/06	1,502	3,618	5,120	8.681
2006/07	1,975	4,148	6,123	8.7943
2007/08	2,399	4,410	6,809	9.2441
2008/09	2,864	4,635	7,499	10.4197
2009/10	2,984	4,667	7,651	12.89
2010/11	3,098	5,619	8,717	16.12
2011/12	3,411	7,290	10,701	17.5

Source: NBE.

Table 8.5 Loans disbursement by lenders, in million USD

Year	Private banks	Public banks	Total	CBE alone
2004/05	538	552	1,090	459
2005/06	839	590	1,429	490
2006/07	1,052	717	1,769	595
2007/08	1,277	1,671	2,948	1,560
2008/09	1,218	1,227	2,445	1,065
2009/10	1,161	1,081	2,242	830
2010/11	1,256	1,362	2,618	1,104
2011/12	1,094	2,111	3,206	1,825

Source: NBE.

in 2011/12, indicating nearly threefold increase compared with the level of loan disbursement in 2004/05 (Table 8.5).

Coverage of MFIs services

Ethiopia's MFIs provide saving mobilization, loan provision and to some extent micro insurance services. By providing such financial services to microenterprise operators both in urban and rural areas, they opened up the start of a more inclusive financial sector. It should be noted, however, that their contribution to these services is still extremely small.

The MFIs' capacity measured in terms of their total capital has been strengthening from year to year to reach $214.6 million in 2011/12, which was a significant increase compared with $65.7 million in 2004/05. However, these capital values are very small relative to the total of the entire banking system. The share of MFIs' capital in the total banking system (including the MFIs and excluding the central bank) was as small as 1.4 per cent in 2004/05 and 1.7 per cent in 2011/12. Also, their total assets increased markedly to $760.5 million from $219.6 million during the same period (Table 8.6), but their share in the

Table 8.6 Performance of MFIs, in million USD

Particulars	2004/05	2007/08	2008/09	2009/10	2010/11	2011/12	Dec. 2013
Total Capital	65.7	145.0	166.7	184.3	182.8	214.6	255.4
Saving	58.9	168.9	201.4	206.3	234.5	311.5	402.4
Credit	171.1	484.1	473.7	451.9	433.7	530.8	653.4
Total assets	219.6	577.7	635.4	617.4	630.0	760.5	930.4

Source: NBE and EMFIA.

total banking system remained small. It was 4.1 per cent in 2008/09, declining to 3.6 per cent in 2011/12.

Financial inclusion

Financial inclusion is facilitating access to saving and transfer services and provision of credit and insurance at an affordable cost to unbanked poor people who have no access to the formal banking system. In dealing with financial inclusion, we took two perspectives: the relationship between banking and inclusion and how financial regulation impacts the size and composition of the financial sector geared towards financial inclusion.

Financial inclusion in Ethiopia is progressing albeit from a weak base. One important aspect of this trend is the progress achieved in the coverage of bank services. One of the indicators for measuring banking access is population per branch. Banks have increased their branches and areas of coverage from year to year and reached 1,376 branches as of first quarter of 2012/13, from just 350 in 2004/05. As a result, the number of people per bank branch has declined significantly, though it is still high even by sub-Saharan African (SSA) standards (Table 8.7).

Table 8.7 Trends in bank branches and access

Year	Public banks	Private banks	Regional states	Addis Ababa	Total	Population in million	Client outreach[1]
2004/05	–	–	235	115	350	71.5	1:204286
2005/06	–	–	273	148	421	73.3	1:173634
2006/07	–	–	302	185	487	74	1:151951
2007/08	264	298	349	213	562	74.9	1:133274
2008/09	273	363	354	282	636	76.9	1:120912
2009/10	273	408	416	265	681	78.9	1:115859
2010/11	483	487	621	349	970	80.7	1:83196
2011/12	675	614	859	430	1289	82.7	1:64158
2012/13Q1	711	665	918	458	1376	84.8	1:61628

Source: Own compilation from NBE.

Note:
[1] Branch to population ratio.

Table 8.8 Access and use of financial services

Indicators	2004	2011
Commercial bank branches per 1000 KM square	0.33	0.96
ATMs per 1,000 KM square	0.008	0.16
ATMs per 100,000 adults	0.02	0.32

Source: IMF, Financial Access Services Database.

Based on the increase in branches and technological changes, access and use of financial services have been improving in Ethiopia. It should be noted, however, that a significant part of branch expansion is in the capital city, Addis Ababa. Of the total number of branches, 33 per cent are found in Addis Ababa. This shows that the formal banks still have limitations in reaching out to the population (Table 8.8).

Despite the developments mentioned above, commercial banks are character-ized by several problems in relation to access to and cost of finance. An IMF staff report for 2013 (IMF 2013:20–21) stated that 'only 7.1 million people have deposit accounts, i.e., less than 8% of Ethiopians have a bank account. The pro-portion of borrowers is even smaller (a mere 112,793)'. The World Bank (2009) has also identified bottlenecks for financial inclusion in the country. In two sepa-rate surveys (2002 and 2006) it found that access to finance is a major constraint to both formal and informal sectors in the country.

More than 80 per cent of the population of the country lives in rural areas with limited access to financial services. The extent to which the rural population have entered into the monetary economy has been very limited. This is due to the fact that most rural people depend mainly on the subsistence economy. The expan-sion of MFIs has brought some changes by reaching some of this population, though very limited. In this respect, one could be of the opinion that this lack of access is believed to adversely affect the possibility of development and growth to be pro poor. Hence, it is imperative for policy-makers to address this issue (by increasing credit and providing bank accounts) if the country is to success-fully implement its poverty reduction development strategies. For this reason, the Ethiopian Government has been paying more attention towards the promotion of financial inclusion. An important step to bring financially excluded people to the formal financial sector has been the promotion of MFIs.

Thus, since the proclamation no. 40/1996 in 1996 that allowed the establish-ment of MFIs, financial services to the unbanked have become a major area of interest for policy actors. The government, in particular, taking financial inclusion as a policy objective, has been trying to build a more inclusive financial system over the years to reach out to the unbanked. Recently, financial inclusion has become an explicit policy objective in Ethiopia as spelled out in the country's five years development plan (2010/11–2014/15) – the Growth and Transformation Plan (GTP). The plan targets to create three million jobs, provide 15,000 hectares of land for working premises and construction of sheds and buildings in the plan period (MoFED, 2010:58). Based on this, in the second year of the GTP, about

Table 8.9 Trends in performance of SMEs, loan and savings in million USD[1]

	2010/11	2011/12	2012/13	2013/14 (9 months)
No. of SMEs (cumulative)	135,897	217,641	295,092	430,653
No. jobs created	650,00	1,290,000	2,020,000	1,710,000
Amount of loan disbursed	61.4	62.3	149.2	124.5
Amount of loan collected	55.2	42.3	96.2	84.4
Amount saved	19.9	83.4	186.9	190.0

Source: Federal Micro and Small Enterprises Development Agency.

Note:
[1] The average exchange rate for 2012/13 is 18.3 (1USD/birr) and for the first nine months of 2013/14 it was 18.9505 (1USD/birr).

81,744 new small and medium-sized enterprises (SMEs) were created together with 1.3 million jobs. The same trend was observed in the third and fourth year of the plan (Table 8.9).

As may be observed from Table 8.9, the amount of loans disbursed by the MFIs (the single dominant lender to SMEs), loans collected and savings of SMEs have reached encouraging levels. Moreover, the figures on repayment of loans and savings indicate that SMEs are performing as expected and using the loans productively.

It should be noted, however, that the average amount of loan per borrower is small though it is increasing over time. For instance, at the end of 2013 it was only $231.6. In addition to this, there are a lot of people who have no access to loans. The Executive Director of AEMFI, one of our KIIs, has noted that there is a huge demand for loans, which goes far beyond the capacity of the existing MFIs. Studies also indicate that about 85 per cent of the Ethiopian rural poor households remain without access to formal financial services; MFIs have reached only 14.5 per cent of the households in the country (Wolday, 2008, as quoted by Wolday and Anteneh, 2013:15).

In addition to the MFIs, low-level financial institutions such as cooperatives and credit unions are critical for financial inclusion. The country has over 8,200 SACCOs in both rural and urban areas, as mentioned earlier. These cooperatives are believed to more easily reach to the lowest segments of the population and also serve as a bridge between the very poor and the formal banks. The problem is that they cannot meet the credit needs of their members from the resources they mobilize from their members.

To recap, it has been observed that the expansion of commercial banks and MFIs is very rapid, albeit from a small base. If we see this from the size of the population the country has, the financial services are still underdeveloped. The overwhelming majority of the population has no access to financial services. It is observed that the supply side of financial inclusion is still poor as witnessed by very high population size per branch and very low number of deposit account holders and much less borrowers. Given this context, the NBE has still to work more towards facilitating the entry of new banks and MFIs and in transforming the existing ones from traditional forms of financial services into technology based services.

Considering that use of technology and innovation in financial service delivery is key to financial inclusion in Ethiopia, the NBE has approved core banking (see next paragraph). It has also issued a directive (Directive No. FIS/01/2012) that governs the operation of financial service delivery through technology based financial services. This is an excellent development that brings the current limited financial service accessibility level to a better position in Ethiopia, and is considered as an important step towards an inclusive financial sector in the country.

Core banking has two components: intra-bank and inter-bank. The first one is networking/connecting of each branch within a given bank at the centre. This facilitates financial services for clients and reduces transaction costs for both the bank and the clients. The second one is networking of all banks at one centre. The NBE, which is responsible for this, has already selected one foreign company among many participants in the bid for implementing the core banking system. For the inter-bank network to be operational, each bank has to network all its branches. The problem, however, is that most banks are not networked within themselves. Very few banks have completed branch network. This has hindered the efficiency and effectiveness of financial services and the implementation of full core banking services. Furthermore, the NBE took almost two years to reach this stage and private banks are of the opinion that it may even take some five or more years to the full implementation of core banking.

The other technology based financial services is channel banking. It includes internet banking, card payment system, mobile banking and point of sales. These kinds of services are the most useful systems for countries like Ethiopia where the overwhelming majority of the population has no access to financial services. The NBE approved these services by its directive no. FIS/01/2012, effective as of January 2013, but still there is not much progress. It is worth mentioning that mobile networks are expanding in the country. The number of mobile subscribers in 2012/13 has reached 23.76 million from 10.7 million in 2010/11 and the target for 2014/15 is 40 million. The percentage of the rural population with access (within a 5-km radius) to a telephone service has also increased from 62.1 per cent in 2009/10 to 84 per cent in 2012/13 and the target for 2014/15 is 100 per cent (MoFED, 2014:53).

From the KIIs with different officials of the financial sector, two basic problems are identified to explain the poor progress of technology based financial services. These are the capacity of the regulatory institutions and status of institutions that provide IT and energy services. Human resources in general for the financial sector is an important issue. There is no financial training institute in the higher learning institutions in the country. From the interviews, it has been noticed that people who accumulate skills through experience and not through formal financial/banking training are managing banks. Because of this, most private banks recruited their high level employees from the public banks. Employees of the NBE are paid very low salary when compared with commercial banks. This left the NBE with young graduates who have not much experience and capacity. This has created a serious capacity gap between the commercial banks and the regulatory institution, the NBE. As it can be observed from the interviews, in most cases it is commercial banks that generate/initiate new policy ideas. The NBE takes much time to understand, conceptualize and issue regulation. Commercial banks are of the opinion that the NBE has not full capacity to provide a speedy response to commercial banks' demands and is slow to adjust to new financial developments and dynamic global changes.

Despite the potential role that existing technology based banking can have, the reality is that it cannot be seen as a panacea. It focuses on creating convenience to account holders. It is not focused on loan services. In addition, in a country where more than 80 per cent of the population live in rural areas and in a scattered manner and where the technology literacy rate is very low, effective use of technology remains questionable. Intensive public education needs to be provided on a sustainable basis.

From our KIIs we have found out that the existing financial system does not provide continued access for SMEs and the poor. Possible explanations for this are the following:

From the commercial banks side:

i) Commercial banks do not have units for SMEs and are not interested in providing loans to SMEs. Because of this, they do not provide continued/ sustained loan access, and when they do, the amount is limited. This limited amount is achieved through administrative arrangements rather than standard regulation. The financial system does not encourage/force commercial banks to provide loans to SMEs.

ii) Private banks have recently raised their paid up capital in order to increase their single borrower limit and hence scaled up their loan portfolio to the large and corporate entities and away from the small borrowers;

iii) The new regulations that have raised the start-up capital for new commercial banks discouraged new banks from joining the industry.

From MFIs side:

iv) Although the efforts and successes of MFIs are encouraging, according to the KIIs, MFIs are also not in a position to ensure continued financial access to SMEs and the poorer segments of society. In addition, the MFIs do not have the financial capacity to meet the vast needs of the rural and urban poor. The overwhelming majority of rural people and urban poor have no access to financial services. The total loans provided by MFIs are supported by a far lower deposit base, which severely limits access.[2] This has even raised sustainability concerns on the MFIs.

From low-level financial institutions (cooperatives and credit unions) side:

v) The presence of low-level financial institutions such as cooperatives and credit unions cannot meet the credit needs of their members, given the limited amount of resources they mobilize from their members' savings.

To address these issues and broaden financial inclusion, innovative mechanisms and proper institutional arrangements are required. To begin with, the infrastructure problem needs to be given prior attention. The existing financial institutions need to exploit their existing capacity and resources through better IT service provisions. Another basic issue is the architecture of the financial sector. According to the KIIs, it seems that the linkage between the commercial banks and MFIs is critical where the former can dedicate a small amount of loans that can be disbursed and managed by the latter. In this regard, the practice of the government owned CBE needs to be encouraged. The CBE regularly provides small amounts to MFIs for on-lending purposes. The NBE needs to encourage private banks to follow the practice of the CBE. There is also a need to link cooperatives and unions with the MFIs. To recap, linking SACCOs with MFIs and MFIs with commercial banks and the development bank seems the right architecture for the financial sector for effective financial inclusion. This needs a clear direction, goal driven strategy and specific guideline at the national level by the regulatory institution.

Financial sector regulations, financial stability and inclusive growth

In this section we explore two relationships:

i) the relationship between the financial sector and inclusive growth and the mechanisms through which financial regulation affect the relationship; and
ii) the relationship between the financial sector and financial stability and the mechanisms through which financial regulation influences the relationship.

Financial sector and inclusive growth

The financial sector has at least three channels that affect growth.

The first channel is physical access to financial services, which is critical for inclusive growth. As discussed in the preceding section, physical access though improving is still very limited. Deposit mobilization and provision of loan is constrained by physical access. For about 90 million people, the country has only 16 commercial banks and one development bank. New entries to the industry are constrained by the directive issued by the NBE that significantly raised the paid up capital. Furthermore, technology based banking is not yet developed in the true sense of financial inclusion.

The second and most important channel is access to finance and its cost. Different studies found that the Ethiopian financial sector is characterized by limited access. The World Bank study (2009), based on two rounds of surveys, one in 2001/02 on 427 enterprises and the other in 2006/07 on 822 enterprises, revealed that formal and informal businesses have ranked access to finance as the second biggest constraint to their investment. According to the 2012 Doing Business Survey, Ethiopia is ranked the 150th hardest country in the world in terms of access to credit (World Bank, 2012). Limited access to finance, therefore, remains a serious obstacle to inclusive growth, employment opportunity creation and poverty reduction.

Limited access to finance has a great deal to do with the existing commercial banks' preference to provide credit to large and well-established enterprises. The World Bank study (2009) has found that banks are providing financial access to well-established and large companies and shy away from SMEs, new and young enterprises. As the World Bank noted, the limited access to finance operates through 'protecting the market share of larger businesses against competition from smaller or younger rivals'. This means that lack of financial inclusion is a serious problem for inclusive growth.

Our KIIs with officials of commercial banks and other major stakeholders in the financial sector support the World Bank findings. The explanation revolves around two factors: one is that commercial banks prefer large borrowers with large volume of transactions since it is easy to administer and has therefore lower transaction costs. This is because small and large loans need somehow the same procedures. The second factor is related to financial regulation. Commercial banks operate through extremely conservative lending policy guided by NBE directives. One of the directives is known as 'know your customer'. This is the first and most important procedure that every applicant should fulfil. For this purpose the NBE has recently established a credit history centre where commercial banks can obtain information about each applicant. In this process the credit history of each applicant will be scrutinized carefully including applicants' personal lives. An applicant who passes this procedure will be subjected to loan appraisal and once this is financially viable then the issue of collateral follows. Due to this very stringent process, a significant number of applicants fail in the first part of the process, and among those qualifying for the first stage, a significant number will fail again due to a lack of adequate collateral. SMEs and new projects cannot pass the stringent loan process, as they have no collateral or credit history. To put it in a nutshell, the credit policy of commercial banks as explained by one of the KIIs is 'for the haves to have more'. Those who are new to the business and those who are in the business but do not have repeated credit history are not eligible for credit. These visible hurdles to the business are attributed to the NBE directives. It should be noted, however, that sustainable lending must find ways of discriminating between creditworthy and non-creditworthy and in most cases large customers and those who stay longer in the business are somehow more creditworthy than the new, young and small ones. The NBE needs to find ways it can induce commercial banks to relax the stringent credit policy and extend their lending to new, young and small borrowers without endangering the viability of commercial banks.

The amount of the collateral required is also one of the major reasons that constrain access to credit with an adverse impact on growth and employment creation. The World Bank in its study found that nearly all loans require collateral and the value of collateral is higher relative to the amount of credit requested and granted.

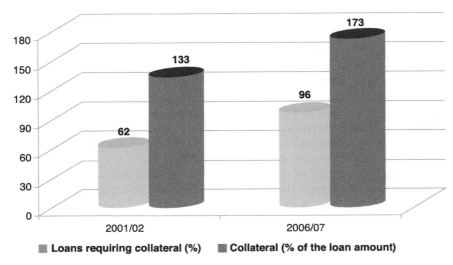

Figure 8.2 Trends in problems associated with access to finance
Source: Computed from World Bank (2009:25).

As can be observed from Figure 8.2, the number of loans requiring collateral and the average value of collateral required relative to loan size has increased unabatedly. In the 2006/07 survey, nearly all loans required collateral and on average each loan required collateral worth 173 per cent of that loan value. This is a significant increase from the 62 per cent of loans to enterprises being collateralized with 133 per cent of the loan value in 2001/02. This figure is one of the highest in the developing world.[3] Currently, projects that pass the stringent credit procedures with high financial viability will require collateral of at least 125 per cent worth of the amount of loan requested (KII with private banks). Ideas are not financed and the collateral requirement is still strong.

Disaggregating collateral requirement by sectors shows an interesting story. About 95 per cent of loans to manufacturing are collateralized with 194 per cent of the loan value while loans to investments in retail/service sectors are collateralized with 157 per cent of the loan value (Figure 8.3).

As can be observed from Figure 8.3, the rate of collateral is higher in the manufacturing sector than in the others. As noted by our KIIs, this is largely because the loan has a long-term nature and the sector is relatively risky. This implies that such sectors that generate dynamic growth and employment opportunities are not in the interest of commercial banks. As noted by most officials of commercial banks, they provide short-term loans to trade and services but not for sectors like manufacturing whose loans often are long term. The Government of Ethiopia (GoE) needs to respond to this financing gap by strengthening the capacity of the DBE, whose aim is provision of long-term loans to sectors like manufacturing.

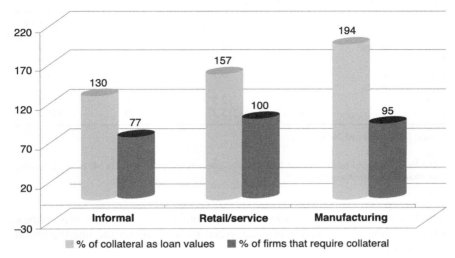

Figure 8.3 Collateral requirement by sub sector
Source: Computed from World Bank (2009).

SMEs in Ethiopia have serious financial access problems as well. The main problem, as our KIIs stated, is not the cost. It is rather availability of funds and access to what is available. With regard to the availability, Wolday (2008, as quoted by Wolday and Anteneh 2013:15) stated that an estimated 10.4 million borrowers will require access to financial services over the next decade, which will require an investment over Birr 106 billion (about $5.5 billion at the time of writing). This amount of money cannot be mobilized by the existing MFIs at the current practice. This has to be facilitated in different ways. One is by encouraging/ incentivized commercial banks to lend to SMEs. The second, and maybe a better solution, is to link MFIs with commercial banks so that banks lend to MFIs for on-lending without endangering the banks, as discussed earlier.

The third channel is the role of Ethiopia's public development banks in providing credit to the private sector, so as to promote poverty reduction and inclusive growth. A central role to this task has been attributed to the DBE. Established in 1909, the DBE is the sole bank in long-term investment financing focusing on the agro processing and manufacturing sector. This is the primary real economy channel through which the banking sector facilitates inclusive growth, mainly by a providing loan to the private sector with a preferential interest rate (8.5 per cent), much lower than the market interest rate.

The major source of loanable fund for the DBE is the 27 per cent NBE bill. That is, on 4 April 2011, the NBE issued a directive requiring all private commercial banks to invest 27 per cent of every new loan disbursement in NBE bills for five years at a very low interest rate, 3 per cent, far below that which banks pay as an interest for the deposit.[4] The Government took this action as a way of

Table 8.10 DBE's loan disbursed by sector, in million USD

Sectors	2009/10	2010/11	2011/12	2012/13
Public enterprises	–	14.6	25.6	22.9
Private	188.1	202.2	223.6	215.8
Cooperatives	7.7	6.3	9.7	3.9
Micro enterprises	0.155	–	–	–
RUFIP[1]	–	12.2	4.1	49.0
Total	196.0	235.3	262.9	291.6

Source: DBE (2011 and 2013).

Note:
[1] The Rural Financial Intermediation Program that channels revolving funds to MFIs for on-lending to microfinance beneficiaries.

mobilizing resources for priority sectors (manufacturing and agro processing), which are not in the interest of commercial banks, through the intermediation of the DBE.[5]

As of December 2013, the NBE bill represented 44 per cent of the total loan advanced by private banks, against 31 per cent in June 2012, thus showing that the amount of NBE bills is growing much faster than the total loan advances. These resources are being channelled to the DBE to finance private sector investment projects.

Despite enhanced lending capacity – see Table 8.10, the DBE still has no reliable and sustainable source of funds, the largest source being the 27 per cent NBE bill. A concern raised by the private banks regarding this particular point is that the NBE bill may be crowding out resources which they could be directing to useful purposes as well. In this context, the creation of other sources of funding for the DBE such as pension funds is worth considering. Furthermore, there is a need to set up an SME financing wing within the bank to alleviate the financing constraint of the sub sector. This will help to enhance its developmental contributions as well as profitability.

Finance, regulation and stability

One major potential source of financial instability is the level of financial services and credit provided. The NBE directives prevent unsustainable extension of credit provided by commercial banks and MFIs by regulating these financial institutions. To this end it has been issuing different directives that limit the level of loan provided to related parties and single borrowers. Directive No. SBB/53/2012 states that the maximum level of credit that commercial banks can provide should not exceed 25 per cent of their total capital for a single borrower and 15 per cent of their total capital for a related party.[6]

The same directive also stipulated the maximum outstanding loan relative to the total capital. That is, 'the aggregate sum of loans extended or permitted to be outstanding directly or indirectly to all related parties at any one time shall not exceed 35 per cent of the total capital of the commercial bank'. To regulate the level of credit provided by the MFIs, Directive No. MFI/18/06 has been issued, stating that MFIs' level of credit to an individual who can provide collateral should not exceed 1 per cent of its total capital and for an individual who can provide group collateral should not exceed 4 per cent of its total capital.

In addition, the NBE has established a unit that provides credit history services to commercial banks on individual applicants so as to reduce ex post risks.

The NBE has also put in place different mechanisms to reduce ex ante risks. The NBE loan provision directive forces banks to craft and work out a Non-Performing Loan (NPL) reduction plan. As a result of NBE directives, commercial banks have prepared and implemented NPL reduction plans over the last couple of years and this led to a successive decline in NPL levels, from 6.8 per cent in 2008 to 1.4 per cent in 2012 (Table 8.11). This is an impressive performance compared with the trend in SSA, which saw a smaller decline between the same period (World Bank, 2013).

The NBE has also issued various directives with the aim of reducing ex ante risks, controlling inflationary pressure and promoting banks' stability. These are reserve and liquidity requirements, minimum capital adequacy ratio, minimum paid up capital and the like. The reserve requirement, for instance, was raised from 5 per cent in 2004 (Directive No. SBB/37/2004) to 10 per cent, effective as

Table 8.11 Indicators of financial soundness, ends June

	2008	2009	2010	2011	2012	2013
Capital adequacy						
Regulatory capital to risk-weighted assets	18.9	18.7	18.7	18.1	13.4	17.9
Capital (net worth) to assets	18.9	18.7	18.7	18.1	13.4	–
NPLs to gross loans	6.8	6.0	3.5	2.1	1.4	2.5
NPLs net of provision to capital	5.6	7.3	0.7	–3.8	–5.6	
ROC	–	31.1	31.3	36.6	47.2	48.0
ROA	–	3.2	3.1	3.2	3.8	3.2
ROE (total capital)[1]	27.7	31.5	42.2	31.5	34.2	–
ROE (core capital)[2]	29.8	34	46.4	34.9	55.8	–
Gross interest income to total income[3]	54.9	57.1	60.1	54.4	54.7	–
Interest margin to gross income[4]	46.1	50.6	38.7	40	45	–
Liquidity asset to total assets	31.5	30.8	32.7	32.7	20.6	–
Liquidity assets to deposit	–	45.5	42.0	43.0	28.8	30.1

Source: NBE and IMF (2013).

Notes:
[1] The average capital used to calculate the ROE includes retained earnings, profits and loss.
[2] The average capital used to calculate the ROE excludes retained earnings, profits and loss.
[3] Total income comprises gross interest income and gross non-interest income.
[4] Gross income comprises net interest income and total non-interest income.

of July 2007 (Directive No. SBB/42/2007), and further to 15 per cent, effective as of April 2008 (Directive No. SBB/45/2008). The liquidity requirement was also revised upwards, which is always 10 per cent plus the reserve requirement. This means that, since April 2008, the liquidity requirement asks banks to hold a further 25 per cent (this is from their total reserve which includes TBs, cash including foreign exchange, etc.) in liquid reserves (only cash deposits). Following the success in reducing national inflation, the NBE revised the reserve requirement downwards to 10 per cent and liquidity requirement to 20 per cent effective as of January 2012 (Directive No. SBB/46/2012). As the inflation pressure diminished further, the NBE revised the reserve requirement downwards to 5 per cent effective as of March 2013 (Directive No. SBB/55/2013). It should be noted, however, that the liquidity requirement remained at 20 per cent, which should have been reduced to 15 per cent. This implies a counter-cyclical use of these instruments, which is an interesting policy tool.

In September 2011, the NBE also issued Directive No. SBB/50/2011 that sets the minimum capital adequacy ratio to ensure financial stability. As per this directive, all commercial banks shall at a minimum maintain capital to risk weighted assets ratio of 8 per cent at all times. As of October 2013, MFIs are required to maintain at all times a minimum capital adequacy ratio of 12 per cent computed as a ratio of total capital to total risk-weighted assets (Directive no. MFI/25/2013). Table 8.11 indicates that indicators set to protect financial stability are within the limit.

With the objective of enhancing commercial banks' and MFIs' capacity to absorb unexpected or unusual losses, the NBE promulgated a directive that sets the minimum paid up capital of Birr 500 million as a minimum start up capital, which was Birr 75 million for new commercial banks since September 2011 (Directive No. SBB/50/2011). Existing commercial banks are also required to raise their minimum paid up capital to Birr 500 million in less than five years, by 30 June 2016. Similarly, since October 2013, minimum start up capital for MFIs has increased from Birr 200,000 to Birr 2 million (Directive No. MFI/25/13). As it is argued that banks with strong capital are in a better position to withstand shocks and enhance the confidence of depositors or borrowers, these actions are expected to help the financial sector to withstand difficulties, preserve its solvency and enhance its lending capacity.

The other bank supervision mechanism which the NBE is trying to implement is the Basel Accords (Basel I, Basel II and Basel III).[7] However, the NBE is currently at the Basel I level only. With regard to Basel II and III, there is no full-fledged implementation. As per our discussion with officials from the Bank Supervision Directorate of the NBE, it is clear that the NBE does not want to implement Basel II and III as a package. It only takes instruments that fit in to the Ethiopian context, which seems a reasonable approach to pursue. For instance, the NBE has drafted a 'good governance directive' which is currently in circulation for comment. This directive has a disclosure requirement that will force all commercial banks to avail information for the market. Each bank has to disclose its external audit reports, which is pillar 3 of Basel II.

It should be noted that more sophisticated methods of supervision requires human and financial capacity which may not be found in full at the NBE. In addition, the absence of foreign banks in the country may have also reduced the incentive and need by NBE authorities to adopt Basel II and III in full (see Chapter 4 in this book).

The role of capital flows

Capital inflows in the form of long- and short-term loans, foreign direct investment (FDI), and other capital flows have been financing current account deficits of the balance of payment in Ethiopia and thereby helping enhance inclusive growth, as some of these flows have led to direct employment creation and income growth.

Following the liberalization of the economy and revisions of the investment code, private capital inflows in the form of FDI have increased significantly in recent years. The total FDI flows has increased from $14 million (0.2 per cent of GDP) in 2002/03 to $1.24 billion (4 per cent of GDP) in 2010/11. Then it levelled at around $1.1 billion in 2011/12. The increasing FDI flow into the economy, particularly in the flower and textile sectors, has contributed to the creation of job opportunities, especially for the unemployed youth and women in the country. In this regard, FDI's contribution to inclusive growth is quite significant in Ethiopia. Other forms of private capital inflow, such as portfolio equity flows, bond flows and cross-border bank lending, are insignificant.

The GoE has been taking measures to encourage long-term capital inflows to Ethiopia such as making the exchange rate more competitive, availing 70 per cent of the capital for FDI investment in priority areas, providing land at lower tariffs for commercial investors in agriculture and providing land for free for the establishment of industrial zones in the country.

Given the increasing capital flows to the country and huge saving and foreign exchange gaps in the economy, the question is how Ethiopia is managing the capital account. The current practice in Ethiopia is more towards quantity based capital account management instruments: prohibition, ceiling or partial permit. Derivative operations and real estate transactions abroad are prohibited. There is a ceiling on net exposure in foreign currency. Foreigners are not allowed to invest in domestic securities and equity investment by foreign firms is strictly regulated. Residents and financial institutions are not allowed to invest abroad and borrow from abroad, respectively. External loan and supplier credit are allowed to exporters and FDI firms only. It should be noted, however, that given the huge financing requirements of the economy, Ethiopia may not afford to restrict capital inflows into the country by imposing a strict capital control regime. In revisiting the capital account management regime, it might be worth considering the following design considerations and potential instruments of capital control:

i)   **Inflows**: Ethiopia might want to broaden the scope for FDI by allowing some sectors (wholesale business, transport, financial sector, telecom, real estate, etc.) to gradually open their doors to foreigners, while being cautious about the risks involved, particularly regarding possible opening of the financial sector to foreign capital, given the sector's still early stage of development. External loan and suppliers' credit could be opened up for import substituting firms as well.

ii) **Outflows**: Given the keen interest to attract greater FDI, it would be beneficial to revisit the current tight requirements regarding profit repatriation by non-resident firms. Restrictions on domestic firms to invest abroad could be gradually loosened to allow some emerging firms to gain global recognition and greater market access. But such investments should be with a limit on the amount to be invested and for selected sectors to which Ethiopian firms have comparative advantage. Indeed, very initial localized steps have already been taken in this direction. With the objective of mobilizing more foreign exchange from abroad, the state owned CBE was allowed to open a branch in South Sudan, which is the first in the history of the country. Currently, such a privilege is not granted to private banks. But to enhance the benefits to the country, it would be wise for authorities to expand the scheme to cover private banks and to explore possibilities of branches in other countries, particularly the neighbouring ones where Ethiopia has a comparative advantage in terms of country knowledge and links.

Conclusion

This chapter has explored the link among financial inclusion, regulation and inclusive growth.

Despite huge progress in the last ten years, financial inclusion is still very low. One of the major problems in enhancing financial inclusion is lack of physical access. Recently, restrictions to physical access have been indirectly exacerbated by the financial regulations issued by the NBE. The NBE has discouraged more financial institutions to join the financial sector by raising the paid up capital for both commercial banks and MFIs. In addition, access to the existing banks has also worsened by the recent financial regulation that led banks to operate through extremely conservative lending policy (know your customer), though this policy may reduce future NPLs for banks, which is very positive. All these measures led banks to shy away from serving SMEs, new and young firms.

The other major problem is the lack/limited use of technology and innovation in financial service delivery. Given this, the NBE has to work more towards facilitating the entry of new banks and MFIs, to transform the existing ones from traditional ways of financial services to technology based services and lighten credit procedures for strategic projects with of course taking into account the possibility of bad debts.

The financial architecture, the linkage between SACCOs and MFIs, and MFIs with commercial banks – as well as identifying reliable and sustainable sources of funds such as pension funds for the DBE – are also other issues worth considering for effective financial inclusion.

On the role of capital flows in the economy, the GoE has been taking different measures to encourage long-term capital flows accompanied by quantity based capital account management instruments. However, there might be potential benefits about loosening some of the current capital account restrictions such as limits and restrictions on external loan and suppliers' credit for import substituting firms, restrictions on domestic firms to invest abroad and restrictions on commercial banks to open branches abroad for more growth and effective resource mobilization.

Notes

1 I would like to thank Stephany Griffith-Jones, Stephen Spratt, Ricardo Gottschalk and Charles Harvey for their insightful comments and participants of 'Making Finance Work for Africa (MFW4A) 2014 Partnership Forum' on 10–12 June 2014 in Dakar, Senegal and 'Workshop and Public Seminar on Financial Regulation in Low-Income Countries: Balancing Inclusive Growth with Financial Stability' on 10–11 September 2013, Accra, Ghana.

2 MFIs also get funds from donors via the DBE. This is a donor financed Rural Financial Intermediation Program (RUFIP). Donors channel RUFIP revolving funds at low interest rates to MFIs for on-lending to microfinance beneficiaries. The DBE manages this program. In addition to this, they also get donations from NGOs and regional governments. The Government owned CBE also provides a small amount for on-lending. This is how they manage their loan provision, which is far beyond their deposit mobilization.

3 For a detailed account of comparison with other developing countries, see World Bank (2009:Figure 22).

4 NBE Directive No. MFA/NBE Bills/001/2011.

5 Private commercial banks have understandably complained about this government measure. The argument is that their deposit mobilization is of a short-term nature while the 27 per cent bill is paid on long-term investment and blocked for five years. Therefore, these resources are not seen as adequate to fund loans for long-term investment projects. The result of the NBE directive is that banks faced liquidity problems to provide loans to their customers.

6 This might seem a high figure. Relative to the total capital each bank has, it is small. For instance, for private banks, on average, it is about $11 million.

7 They are named after the secretariat located at the Bank for International Settlements in Basel, Switzerland.

References

DBE (2011) DBE Annual Report, Development Bank of Ethiopia, Addis Ababa.

DBE (2013) DBE Annual Report, Development Bank of Ethiopia, Addis Ababa.

IMF (2013) IMF Country Report No. 13/308, The Federal Democratic Republic of Ethiopia, Staff Report for the 2013 Article IV Consultation.

MoFED (2010) Growth and Transformation Plan 2010/11–2014/15, Volume 1, Main Text, Addis Ababa, Ethiopia.

MoFED (2014) Growth and Transformation Plan Annual Progress Report for F.Y. 2012/13, Addis Ababa, Ethiopia.

Wolday, Amha and Kifle Anteneh (2013) AEMFI Performance Analysis Report, Bulletin No. 9.

World Bank (2009) Towards the Competitive Frontier, Strategies for Improving Ethiopia's Investment Climate.

World Bank (2012) Doing Business Survey, 2012.

World Bank (2013) Ethiopia Economic Update II: Laying the Foundation for Achieving Middle Income Status, June 2013.

9 Conclusions

Stephany Griffith-Jones, Ricardo Gottschalk and Stephen Spratt[1]

Introduction

The aim of this book was to see how the financial systems and their regulation in African low-income countries (LICs), still in their early stages of development, could be better shaped to achieve simultaneously the goals of financial stability and inclusive growth. This draws on understanding the features of financial systems in LICs, both their challenges and their relative strengths, and on possible lessons arising from the global financial crisis, as well as previous experiences of crises in emerging economies.

Finance is crucial for development. Without a well functioning financial system that channels finance to the right places in the right form, inclusive growth is impossible. This is not just a question of the quantity of finance, though this is extremely important, but also what we might call its *quality*. Different types of economic activities (and actors) require different types of finance in terms of cost, maturity and risk characteristics. The more financial systems are able to meet these needs, the more likely they are to be supportive of inclusive growth. As well as its potential to foster growth, however, the financial sector can also generate instability and crises, with devastating consequences. Increasing understanding of the role that financial structure and regulation can play in balancing these objectives in LICs was the aim of this research project and resulting book.

LICs have the greatest need for financial systems that can support inclusive growth. In 2013, aggregate per capita income for LICs was US$722, compared with US$4,814 in middle-income countries (MICs), and US$39,116 in high-income countries (HICs).[2]

Table 9.1 describes average financial sector depth by income group, highlighting how the total size of the financial sector relates to income level of countries, and the scale of financial sector development required in LICs.

Table 9.2 shows that just 12.5 per cent of people in LICs have deposit accounts at commercial banks, compared with more than 50 per cent in MICs. The figures for HICs are close to 100 per cent. These differences are reflected in the number of bank branches, which are five times greater in MICs than LICs, and ten times greater in HICs.

While credit is scarce in countries at lower levels of income, it is also expensive. As shown in Table 9.3, average lending-deposit spreads in LICs are nearly

Table 9.1 Arithmetic average financial depth indicators by income group, 2013

	LIC	*MIC*	*HIC*
Private credit by deposit banks to GDP (%)	18.54	41.19	101.87
Financial system deposits to GDP (%)	26.70	45.93	93.32

Source: WDI.

Table 9.2 Average financial access indicators by income group, 2011

	LIC	*MIC*	*HIC*
Bank branches per 100,000 adults	3.62	17.03	32.67
Depositors with commercial banks (per 1,000 adults)	124.9	504.9	–

Source: WDI.

15 per cent, compared with 7.65 per cent and 4.44 per cent in MICs and HICs respectively (we return in some detail to this issue below).

It is unlikely that these differences in spreads simply reflect greater risks. If this were the case we would expect to see a roughly similar level of profitability across country income groups. Instead, Table 9.3 shows that average profitability of banks is much higher in LICs. Returns on both assets and equity are roughly three times higher in LICs than in HICs.

As well as risk, higher spreads could be because of higher costs. As shown in Table 9.4, overhead costs are far higher as a share of assets, but the difference is small when total costs are compared to income.

Table 9.3 Average financial sector profit and spread indicators by income group, 2013

	LIC	*MIC*	*HIC*
Bank return on assets (% after tax)	2.15	1.40	0.80
Bank return on equity (% after tax)	19.17	13.04	6.20
Bank lending-deposit spread (%)	14.87	7.65	4.44

Source: World Bank Global Financial Development Database (GFDD).

Table 9.4 Average financial efficiency indicators by income group, 2011

	LIC	*MIC*	*HIC*
Bank cost to income ratio (%)	60.99	56.27	55.52
Bank overhead costs to total assets (%)	5.54	3.82	2.07

Source: GFDD.

Table 9.5 Average financial competitiveness indicators by income group, 2012

	LIC	MIC	HIC
Bank concentration (%)[1]	75.74	66.06	74.29
H-statistic[2] (closer to 1 implies greater competition)	0.46	0.63	0.64

Source: GFDD.

Notes:
[1] The assets of three largest banks as % of total banking assets.
[2] "A measure of the degree of competition in the banking market. It measures the elasticity of banks revenues relative to input prices. Under perfect competition, an increase in input prices raises both marginal costs and total revenues by the same amount, and hence the H-statistic equals 1. Under a monopoly, an increase in input prices results in a rise in marginal costs, a fall in output, and a decline in revenues, leading to an H-statistic less than or equal to 0. The closer the H-statistic is to 1, therefore, the greater the implied competition" (GFDD Database explanatory notes).

Conventionally it is argued that excessive spreads (and profits) result from a lack of competition. Two measures used to measure competitiveness are shown in Table 9.5. These results appear less conclusive. While bank concentration is higher in LICs than MICs, there is little difference with HICs. Other indicators also suggest that competition is somewhat lower in LICs, but the orders of magnitude are unclear and competitiveness in HICs is not generally higher than that in MICs. Furthermore, as reported in the case studies, though the number of banks has increased significantly in recent years, in countries like Ghana, spreads have hardly fallen.

To summarize, compared with countries at higher levels of income finance is more scarce in LICs, but also more expensive. Financial intermediaries are less efficient, but also much more profitable, and competitive pressures may be less. Financial exclusion remains the norm for most people. The scope for financial sector development is thus very large in LICs. The potential for this to contribute to inclusive growth is similarly large. In this context, it is important to welcome that growth in the recent period in Sub Saharan African LICs has been significant, which is very positive, but it has not been inclusive; furthermore, there are concerns whether this growth can be sustained, if the global economy continues to grow at a slower pace, and at a time when commodity prices seem likely to remain at lower levels. In this context the challenges for sustained growth are larger and may therefore require a better and better functioning financial sector.

At the same time, the potential risks of financial instability are also significant. This is evidenced by the numerous and costly crises that have occurred in recent decades, both in emerging and high-income economies. Sub Saharan African LICs have suffered very few banking crises in the last decade, which is also positive, but this does not imply that there is room for complacency, especially if financial sectors grow significantly and fast. There is no reason why Sub Saharan African LICs should be different from other regions, unless careful prudential measures are taken.

A difficult balancing act is therefore required. Financial sector development is crucial for inclusive growth, but it also brings greater risks of instability and crises. Effective regulation is the key to achieving and maintaining this balance. The research described in this book has sought to better understand how regulation in LICs should be designed to balance inclusive growth with financial stability.

There have been two main elements to this research. Part 1, which is covered in the earlier chapters of the book, entailed reviews of the literature. The aims were to a) identify and review the literature on the most important issues with respect to financial regulation, growth and stability in LICs, and b) identify the most important research gaps. The second part of the research built upon this foundation with four detailed case studies. These explored how key issues of financial regulation, inclusive growth and stability manifest in different country contexts. The studies were undertaken in Ethiopia, Ghana, Kenya and Nigeria. The country studies show that, although all in the early to middle-stages of financial sector development, their financial systems are already significantly different from each other. Ghana and Kenya have systems with open capital accounts, which are dominated by private banks. Nigeria is a large, oil-based economy, with a more sophisticated financial system and domestic banks penetrating other African markets. Kenya also has a large number of banks in neighbouring countries. Ethiopia has a heavily regulated bank-based financial sector in the early stage of development, with a large (though decreasing) role for government owned banks – including a large public development bank – and restricted capital account opening. These differences are partly due to previous policy choices, and partly because initial conditions, such as economic structure, are different as well.

Despite these large differences, there are also similarities, as detailed in the country chapters in the second part of the book. The lessons we can learn from these national differences and similarities are distilled in this concluding chapter. Before doing so, however, we first recap the key findings from the general analysis and review chapters contained in the first part of the book. After examining the most important results from the country chapters, the chapter concludes with some policy recommendations and suggestions for future research.

Key issues arising from the literature

For the issues of financial stability referred to in this book, a significant event in recent times was the financial crisis of 2007/8. Most refer to this as the 'global financial crisis', while others – more accurately – term it the 'North Atlantic financial crisis'. The latter description captures the fact that the crisis emanated from the US, spread to Europe, and resulted largely from the practices of US and European financial institutions. The former description captures the fact that the effects of this crisis have been global, though unevenly distributed.

As well as financial and economic impacts, the crisis has had other global effects, notably on academics', policy-makers' and regulators' views on financial sector development in general, and financial regulation in particular. On structure, the financial institutions, mechanisms and markets that developed in the world's major financial centres could no longer be viewed always as an example to which developing countries should aspire. Similarly, the 'sophisticated' risk-management practices of these financial centres proved to be ineffective at best, and highly problematic at worst while the 'light-touch' regulation that accompanied these sophisticated techniques had disastrous consequences. For both financial sector structures and regulation, therefore, policy-makers in countries at all levels of development have had to think again.

In Chapter 1, Griffith-Jones et al. describe some of the most important findings of recent analysis. An important recent finding, now rather widely accepted (anticipated earlier by only a few prescient academics), is that there are limits to financial sector development beyond which expansion begins to have a negative impact on growth. Recent research, for example at the Bank of International Settlements and at the International Monetary Fund, estimates this to be between 80–100 per cent of private credit to GDP. As shown in Table 9.1, this is about the average level of HICs today, double that for MICs and five times the average level in LICs. Therefore this link is less relevant for LICs than for countries with higher incomes. However, the link has some relevance for countries at all income levels for three reasons.

First, knowing that expansion of the financial sector begins to constrain growth beyond a certain point allows developing country policy-makers to take a long-term view of financial sector development. Second, income-group averages mask wide variations. While the average figure for HICs for the private credit to GDP is around 100 per cent, the highest is 284 per cent. For LICs, the highest level is 50 per cent. Although the 'limit' remains above what exists in any LIC, the lower end of the range (i.e. 80 per cent) is not so far away for some LIC countries. LIC country policy-makers need to note this.

The third reason why this matters is that the optimal size of the financial sector will not be the same for all countries. As described by Spratt (Chapter 2), a relatively small financial sector providing affordable and appropriately structured finance to the real economy will be more developmentally beneficial than a large financial sector focused on trading esoteric financial products. Credit to enterprises seems to have greater growth impacts than credit to households. This may be more the case in LICs which may suffer more from supply constraints than demand constraints. As the economy develops, and becomes more diversified, this may change. The composition of the financial sector is an important determinant of its activities, and policy and regulation have a major role to play in helping to shape this composition.

Griffith-Jones et al., in Chapter 1, discuss the potential importance of public development banks as part of this mix as one of the insights that has been 'rediscovered' since 2008. The crisis showed how development banks could play a crucial counter-cyclical role, stepping in when private finance dried up. This prompted a broader re-assessment of their record and potential. Once common in many countries, the record of development banks has not always been positive. Following a series of influential studies linking government-owned banks to lower growth, many development economists assumed they were a thing of the past.

But this was never true. Development banks have been central to the growth of large emerging economies (e.g. Brazil, India and China), and remain integral to the financial landscape in highly successful developed economies like Germany. As well as playing a counter-cyclical role, these institutions can help provide the long-term 'patient' finance that is key to the development process, but which the private sector rarely provides at the scale needed. Furthermore, they may be valuable for funding structural transformation, essential for long-term growth. More recent research, which controls properly for institutional quality, does not find that government ownership of banks is associated with lower growth. Indeed, when the crisis period is included, the opposite may be true.

As argued by Griffith-Jones et al., and supported by the evidence by Spratt (Chapter 2), there thus remains a strong case for public development banks. There are risks, but the experience of some countries shows that these can be overcome. The question may therefore be not whether to create a development bank per se, but how to design and run a *good* development bank.

The final issue, highlighted in Chapter 1, seems to be the most important one. As understood by those working on financial crises in developing and emerging countries for many years, this relates to the importance of the *rate* of credit growth. An overly rapid expansion of credit – regardless of the starting level and the exact form this credit assumes – is strongly associated with financial crises.

Whether in the 2007/8 crisis, in the Nigerian financial crisis of 2009 described in this book, or many of the financial crises that have occurred around the world since the 1980s, rapid credit expansion tends to see finance allocated in-efficiently (lowering long-term growth prospects), and asset price bubbles inflated, triggering instability and subsequent collapse. Given the perennial nature of such events, with us in one form or another for hundreds of years, there is every reason to think they will continue, unless financial regulation is far more effective. Rather than assuming that 'this time it's different', Griffith-Jones et al. argue strongly that regulation needs to counter these trends, with counter-cyclical (often called macro-prudential) mechanisms deployed to dampen credit growth when this becomes excessive, and vice versa.

In an extensive review of the literature in Chapter 2, Spratt examines the evidence on how financial structures affect inclusive growth and stability in LICs, and how financial regulation affects these structures, as well as the behaviour of financial sector actors. The evidence can be organized into three categories: the supply of finance (including access to finance); the cost of finance; and the maturity of finance.

Chapter 2 assesses these categories with respect to three actors – firms, households and governments. In each case, evidence is assessed on what financial structures and behaviours are most likely to balance growth with stability, and how financial regulation could be designed to encourage these structures and behaviours.

Given the dominance of banks in LIC financial systems, and the importance of credit in determining growth and stability outcomes, the chapter focuses largely on bank credit. The potential of capital markets with respect to inclusive growth and stability is also reviewed. As LICs generally lack the structural features required to obtain the benefits of capital markets – such as sufficient liquidity, for example – the chapter argues that policy-makers in LICs should focus on improving the impact of the banking sector on growth and stability, and ensuring that the capital account is managed carefully to support this goal.

The first area to consider is the supply of finance to firms and households. In both cases, access to finance (of any kind) is a major issue in LICs. Firms, particularly small-and-medium-enterprises (SMEs), regularly cite lack of external finance as the major constraint to growth. Financial inclusion of households in LICs is also the exception rather than the norm. Many of the reasons are the same: information on creditworthiness is rarely available in third-party form; transaction costs of lending small amounts are high; borrowers may be located in relatively remote rural areas. As we saw in the tables earlier in this chapter, the total size of the financial sector – i.e. total credit available – is relatively low, and bank branches are few. As a result, finance tends to flow to activities less affected by these problems, such as blue-chip corporates and government.

Regulation can be used to reduce these problems for incumbent institutions: encouraging information sharing and credit bureau, and fostering innovative practices to reduce transaction costs, for example. Using regulation to affect the composition of financial institutions may also be very important. As proposed in Chapter 1, and supported by evidence gathered in Chapter 2, increasing the supply of finance to diverse sectors is likely to be easier with a diverse set of financial institutions: large and small banks; diversified and sector-specific; commercial and development-oriented. Microfinance Institutions (MFIs), credit unions, cooperative banks and mobile banking will be a part of this. As well as supporting financial inclusion (households) and inclusive growth (SMEs), such an 'ecosystem' may also be positive for financial stability, as institutions will be exposed to different sectors and risks.

The argument for diversity also applies to large-scale infrastructure projects, which also face severe – though different – financing constraints. The case made for development banks is also relevant here. There is more potential to involve external financial institutions in infrastructure. Often these will be multilateral or bilateral development banks, with commercial institutions also participating in projects. The presence of an effective national public development bank is likely to increase the likelihood of successfully financing such projects, and improve their development outcomes.

Chapter 1 makes a case for comprehensive regulation of all financial institutions. This is supported by evidence presented in Chapter 2, where it is also argued that regulation should be tailored to the specific characteristics of different sectors. If the aim is to encourage institutions to act in different ways, then regulation should be designed to support rather than stifle this. Though regulation should be comprehensive, it should be proportionate to the scale and the systemic risk of financial institutions, as well as their specific features.

The supply of credit to government is considered in the context of 'crowding out' and, above all, debt sustainability.

As mentioned previously, the cost of credit in LICs is also important, including for small borrowers, due to the high rates charged by commercial banks but also by many MFIs. While not certain, it is more likely that MFI rates more accurately reflect risk than is the case with commercial banks. This does not mean that the resulting debts are sustainable, however. Credit will only be developmentally beneficial – to firms, households or indeed governments, if invested in activities with returns greater than the rate of interest charged. Increasing levels of non-performing loans (NPLs) in the microfinance sector suggest, at the very least, that this is not always the case. Debates on whether MFI rates should be capped continue.

As we saw very clearly in the US sub-prime market, extending credit to the financially excluded is not an end in itself. It will only be beneficial – for both inclusive growth and stability – if borrowers can invest this finance productively, and if they have the financial capacity to pay them back. If not, the extension of credit is liable to make matters worse, not better, for poorer borrowers, as well as for financial system stability.

As for governments' borrowing, if their costs are very high, the resultant debt service payments reduce their ability to fund other activities. If financial institutions in LICs can obtain very good returns by just lending to government at high, risk-free rates, they will be less inclined to lend to the other parts of the economy. By providing financial instruments and building a yield curve, government borrowing is an important driver of financial sector development in LICs.

The final area to consider is the maturity of finance. Much of the finance that is available in LICs is short-term and expensive. As well as designing regulation to encourage banks to take a longer-term view, domestic investors such as pension funds that naturally take a long-term view, also given the long-term nature of their liabilities, should be encouraged to channel more of it to long-term investment, e.g. in infrastructure. This is a long-term process, but infrastructure needs in LICs are pressing and immediate. Again, we have a strong case for public development banks to help fill this gap, as well as help channel long-term funds, such as from institutional investors to long-term investment.

External finance can also play a role, but international direct investors may demand very high returns to offset the risks they associate with LICs. This does not mean that there is no scope for such investment, but is probably best deployed in conjunction with multilateral and bilateral development finance institutions, either as co-investors or as suppliers of risk mitigation.

Chapter 3 by Isabella Massa examined the issue of private capital flows and capital account management in LICs in detail. In particular, this chapter surveys the literature on the growth benefits and risks of private capital flows as well as on capital account management tools and their effectiveness. Overall, the analysis confirms that private capital flows, in some cases and under certain conditions, may carry important growth opportunities. A significant share of the literature focuses on the growth impact of foreign direct investment (FDI) flows on growth in LICs, while much less quantitative work has been done on growth benefits of other types of private capital flows, especially bond flows and international bank lending. This is a cause of concern, as bond flows (especially to sovereigns) are becoming an important part of private capital flows in several Sub Saharan African LICs.

Notwithstanding their growth benefits, private capital flows are also found to be a significant source of risks. Indeed, sudden surges in capital flows can lead to appreciation and volatility of real exchange rates, to inflation, stock market booms and to credit expansion. Moreover, sudden capital flow reversals or stops can lead to depletion of reserves, sharp currency depreciations, as well as to currency and banking crises. Private capital flows are thus a double-edged sword, and therefore it is important to develop adequate and effective capital account management policy tools.

A number of policy measures may help manage surges in capital flows, as Massa discusses. These include capital controls, macroeconomic measures (i.e. official foreign exchange intervention, exchange rate intervention and fiscal policy) and structural reforms (i.e. financial sector reforms including prudential regulation and supervision, and easing restrictions on capital flows). The evidence on the types of capital account management tools that have been used in LICs over time is still limited and much more detailed information on the issues that might arise in implementing specific capital account management tools in LICs is needed.

The debate on the effectiveness of capital controls regained momentum in the aftermath of the 2008/9 crises. A broad consensus is emerging that capital controls may be a good tool to moderate the impact of capital flows (e.g. to prevent the build-up of financial sector risks), but they should be used in coordination with other macro-prudential tools to prevent asset inflation and overvaluation. An important development is the significant change in position of the International Monetary Fund (IMF), which until not long ago had a position broadly against capital controls and favoured capital account liberalization, while in the aftermath of the 2008/9 crises, it decided to endorse the use of capital controls under certain circumstances.

A number of structural reforms may help manage capital flows, as Massa discusses. Financial sector reforms, which include among others prudential regulation and supervision, are a capital account management tool that aims to influence indirectly capital inflows or outflows with the objective of reducing the vulnerability of an economy to systemic financial crises. Particularly relevant in this context are regulations on currency mismatches in the balance sheets of financial and non-financial agents. In this context, it is important to examine whether regulatory measures should be done via domestic prudential policies (e.g. regulating currency mismatches in the balance sheets of banks) or through capital controls, by analyzing their respective advantages and disadvantages. More precisely, domestic financial regulation may work for loans channeled through the banking system, whereas loans lent to nonfinancial companies directly may require capital controls, if they become too large.

The evidence on the effectiveness of macroeconomic measures to manage capital flows is mixed across the different types of policy instruments, with fiscal tightening appearing to be the most effective macroeconomic policy tool, although it is difficult to implement. The evidence on the effectiveness of prudential regulation is instead still relatively scarce. In particular, there is a research gap on whether regulatory and supervisory practices originated in the developed world may be successful in LICs that are characterized by different structural features, stage of development and institutional capacities.

Chapter 4 by Ricardo Gottschalk discusses the regulatory challenges facing LICs, with a focus on capacity issues. Its starting point is that African LICs are not insulated from financial globalization despite their relatively low levels of financial integration, and therefore are vulnerable to destabilizing effects of financial shocks generated elsewhere. Given this context, the chapter discusses in particular the challenges this grouping of countries face in adopting complex regulatory approaches developed internationally, how to deal with foreign banks in their jurisdictions and how best to manage risks arising from financial integration, as a result of capital account liberalization.

The chapter shows that African LICs are responding to complexity in financial regulation by slowing down on the implementation of the most challenging aspects of it, particularly on Basel rules. Moreover, they are choosing regulatory tools that are simpler and more suitable to their needs. Also, they are investing in regulatory capacity, although important regulatory and supervisory gaps remain – for example, they still lack counter-cyclical tools to address systemic risks and insufficient assessment of the foreign exchange position of banks, although interviews with African regulators indicate that they are making progress in these areas, as reported towards the end of Chapter 4 and later in this chapter.

The chapter makes the point that the issue of capacity should be addressed with caution. Capacity to deal with complex rules may indeed be missing. However, complexity has recently been challenged both by developed country and developing country regulators, on grounds of ineffectiveness and inappropriateness. The chapter concludes that if simpler – and more effective – regulation is adopted by African LICs, then there is evidence summarized in the chapter showing that such countries do, on the whole, have the capacity to put in place a regulatory system appropriate to their needs and that is sufficiently good to ensure the safety of their financial systems. The few financial crises that the region has suffered more recently have had more to do with inappropriate policy choices than with capacity for effective banking regulation, as the Nigerian case discussed later demonstrates.

Having explored what the literature tells us about financial regulation, inclusive growth and stability in LICs, we now consider the most important conclusions and lessons emerging from the country study chapters, which form the second half of the book.

Case study findings

The broad analysis outlined in the first section allowed us to identify the key questions that would help frame the case studies; these questions were outlined in Chapter 1. Now we first explore what we have learnt from the case studies, both broadly and in relation to the specific questions addressed. We split here the discussion first in terms of the domestic sector, before examining later issues with respect to the external sector.

Domestic credit, inclusive growth and stability

The case studies show that LIC banks are well-capitalized and very profitable (see Tables 9.3, 9.9 and 9.10 in this chapter, the first for average of LICs, and the latter two for indicators for our four case study countries, which all have higher return on equity than the already very high average for LIC countries, at 19 per cent, in contrast with average for HICs at 6 per cent). This is clearly positive, as the former provides a valuable buffer against financial instability. However, their very high levels of profits show that banks are charging their clients excessively, mainly through high spreads (see Tables 9.3 and 9.6). The resulting high cost to borrowers is a clear problem for the growth of the rest of the economy. In a recent empirical study, Aizenman et al. (2015) show that for Latin America and Asia, the faster the growth of financial services and the larger the lending-deposit interest spread, the slower the growth of the manufacturing sector. The authors call this a financial Dutch disease, which could have similar effects in African LICs. Further research is clearly required on this important issue.

A common feature among the countries under study is the extremely high levels of spreads, although this is reportedly less so for Ethiopia. In Ghana and Nigeria, but also in Kenya, spreads are not only high but have not come down through time (see also data presented in case studies), despite a growing number of banks, including foreign banks, which should lead to increased competition. There are some exceptions, like Tanzania, where spreads have come down significantly in the last ten years to around 5 per cent. High spreads, however, occur for most LICs (the average spread for LICs was 14.87 per cent in 2013, and 11.4 per cent in the 1990–2012 period, see again Tables 9.3 and 9.6).

Our case studies also see spreads remain high despite technological improvements and, in the case of Kenya, creation of credit reference bureaux to reduce asymmetries of information and the establishment of branchex across the country to reduce costs associated with transportation of cash.

The common culprits suggested by banks to explain this phenomenon include: high transaction costs, difficult business environment, poor infrastructure

Table 9.6 Spread (lending rate–deposit rate) in per cent, 2013

	Kenya	*Ghana (*)*	*Ethiopia*	*Nigeria*	*LICs (**)*
General	9.5	21.8	6.5	15.6	11.4
SMEs	12.0				

Source: Central Bank of Kenya, Bank of Ghana, Central Bank of Nigeria, Central Bank of Ethiopia.

Notes:
* Year 2012.
** LICs: 1990–2012 average.

services, high salary costs (the latter especially among foreign banks) and high default rates.

However, in relation to the role of default rates, the evidence is that banks in Africa lend to creditworthy borrowers, whose default rates are low, not high, and which therefore do not justify high spreads (see case study chapters for default rates). The high profitability of banks would support this, as high default rates would sharply reduce profit margins.

This is illustrated by the case of Kenya (see Chapter 5). In Kenya, total bank profits before tax increased from about US$70 million in 2002 to US$1,256 million in 2012, an average annual growth rate of 38.7 per cent. The main sources of income were interest on loans and advances (average of 49.6 per cent of total income during the period), which increased over time reflecting an increase in their spreads. This increase in profits seems excessive.

As described in Chapter 2, a common policy recommendation to lower interest rate spreads is to increase banking competition, especially by attracting foreign banks to domestic markets. The expectation is that foreign banks bring new technology, introduce better management practices and have lower transaction costs. But if more competition in the system, including from foreign banks, does not contribute to lower spreads, as the evidence seems to suggest, then regulatory measures might be a way to tackle the problem.

The chapter on Kenya reports that a committee set up by the Kenyan National Treasury recommended the introduction of a common reference rate, which banks would have to follow. Where they charge above the reference rate, they would have to explain this. Even if this measure does not reduce spreads, it would at least increase transparency and help uncover the factors underlying high spreads, thus facilitating further corrective measures, which may even contemplate capping if all else fails. Indeed, other countries might wish to consider adopting common reference rates, and possibly contemplate capping as well.

Together with cost, the supply of finance (or access to finance) is a major issue in Africa. As Table 9.7 shows, credit to GDP in the case study countries is relatively low, especially in Ghana and Ethiopia. Amongst the case study countries, Kenya is making progress in expanding credit to SMEs as well as providing basic banking services to the wider population, the latter particularly through its innovative mobile banking operator M-PESA. The combination of competition and new technology is driving local banks to reach the lower end of the market. They are able to make significant profits, while taking calculated risks. Interestingly, foreign banks are starting to follow local banks in trying to expand their client

Table 9.7 Credit to the private sector/GDP in per cent, 2010

Kenya	Ghana	Ethiopia	Nigeria
33.8	15.3	17.2	24.9

Source: African Development Indicators, World Bank database, except for Ethiopia which is World Bank (2013).

base. However, even in Kenya, 25 per cent of the population remains excluded from financial services.

While MFIs partly fill the gap, they are focused more on individuals and micro-entrepreneurs. Medium-sized and even many small enterprises are not served by MFIs, in what Justin Lin has called the 'missing middle' (Lin, 2013). As suggested by literature reviewed in Chapter 2, there may be a case for smaller and more decentralized banks being better at providing credit to SMEs, as they have fewer asymmetries of information and lower transactions costs, partly as they may pay their staff more reasonable salaries.

As well as a more diverse mix of financial institutions, the way that these institutions are regulated is important. Banks are required to set aside capital for all the loans they make. The introduction of the Basel Capital Accord in the 1980s, and its subsequent adoption as the international standard, provided an important mechanism to prevent international competition resulting in a lowering of capital adequacy over time.

As we can see from Table 9.8, capital adequacy levels in our case study countries remain far above the required Basel level. There are good reasons why regulatory capital should be higher in LICs, as risks to the banking sector are also higher, for example from external shocks. While stability may be furthered by capital requirements at high levels, they may discourage credit, particularly for borrowers deemed to be relatively high risk – i.e. the crucial SME sector. More research is needed on the appropriate level of capital in different LICs.

The final issue identified is maturity. Bank credit in Africa is mostly short term, in the form of consumer credit to households and working capital to businesses. So the challenge is how to increase provision of long-term finance to support investment in sectors, such as infrastructure, agriculture and manufacturing. Ghana, Kenya and Nigeria have capital markets, but these are not sufficiently

Table 9.8 Capital adequacy in per cent, 2013

Kenya	Ghana	Ethiopia	Nigeria
23.2	18.6	17.9	17.2

Source: Bank of Ghana, National Bank of Ethiopia, Central Bank of Kenya, Central Bank of Nigeria and IMF.

Table 9.9 Return on assets in per cent, 2009–2012 average

	Kenya	Ghana	Ethiopia	Nigeria
Foreign and local private banks	4.6			
Banks with state ownership	3.7			
State-owned banks	3.1			
Average total banks	3.4	3.7	3.3	1.9

Source: Central Bank of Kenya, Bank of Ghana, National Bank of Ethiopia, Central Bank of Nigeria and IMF.

Table 9.10 Return on equity (total capital) in per cent, 2012

Kenya	Ghana	Ethiopia	Nigeria
34.2	26.7	34.2	20.2

Source: Central Bank of Kenya, Bank of Ghana, National Bank of Ethiopia, Central Bank of Nigeria and IMF.

Total capital: average capital used to calculate the ROE includes retained earnings, profits and loss.

Table 9.11 Return on equity (core capital) in per cent, 2009–2012 average

	Kenya	Ethiopia
Foreign banks	46.3	
Local private banks	44.6	
Banks with state ownership	34.1	
State-owned banks	24.6	
Average total banks		42.8

Source: Central Bank of Kenya, Bank of Ghana, National Bank of Ethiopia and IMF.

Core capital: average capital used to calculate the ROE excludes retained earnings, profits and loss.

developed to provide longer-term financing to the extent required. The banking system will remain the most important source of finance in African LICs, and should provide long-term finance to sustain rapid growth.

Among the case studies, Ethiopia can be singled out as a country with a strategy for long-term credit provision, via its public development bank, with funding coming from private banks and the government owned commercial bank. Although the mechanism to achieve this in Ethiopia appears to work well, in that the development bank is able to serve priority sectors including manufacturing and infrastructure, it seems idiosyncratic and may only be possible due to a strong state and the very early level of development of its financial system. In any case experiences like that of the Ethiopian development bank need further research, to evaluate in more detail its effectiveness, both in terms of funding long-term growth and structural transformation and in terms of commercial returns. Whilst it may not be directly replicable in other countries, it does suggest that other African countries could find their own ways to tackle the problem of long-term finance and support long-term growth.

Given the concerns about financial inclusion and lack of sufficient availability of long-term finance, and support for sectors such as SMEs, African policy-makers and regulators know more needs to be done. What they envisage are financial systems that can provide more and cheaper finance, and long-term finance for larger productive and infrastructure projects, and that finance reaches the poorest. Their view is that, to this end, their financial systems should become more diversified, as clearly supported by the literature. Within this common vision, a greater role could be played by well-run public development banks, especially in the provision of long-term credit, as is the case in many successful countries in Asia (Hosono, 2013), Latin America (Ferraz, Forthcoming) and Europe (Griffith-Jones and Karwoski, 2015).

External credit, growth and stability

To the extent that countries such as Ghana and Kenya are graduating towards middle-income status, they will increasingly use private foreign finance for funding. Too much dependence on foreign capital is risky, especially if it is of a short-term nature and/or that currency mismatches become significant. In all, foreign capital creates the risk of excessive external debt and vulnerabilities in their financial systems, whilst having an unclear effect on growth (see Chapter 2 for discussion of external debt sustainability and Chapter 4 for in-depth analysis and review of the evidence for LICs).

As capital flows are an important conduit of risks and source of financial vulnerability, the country studies examined carefully the issue of capital account management. In the Ethiopian case this sort of risk is very limited, because the country has a fairly restricted capital account, which essentially allows only for FDI and some borrowing by the government on the international bond market. Portfolio flows are not permitted, and banks are not allowed to borrow from abroad.

In Ghana, Nigeria and Kenya, capital accounts are fairly liberalized, letting in all forms of capital, including short-term bank lending and portfolio flows. The country studies show that this policy stance has created important vulnerabilities in all three countries. The Nigeria case is interesting, as the drying up of capital flows to the country in late 2008 and early 2009 was a major contributory factor to the banking crisis the country suffered in 2009. The country studies also show that both Kenya and Ghana have large current account deficits and are therefore vulnerable to a sudden reversal of capital flows.

In Kenya, more than half of its current account deficit is financed with short-term capital flows. Given the close links between such flows and domestic financial systems, the latter are vulnerable as well. So, although volatility of capital flows is a balance of payments issue in the first instance, what is particularly worrying from the perspective of this book is that it constitutes a critical source of instability for their financial systems. This can be true, for example, not just in terms of direct impacts due to currency mismatches of banks themselves, but also in terms of currency mismatches of companies. Where companies borrow from banks in foreign currency, but sell mainly in local currency, they are exposed to foreign exchange risk, which can indirectly also cause problems for the banks' stability.

If standard indicators, such as the capital adequacy ratios given above, show that financial systems are in good shape, there may, however, well be a problem with the indicators being used for financial stability assessment. These indicators should be broadened and measures should be undertaken to gradually reduce vulnerabilities.

As a contrasting example, Ethiopia may also have balance of payments' financing problems, but it is not resorting to easy foreign capital due to the risks it creates. This at least keeps its financial system, still underdeveloped, insulated from external shocks.

Returning to the issue of a more diversified banking structure, there are important questions on the best composition of such a structure, as well as how it is achieved. African regulators envisage a diversified financial system, as mentioned above, but does this imply less (rather than more) consolidation? And if foreign banks are allowed in, thus contributing to a more diversified system, does it matter whether these banks are Pan-African or from developed countries? More broadly, do foreign banks contribute to financial stability or make countries more vulnerable to financial instability? Beck et al. (2014) summarizes the recent empirical evidence well, by saying cross-border banking can help mitigate the impact of local financial shocks, but exacerbates global financial shocks.

In addition to the role that external capital had on Nigeria's banking crisis of 2009, the Nigeria chapter further suggests that in a LIC context a more consolidated banking system, which the country had attained prior to the crisis, does not necessarily make the system safer. Despite consolidation, Nigeria did not close down its development and specialized banking institutions. However, the past track record of these banks has been perceived as not good. Nevertheless, Nigeria has recently created new development financial institutions and mechanisms, which hopefully will be more efficient. As with the point made about development banks above, it may not be the precise form that a financial institution takes that is most important, but whether it operates effectively and efficiently with appropriate safeguards against excessive bureaucracy and/or capture by corrupt practices. Important lessons can be learned here from successful development banks in both developed and developing economies. The ideal may be a diversified system, but only if the components of this system operate effectively.

A lesson from Nigeria's recent experience is that what a natural resource rich country like Nigeria needs to achieve may not just be more or less consolidation, or more or less development banking. No approach is likely to succeed without institutional mechanisms that are more accountable and better governed so that natural resources wealth can be effectively channeled to support pro-poor and pro-growth projects.

Though development banks, as well as sovereign wealth funds, may play an important positive role, especially in channeling resources into long-term and strategic private and public investment for structural transformation, it is important that they are well designed and well run. It is also important they complement, as well as work with, private banks and capital markets, where these function well, and do not attempt to substitute them. On this point, the Ethiopian chapter reflects some concerns about public banks excessively drawing on resources from private banks, even though it seems the public development bank does seem to channel its resources efficiently towards long-term structural transformation.

Interviews conducted in the context of the research project that resulted in this book point to divergent views on whether foreign banks from developed countries or Pan-African banks are preferable.[3] Although foreign banks are currently not permitted to operate, Ethiopian regulators would give preference to those from developed countries if this were to change. These are seen as stronger, better managed and subject to better regulation and supervision. They are often large and have more capital. If they came to Ethiopia, they would need to comply with the high national capital requirements shown above.

Regulators from other African countries express a different opinion. For them, banks from developed countries would just be more of the same: acting conservatively and following a banking model already practiced by the established foreign banks in their countries. In contrast, they believe that Pan-African banks would lend more, and cheaper, as has reportedly already been the case in Kenya, Tanzania, Uganda, Rwanda and other African countries where these banks have a presence. The lower spreads charged in the East African Community countries by Pan-African banks (both in their home and host countries) than either foreign banks from outside the region or domestic private banks is confirmed empirically by evidence provided by the World Bank (2013) in the Financial sector Assessment Program led by the World Bank (see also Beck et al., 2014). It should be noted, however, that even the relatively lower spreads reported charged by the East African Community cross-border banks are still high, at an average of almost 12 per cent for 2012.

The Ghana chapter, in contrast, suggests that the presence of Pan-African banks may generate important cross-border risks at the regional level, which their regulatory framework is not equipped to deal with. It also makes the point that regional colleges of supervisors, discussed later, are good for information sharing, but not very useful for addressing crisis resolution problems, which would arise in case of failure of a Pan-African bank. The Nigerian chapter, moreover, alerts to the fact that supervision of operations of Nigerian banks with branches and subsidiaries abroad has been largely deficient so far, which poses risks both for Nigeria as a home country of several Pan-African banks and for countries hosting such banks.

Regulatory challenges facing African countries

The book chapters and the country studies, in particular, show that African regulators are investing time and resources to be fully compliant with the Basel Core Principles, and are submitting their banks to strict capital adequacy requirements. Some countries are still firmly under Basel I, while others are moving to Basel II and III.

However, despite their efforts and recent achievements in terms of having a good regulatory framework in place, and being up to date with recent international regulatory developments, all LIC regulators see it as a challenge to adopt financial standards designed internationally. The first reason has to do with their complexity. Indeed, even in developed economies, there are influential voices, such as that of Andy Haldane, Chief Economist at the Bank of England, who have persuasively argued that excessive complexity of regulation seems undesirable. Second, they lack sufficient capacity (human, technical) to do so. In the face of this challenge, their response has been, first, to adopt a gradual approach and, second, be selective, going for parts of regulation that are appropriate to their needs and the features of their financial systems. The country studies confirm this has been the case. Second, they are investing heavily in capacity building on a continuous basis, and for that purpose they are allocating the resources needed to support this investment.

In relation to Basel rules, which arguably are the part of banking regulation that is particularly complex and whose complexity has only increased, all countries are adopting a gradual approach. Kenya, for instance, fully complies with Basel I and with Pillar 1 on credit risk of Basel II. It is considering what aspects of Basel III they want to adopt, coordinating with its neighbours.

Systemic risks have been part of their regulatory concerns. Some countries are considering adopting some aspects of Basel III, in order to address systemic risks relating to bank size and pro-cyclicality of credit. Risks of loans to a single borrower are an older issue facing African regulators, for which they have in place quantity limits. Finally, African regulators have quantity limits to address currency mismatches, which can create important risks for countries with open capital accounts. This is positive, but as pointed out above, indirect effects of such currency mismatches (on the companies to whom banks lend) also need to be considered by regulators.

Despite all their efforts, African regulators may need to do more to address adequately systemic risks. Their focus has traditionally been on micro-prudential rather than macro-prudential regulation. Although these measures are important, they might give regulators a false sense of safety. It is encouraging that regulators acknowledge in interviews that it is important to develop more regulation of systemic risks.

What might be needed is a more robust analysis and understanding of the links between the macro-economy and the financial sector. Counter-cyclical (or macro-prudential) regulation is one concrete way in which these links can be established. It is an important innovation of Basel III that should be adopted in LICs, though its features would need to be adjusted to the needs and features of their financial systems.

A step forward in this area might not be just in the form of more investment on regulatory capacity in a narrow sense. Instead, what seems needed is to approach these risks differently. The safety of a country's financial system should not be just the responsibility of regulators, but of other government officials as well, so that issues arising from macro-financial links can be quickly spotted, understood and adequately addressed. In their efforts to build capacity, African countries need new and different skills to be able to keep up with the regulatory developments and to have effective regulation and supervision in place.

Main policy conclusions and research challenges

Clearly there is not enough finance to support inclusive growth in LICs. It is not just the quantity of finance that matters, but its maturity and cost. The quantity *and* the quality of finance in LICs are both problematic. There is insufficient finance, and that which is available tends to be short term, expensive and not well suited to the needs of borrowers. This is especially true for SMEs, 'the missing middle'.

An area of focus of this project has been the cost of loans, which remains high in many LICs. This restrains growth and fosters financial instability. Solutions have proved elusive. Numerous reforms to increase competitive pressure and efficiency in the banking sector have had little impact upon spreads. Identifying and addressing the determinants of reducing the cost of finance, for individuals and firms in LICs, including through greater transparency and possible regulation, such as capping interest rates, is a crucial area of future research.

The structure of the banking sector is important. A first feature should be that the financial sector should be simpler, in the sense that, for example, the type of instruments used should not be complex or opaque, and thus the risks could be more easily assessed by the institutions themselves, and by the regulators. This facilitates regulation itself to be simpler. Furthermore, simple arrangements and institutions that increase and share information, like credit bureau, can play a very positive role to both increase access to credit and to enhance financial stability.

Evidence suggests that a diverse set of banking institutions would improve both the quantity and quality of finance for different borrowers, and thus have positive impacts on inclusive growth and stability. As regards the latter, the benefits of diversification for reducing risk is well known, within institutions, but should also be applied across institutions. Further research and policy discussion seems needed for the desirable composition of the financial system in LICs, for example the balance between public and private banks, large and small institutions, domestic and foreign, and between more universal banks and those focused on particular sectors such as SMEs.

While the potential for development banks to foster inclusive growth in LICs is significant, there are some risks. Our understanding of how to design and run 'good' development banks that can fulfill this potential while avoiding risks is growing, but remains at an early stage. The need for development banks is not new, but new challenges and what we have learned about successful development banks make this a new area of research in development finance. Focusing on LICs, where the need for development banks seems large, but the risks they create may also be large, seems a particularly important area of research.

Regulation is fundamental. If we know more about the types of financial institutions that are best suited to balancing inclusive growth and stability in LICs, it is necessary to design regulatory frameworks and other measures to encourage/support the emergence of these institutions. A second issue is how different types of institutions should be regulated and supervised in LICs. The benefit of a diverse set of finance institutions is that they can offer different services to different groups of customers. It is important that regulation is designed to support – rather than stifle – the services different financial institutions can provide. Furthermore, though regulation may be diverse, it should be equivalent, to avoid regulatory arbitrage. It should also be comprehensive, so all financial institutions providing credit are regulated, but such regulation should be proportional to the level of systemic risk different financial institutions are likely to generate.

A diverse mix of heterogeneous institutions is very unlikely to evolve naturally, or to survive if it does so. Understanding how regulation can help support and maintain this process in LICs is another new area of research.

Macro-prudential regulation is an important area for regulation that has been mainstreamed since the global financial crisis. It requires better understanding on how domestic regulation interacts with the macroeconomic and external environment in a LIC setting, including which tools are most appropriate (whether, for example, focusing on domestic financial regulation or managing the capital account) to deal with this interaction such that stable, inclusive growth is supported.

Simply importing frameworks from developed and emerging countries, such as Basel II–III, is not the solution. If LICs are to use financial regulation to help strike the right balance between growth and stability, this will need to be designed explicitly for the circumstances of LICs. Again, more research is required.

We have focused more on the banking sector; however, capital market development, especially local currency bond market development, is also an important area, both for policy and research.

Financial sector development is crucial for inclusive growth in LICs. However, financial instability can have devastating consequences, especially for poor people. How finance can help achieve the optimal balance between growth and stability in LICs, and the role that regulation should play in this, is among the most pressing development questions policy-makers and researchers face. We hope to have contributed to an understanding of these issues with this book, by providing some answers, but many more questions.

Notes

1 We thank Francis Mwega, Olu Ajakaiye, Getnet Alemu, Charles Achah and Isabella Massa for their excellent research reflected in their chapters, as well as their and Dirk Te Velde's valuable comments on this chapter. We also thank Noe Nsemi and Edward Griffith-Jones for excellent research assistance.
2 Current US$. Source: World Bank's World Development Indicators (WDI).
3 These interviews were conducted in February 2015 and are reported in Gottschalk (2015).

References

Aizenman, J. et al. (2015) Financial Development and Output Growth in Developing Asia and Latin America. NBER Working Paper 20917, www.nber.org/papers/w20917

Beck, T. et al. (2014) Making Cross-Border Banking Work for Africa. GIZ (German Cooperation), Bonn.

Ferraz (Forthcoming) "The Role of Development Banks in Development Finance". In: Noman, A. and Stiglitz, J. (eds) *Efficiency, Finance and Varieties of Industrial Policy*. New York: Columbia University Press.

Gottschalk, R. (2015) What Financial Regulation for Stability and Financial Inclusion in Africa? The Views of Regulators of Ethiopia, Kenya and Lesotho. ODI Working Paper 414, March.

Griffith-Jones, S. and Karwoski, E. (2015) "Can the Financial Sector Deliver both Stability and Growth in Sub-Saharan Africa?". In: Norman, A. and Stiglitz, J. (eds) *Industrial Policy and Economic Transformation in Africa*. New York: Columbia University Press.

Lin, J. (2013) *Against the Consensus: Reflections on the Great Recession*. Cambridge UK: Cambridge University Press.

Hosono, A. (2013) "Development Finance for Structural Transformation and Inclusive Growth: Asian Experiences". In: Te Velde, D. and Griffith-Jones, S. (eds) Sustained growth and structural transformation. DGRP Policy Essays. ODI. December. https://static1.squarespace.com/static/5167f6a2e4b0f1cbdee8d1c0/t/529e208de4b0e7dbabb0449c/1386094733976/DEGRP+Policy+Essays+Sustaining+growth+and+structural+transformation+in+Africa+03+Dec+2013.pdf

World Bank (2013) Domestic Credit Provided by Financial Sector (% of GDP). World Bank, http://data.worldbank.org/indicator/FS.AST.DOMS.GD.ZS

Index

For Product Safety Concerns and Information please contact our EU
representative GPSR@taylorandfrancis.com Taylor & Francis Verlag GmbH,
Kaufingerstraße 24, 80331 München, Germany

Printed and bound by CPI Group (UK) Ltd, Croydon, CR0 4YY

01/05/2025

01858348-0002